GHOST TOWNS OF THE COLORADO ROCKIES
Sectional Map

R.L. BROWN

W9-AJO-379

GHOST TOWNS
OF THE
COLORADO ROCKIES

GHOST TOWNS
of the
COLORADO
ROCKIES

By

ROBERT L. BROWN

ILLUSTRATED WITH PHOTOGRAPHS

The CAXTON PRINTERS, Ltd.
CALDWELL, IDAHO
1969

First printing February, 1968
Second printing February, 1969

Standard Book Number 87004-020-0

Library of Congress Catalog Card No. 68-10099

Printed and bound in the United States of America by
The CAXTON PRINTERS, Ltd.
Caldwell, Idaho   83605
111654

For
EVELYN McCALL BROWN
My wife and companion for more than two decades

PREFACE

ROUGHLY THREE YEARS have elapsed since work was started on this project. Doing research in and writing about Colorado's early history, with particular reference to the mining period, has been an immensely satisfying experience. Several time blocks during vacations, many, many weekend jaunts, and not a few holidays have been spent in relocating and exploring these early towns by Jeep, on foot, and occasionally on snowshoes.

Two rather annoying frustrations have persisted throughout the preparation of the volume with regard to the selection of places to be included. In some instances there are rather good pictures of towns, but insufficient or conflicting information has precluded the writing of a chapter. There are other locations where a veritable wealth of information exists, but apparently no photographer ever recorded how the place looked for posterity. In no instance has a town been included without pictures. Likewise, in no case have I included towns that I have not visited personally.

In duplicating the angles from which the early photographs were made, wide-angle lenses were used far more than optics of a normal focal length. Due to the growth of trees, changes in the terrain, and for other like reasons, several fine old pictures could not be matched and were therefore excluded. For those persons interested in photography, the pictures were made with Leica and Pentax equipment, using green or yellow filters in most cases. The film was Plus-X. All prints were made on Luminos enlarging paper.

A word of special gratitude is due to my wife, Evelyn, and to our two children, Diana and Marshall, for their patience during many long trips to remote locations, and for their help in the identification of photographic angles. Thanks should also go to Dianne Zahller, Kathleen Brandel, and Evelyn Brown for typing all of these chapters. Freda and Francis B. Rizzari gave generously of their time, ingenuity, and understanding by proofreading the completed manuscript for errors and omissions. Virginia McConnell checked the historical accuracy of my chapters dealing with the South Park towns. Arthur Abe and Jessie Bingham assisted with technical photographic problems. Fred and Jo Mazzulla were most generous in supplying a large number of early photographs from their superb collection. Many additional pictures were secured from the fine collections of Richard A. Ronzio, Francis B. Rizzari, Jack Thode, Malcolm E. Collier, George A. Dumont, and Velma Churchill. The photographic library of the State Historical Society of Colorado and the Western History Department of the Denver Public Library filled a number of other photographic needs with rare old pictures.

Erl Ellis, Allison Chandler, Joe Tomsick, Harry Simcox, George Dumont, and many others furnished me with information by letters, tape recordings, and personal interviews. Mrs. Enid Thompson, Mrs. Laura Ekstrom, Mrs. Kay Pearson, and Mrs. Louisa Ward Arps spent many long hours and were of tremendous assistance to me in researching information at the library of the State Historical Society of Colorado. Mrs. Alys Freeze and her staff at the Western History Department of the Denver Public Library also devoted a great deal of time to my many requests. Mrs. Opal Harber, James Davis and Mrs. Hazel Lundberg were particularly helpful.

Finally, in alphabetical order, the following references were used in the preparation of this book. The *Alamosa Journal* for February 28, 1884; the *Boulder Daily Camera* for March 8, 1946, and August 13, 1953; Samuel Bowles, *The Switzerland of America* (New York: Samuel Bowles and Company, 1869); the *Canon City Mining Gazette* for August 23, 1882; the *Carbonate Chronicle* for February 27, 1939; the *Central City Register-Call* for April 26, 1897; the *Colorado Business Directory* for 1885 and 1877; the *Colorado Graphic* for October 29, 1887; the *Colorado Miner* for September 14, and 21, 1878, February 1, March 29, and August 2, 1879; the *Colorado Mining Directory* of 1883; George Crofutt, *Grip-sack Guide to Colorado* (Omaha: The Overland Publishing Company, 1881); the *Denver Daily News* for February 3, 1883, and March 15, 1884; the *Denver Post* for February 11, 1899, October 28, 1900, December 19 and 31, 1941, October 23, 1954, and November 17, 1957; *The Denver Republican* for February 4, 1867, January 17, 1882, June 25, 1893, May 17, and September 9, 1897, February 3, and 4, 1899, January 2, July 20, and August 6, 1900, January 23, and September 29, 1901; *The Denver Times* for December 16, 1874, November 1, 1881, December 31, 1896, August 16, 1898, January 4 and 25, February 4, 6, 9 and 21, May 13, June 28, October 22, and December 21, 1899, October 30, 1900, January 19 and November 28, 1902; the *Denver Tribune* for December 20, 1880; John L. Dyer, *The Snow-Shoe Itinerant* (Cincinnati: Cranston and Stowe, 1890); the *Eagle Valley Enterprize* for April 12, 1940; Perry Eberhart, *Guide to the Colorado Ghost Towns and Mining Camps* (Denver: Sage Books, 1959); the *Elk Mountain Pilot* for July 18, 1935; the *Fairplay Flume* for July 17, 1879; Frank Fossett, *Colorado, Its Gold and Silver Mines* (New York: C. J. Crawford, Printer and Stationer, 1880); Don and Jean Griswold and Fred and Jo Mazzula, *Colorado's Century of Cities*, published by the authors (Denver: 1958); the *Gunnison News Champion* for November 30, 1939; Frank Hall, *History of Colorado*, four volumes published between 1889 and 1895 by the Blakely Printing Company of Chicago; Ernest Ingersoll, *Knocking Around the Rockies*

(New York: Harper and Brothers, 1883) ; Sidney Jocknick, *Early Days on the Western Slope of Colorado* (Denver: Carson and Harper Company, 1913) ; David Lavender, *The Big Divide* (Garden City: Doubleday and Company, Inc., 1948) ; and *One Man's West* (Garden City, N.Y.: Doubleday and Company, Inc., 1956) ; *Leslie's Illustrated Weekly* for March 23, 1899; Virginia McConnell, *Bayou Salado* (Denver, Colorado: Sage Books, 1966) ; L. L. Nunn, *A Memoir* (Ithaca, New York: The Telluride Association, 1933) ; the *Pueblo Chieftain* for May 16, 1955; the *Rocky Mountain Miner* for October 11, 1902; the *Rocky Mountain News* for November 14, 1860, February 6, May 4, and October 19, 1867, June 9, 1877, April 10, September 24, and November 16, 1880, August 12, and December 12, 1881, January 13, and October 17, 1882, March 18, and 21, 1883, October 10, 1891, July 12, 1897, January 1, and January 28, 1898, and March 10, 1958; the *San Juan Prospector* for July 2, 1887; Marshall Sprague, *Money Mountain* (Boston: Little, Brown and Company, 1953) ; and *The Great Gates* (Boston: Little, Brown and Company, 1964) ; the *Steamboat Springs Pilot* for April 17, 1936; the *Summit County Journal* for August 14, 1936, and November 19, 1937; Warren and Stride, *Cripple Creek and Colorado Springs Illustrated* (Colorado Springs, 1936) the *Wason Miner* for December 12, 1891; Frank Waters, *Midas of the Rockies* (Denver: University of Denver Press, 1949) ; Albert N. Williams, *Rocky Mountain Country* (New York: Duell, Sloan and Pearce, 1950) ; George F. Willison, *Here They Dug the Gold* (London: Readers' Union, 1952) ; and last but far from least, Muriel Sibell Wolle's magnificent and monumental *Stampede to Timberline* (Boulder, the Author, 1949) and *The Bonanza Trail* (Bloomington: Indiana University Press, 1953).

By far the most trying problems in the preparation of this book were encountered in my efforts to disassociate fact from fiction, folklore, and downright deliberate errors. In one instance, the son of a former publisher of the *Animas Forks Pioneer* admits that his father often made up his own news stories to fill the columns and sell papers when news was short. Likewise, even first-person accounts of pioneer happenings, early mine production figures and population statistics—to name just three—vary widely from source to source. In all instances my work has been the often impossible task of finding out what really happened.

In no instance have I knowingly presented events as facts without good authority, or have I intentionally colored what happened by my own literary style or ideas of what might have been. Whenever a "story" has been included, it has been labeled as such. For all unresolved statements and figures that have eluded careful checking, and for any other errors, genuine or imagined, that may vary from what the reader has seen or heard, the author apologizes in advance. In several cases within these chapters, the truth has been stranger than fiction.

R. L. B.

$\mathcal{G}$

INTRODUCTION

SINCE THE PUBLICATION of *Jeep Trails to Colorado Ghost Towns* (Caxton, 1963), I have often received letters from and been confronted by many persons who have neither the desire nor the audacity to own or operate a four-wheel-drive vehicle. Nevertheless, these same people express a profound interest in Western history, an incidental concern with the mining period, and a specific fascination with the mystery associated with our ghost towns. With only minor variations in their approach, the desire has almost always been expressed for information about ghost towns and early mining camps that can be reached on a weekend or single-day outing in the family sedan, or perhaps this coupled with a very short, easy hike.

The idea seemed appealing to them, and to me, and a file of materials for possible inclusion began to grow during the preparation of another book (*An Empire of Silver*, Caxton, 1965). Serious work started on this project in October of 1964. A wide variety of communities with interesting histories grounded in the mining period were considered. Some, like Leadville and Central City, were rejected as being too obvious. Others were deleted due to my failure to find enough interesting material that could be documented in the text, to geographical conditions, to the present status of the site, or to changes in routes—to name just a few.

Although most of the towns in this book were selected for their accessibility, a smaller number of prime places where a four-wheel-drive vehicle is needed for access have been included just to keep things interesting. I might add, however, that a hike to these locations is not out of the question.

Seeking the locations of Colorado's myriad array of true ghost towns is often a frustrating experience. The multiplicity of old and unlabled mountain roads or trails may lead you up countless blind alleys, and it may require hours or even days for you to reach your destination—and this only by the complicated process of elimination. Often these "freeways" wind about in all directions at once and a compass actually becomes more useful than your road map, or the directions from natives. And then, assuming that you finally do get there, your town may have been totally obliterated by the natural environment indigenous to our Colorado mountain winters. The history of most early Colorado mining camps is liberally punctuated with an extremely high incidence of their destruction by rockslides, snow avalanches, fires, mud slides, and a few floods. Assuming that a given camp may have escaped, to a degree, the rigors of these destructive forces, its remains must still somehow survive contemporary Colorado's high mountain winters.

Woodstock was obliterated when a train, approaching the western portal of the Alpine Tunnel, started a snowslide which took the lives of fourteen of the town's seventeen inhabitants who, unfortunately, were in the right place at the wrong time. A mud slide buried Brownsville, just west of Silver Plume. Three mud slides thus far have submerged parts of Marble and the end is not yet. Three fires and two Hollywood motion picture companies on location have left a sadly depleted shell of once attractive Rosita. Snow avalanches terminated the life of Tomichi and were so common in southwestern Colorado that the "white death" became the most dreaded single aspect of living in the San Juan camps. Rockslides interrupted the way of life at Eureka with a frightening degree of regularity. Colorado's history is replete with many other similar examples but these few should suffice to make the point. What one may or may not find at any given location may change radically from year to year or, in a few instances, from day to day.

Searching for ghost towns may also be rewarding. There's a real thrill in store when one tops a ridge or rounds that last curve to find an abandoned town spread out below in some remote meadow. It's a silent and empty place now with streets overgrown by grass and weeds. Tiny fenced yards, once proudly kept, are now filled with restless, ugly spheres of sagebrush. Once upon a time, hundreds (or thousands) of people like ourselves lived here. Now there is no one.

By way of providing a modicum of background material against which this book is to be read, I'd like the reader to consider with me a series of four questions which, it is hoped, will enrich and enhance your enjoyment and appreciation of what has been attempted in this book.

First of all, what is a ghost town? There are many definitions. Some insist that the only true ghost town is one that is completely gone; a town like Parkville or Quartz, that simply is no more. Some academic objections have been raised with reference to labeling as ghost towns those locations where buildings still stand, even though no population currently exists. To many of us, an empty town that is not all that it used to be, qualifies as a ghost town. Various other sources have included in their definitions those towns that are only partly ghost or empty, but which have small numbers of people living in some of the structures within the community. Accepting this last definition would allow inclusion of Leadville, Central City, Cripple Creek, and a variety of similar communities. One author said, "A ghost town is a shadowy semblance of its former self." Obviously, there will be borderline cases within whatever definition you accept. My own ideal example is a town completely abandoned by all business and permanent residents, preferably with buildings still standing. Oriental City, Dyersville, or Animas Forks would qualify here.

Second, how does a community become a ghost town?

Probably the greatest single cause was repeal of the Sherman Silver Purchase Act in 1893. Destroying the basic economic value upon which the community was built inevitably destroyed the purpose for its existence. Pegging the price of gold at thirty-five dollars an ounce wiped out many towns early in the present century. With rising costs of mining equipment, unemployment insurance, higher taxes at all levels, union wages, social security and other similar items, the price of gold is nevertheless still only thirty-five dollars an ounce. This largely negates the efforts of an American mining industry and there are almost no new mining towns being started.

In 1861 the Civil War brought about a collapse in the speculative mining boom, depopulated the towns, and resulted in a decided chill that developed between Eastern risk capital and Colorado deep-mining ventures. High transportation costs for travel over difficult terrain killed the otherwise promising camp at Ruby. Floresta became a ghost town when there was no longer a market for its fine anthracite coal. A similar ending engulfed Coal Basin, and the railroads were taken out in both instances. Today, huge trucks haul coal down over the old grades from Coal Basin and a measure of prosperity has returned to the industry, but the town will probably never be rebuilt.

By no means were all early towns built as a result of mining, or died as a consequence of it. Eastonville expired when the railroad was abandoned and its taxes no longer supported the town. Jefferson was once a big railroad shipping point for sheep and South Park hay. The same circumstances applied to the now extinct town of Michigan. Bent's first stockade was abandoned after only two years 1826-28) when it was discovered that it had been built in the middle of a no-man's-land between hostile Ute and Arapaho territories where no Indians dared venture for purposes of trade. Robinson, a beautifully preserved gem among ghost towns, was buried under the vast, ever-expanding dump of the Climax Molybdenum Company. Montgomery is in a watery grave at the bottom of a reservoir storing water for Colorado Springs. Marble faded when its product became too expensive. In Vermont, quarries were more accessible and, therefore, transportation costs were minimized. Later use of synthetics hurt the market for marble in both states. The previously mentioned mud slides were no help.

Wagon Creek and Garland City on the Denver and Rio Grande Railway, expired when the line was extended to Fort Garland. Wagon Creek, in fact, lasted only six months. Trail City, in eastern Colorado, folded when the great cattle drives stopped concurrent with the end of the open range cattle industry. Many twentieth-century ghost towns were created on the Colorado and Kansas prairies in the 1930's. Mainly, a town dies from lack of business.

Some towns went out of business by becoming a part of another community. In Gunnison County Irwin and Ruby got themselves annexed and ceased to exist as separate entities. Recen and Kokomo joined forces after a fire destroyed the latter. Old Congress Town and Red Mountain were abandoned due to location. Both apparently merged later into Red Mountain Town in a new location just off the top of Red Mountain Pass. Then in 1892 the town burned. Again in 1896 the fire laddies were called out as history repeated itself. Red Mountain, however, rose once more from its ashes. A destructive forest fire nearly finished the job in 1937. Rosita also had three fires. No Colorado mining camp worthy of note escaped the ravages of at least one fire. In some instances, fires became a stimulus to accelerated growth—Nevadaville being a case in point. At other times they became a secondary reason contributing to abandonment.

A better road which was bladed into Leavick from the Fairplay side hastened its destruction by vandals. Conversely, the wretched road into Carson has left us a well-preserved town. Notoriety is sometimes the downfall of a town. Following the publication of a fine illustrated article in a Denver paper about the old Victorian two-story house at Rosita, vandals burned it to the ground that next weekend. A few towns have been burned by the Forest Service as fire hazards. Bowerman was founded on a hoax and died following the exposure.

Third, where are the ghost towns? Most seem to have been founded up nearly every little creek where gold and silver were thought to exist in paying quantities. The mining towns were in the mountains, often high up since gold and silver deposits were forced into seams and faults during the prehistoric period when volcanic pressures wrinkled the earth's crust and formed our Rocky Mountains. Where there are no mountains, gold is not likely to be found except in the form of placers which have washed down via stream beds which in turn are fed by lofty melting glaciers which erode away the high canyons.

Fourth, and last, are any new ghost towns being created today? The answer is very definitely, "Yes. Como is dying from a combination of the mining collapse coupled with railroad abandonment. The original Dillon had to be abandoned when Denver built its new reservoir. A new town was built on higher land and took the old name. New highways have isolated some communities and left them to wither away on old vines. Henderson and Bayfield are two examples. Neither is dead yet by any means, and who knows what tomorrow may bring? Depletion of oil reserves in the Denver-Julesburg basin will undoubtedly cause some population shifts here as it did in Oklahoma and Texas.

It has long been the hope of this writer that one of these towns might be set aside and preserved, perhaps as a state park, at some time in the near future. Massachusetts has its old Sturbridge, Virginia has restored both Williamsburg and Jamestown. Since our mining period ranked high on any list of priorities responsible for bringing people here in large numbers, what could be a more fitting monument than a well-preserved mining camp to show future Coloradoans how people lived during the nineteenth century in the Centennial State? A possible choice might be St. Elmo, which is centrally located, accessible, scenic, well preserved, endowed with adequate water and sufficient space for a park and campground. The mining period is unique in Colorado history. Its priority in time and its short life combined to furnish most of the true ghost towns.

In the meantime, tread easily on your visits to the past. The old relics are fragile and tinder dry. Vandalism, a carelessly discarded match, or a thoughtless act may erase these historic and interesting places forever.

R. L. B.

ॐ

CONTENTS

22   CONTENTS

ILLUSTRATIONS

GHOST TOWNS
OF THE
COLORADO ROCKIES

1.

ALMA

SLOWLY THE LAST warming rays of the setting sun fanned out behind the majestic peaks of the as yet unnamed Mosquito Range. In their place a high-altitude chill spread across the Bayou Salado. It was a typical evening in late June of 1844 and the party of men who had just made camp were busily building fires to ward off the cold. Presently their leader returned from tethering his mount and sat down to record entries in his log by the flickering firelight. John C. Frémont, erstwhile pathfinder of the early West, was only thirty-one years old. Now he was on the return leg of a trip to California, having been charged with mapping the territory from the South Platte River to the Pacific Ocean.

Some minutes after darkness had enveloped their camp, the mournful howl of a distant timber wolf shattered the mountain stillness. Frémont is said to have remarked that at some time in the future, even this very spot would probably be settled. He further speculated that the forlorn animal had merely scented the path of progress and was doubtless raising his voice in protest. Already, a band of Utes had started camping on Sacramento Flats nearby, and now a band of whites was busily tramping the alpine meadows.

Within the brief span of white man's recorded history, the Bayou Salado, now known as South Park, had experienced many explorers prior to Frémont. Among others, it was well known to such men as Jim Bridger, Zebulon Pike, Lan-

caster P. Lupton, and Jim Beckwourth. Under the circumstances, Frémont's prediction had a better-than-average
chance of proving to be accurate. Ultimately, a whole
series of camps grew up in the neighborhood, largely as
satellites of Fairplay and Alma. Some legends insist that
Fairplay was actually built over the site of the Frémont
campsite.

Park County was established by an act of the First Territorial Legislature when it met in 1861.

Alma seems to have had its beginnings in the very early seventies. Hall's *History of Colorado* states quite positively that
it was established in 1872. J. B. Stansell and Abram Bergh
put up the first house in town for a Mr. James who had
kept a general store at Fairplay. James also planned to open
a branch at Alma. His wife, Alma James, is often mentioned as the source of the town's name. From another quarter we hear that several other ladies in town all shared the
same given name and that the settlement was called after,
"All the Almas in town."

Before going into the contracting business, J. B. Stansell
had been an early partner of Joseph Higginbottom at Buckskin Joe. After he had completed the James home, he also
built a large ore storage building of rough log construction.
By that time Alma was booming and by 1873 it already
boasted a population of five hundred people.

Initially, the impetus for the establishment of a town
at this point came from the discovery of placer gold. Both
placer mining and extensive hydraulic dredging were tried
here. Huge ugly piles of smoothly polished boulders still
bear mute testimony to this most destructive of all mining
methods. Dredging is now mercifully outlawed in Colorado. As time passed, the gold search was expanded to include silver, copper, and lead. All of these metals were found
near Alma. Among the better known properties were the
Dolly Varden, Sweethome, Fanny Barrett, Sacramento, Silver Gem, Moose, and Security.

Looking west toward the Mosquito Range, this early photograph
shows Alma at the height of the mining boom.

Alma today appears to be fully as large as it was in the old picture above

Alma's location proved to be an extremely fortunate one. In 1879-80, silver discoveries were made at a number of locations on the slopes of Mount Lincoln and Mount Bross, both of which are 14,000-foot-class peaks. Alma was built almost at the base of these two adjacent mountains where Buckskin Creek flows down into the Middle Fork of the South Platte River.

George Crofutt, energetic chronicler of early-day Colorado communities, also visited South Park and recorded that Alma had one sampling works, a newspaper called the *Alma Eagle,* the St. Nicholas, the Southern, and several other hotels, and twice-daily stagecoach and mail service to and from the surrounding communities. He also recorded its proximity to other camps as being twenty miles from Breckenridge, five miles from Fairplay, and only seventeen miles from Leadville. This latter distance involved a crossing of lofty, rocky, Mosquito Pass which tops the rugged range to the west at an elevation well in excess of thirteen thousand feet.

On March 23, 1937, long after it had passed its prime as a mining camp, Alma fell victim to that most common and most destructive scourge of mountain boom towns, the fire. Here, as in so many camps, the blaze seems to have started from an overheated stove located in the back room of the Budd and Beck Recreation Company, a beer parlor. The time was about 4:00 A.M. Only the bank at Alma was of masonry construction, all the rest were frame buildings. As a result the business section was virtually destroyed. Overall damage amounted to fifty thousand dollars.

It now seems likely that a chance spark from the stove was fanned into flame by a fifty-mile-an-hour wind that had been blowing across South Park. Within a few minutes the structure was ablaze, destroying a pool hall and the Williams Barber Shop which were also housed in the Budd and Beck Building. Next door, Clark's Restaurant caught fire and in turn ignited the Red and White Building. A grocery store went next as the blaze spread along the town's single business street. When an automobile dealership went, this was the greatest loss in the fire.

In 1937 the population of Alma was about five hundred. The town had no fire department of its own. Five miles away, the Fairplay Fire Department heeded the call for assistance and sent their equipment. By that time most of the damage had been done and little could be accomplished beyond preventing any further spread. Since Alma had no community water system, the people depended upon wells. To further complicate things, Buckskin Creek was frozen solid. The same high winds that had whipped the flames also blew down the telephone lines that night.

When the fire broke out again in the center of town, a bucket brigade tried but could do little beyond concentrating on saving the rest of the village. Surprisingly, much of Alma still stands today. Some new construction has gone up in places over the old scars.

Alma is one of the simplest of all places to find, and excellent roads enter it from two directions. From Denver, U.S. 285 will take you southwest through South Park to Fairplay. Alma is five miles to the northwest on State Highway 9. From Dillon and Breckenridge, State Highway 9 comes across scenic Hoosier Pass and south into the town.

Alma was of considerable importance in the gold and silver mining history of Colorado. Here, even in the early days, miners washed huge fortunes from the earth. The Alma district, however, was never a hard-rock country. In many instances, precious metals were placered from the creek beds by the same men who had panned the waters of Cherry Creek near Denver. By any measure, the Alma district is a region notably rich in memories.*

---

* In this same general area, see also Buckskin Joe, Fairplay, Puma City, Quartzville, Montgomery, Leavick, and Sacramento.

2.

ALPINE AND ALPINE TUNNEL

FOR MANY YEARS Colorado had not merely one but two communities called Alpine. Since they are reasonably close together and are now ghost towns, each will be treated in this chapter. Our first Alpine was, and still is, about twelve miles west of Nathrop, southwest of Buena Vista on State Highway 162, a very good dirt road. Today, only a few original cabins and the ruins of the smelter remain. Summer cabins now dominate the area about one mile off the present road.

Although the first house was built at Alpine in 1877, the town was not incorporated until two years later. For many years its population hovered around five hundred people. In the course of the town's growth, the Tilden Smelting and Sampling Works moved into Alpine and erected a fair-sized mill. Colonel Chapman, who owned and operated the plant, employed about forty men. In an incredibly short time the Tilden was processing thirty tons of ore per day. Among the better producing mines which contributed to the welfare of Alpine were the Tilden, Livingston, and Britenstein. Ores from these properties averaged from fifty to one hundred and twenty-five dollars per ton.

Alpine was located along the track of the beloved narrow-gauge Denver, South Park and Pacific Railway. Incidentally, the fare from Denver in those days cost $12.85. When George Crofutt visited the town he said that it consisted of "A number of stores, hotels, restaurants, two saloons, and other buildings." The hotels were called the Arcade and the

Badger. Crofutt was conservative on the subject of saloons; there were twenty-three. Within the town's short life span, a newspaper developed, the *True Fissure*. Alpine lost out to St. Elmo when the owner-editor chose to migrate upstream and publish in the new location.

Three banks took care of all financial demands at the town. George Knox opened a school at Alpine in 1881. One source tells us there was never a church in the town, while another insists that one church was built and did flourish for a time. Since Alpine had gained a rather rough reputation for itself, this single church among those twenty-three saloons must have seemed as out of place as a cow on the front porch.

Suddenly Alpine went into a slump from which it never recovered. Actually, its life span was extremely short. When St. Elmo was booming in 1882, most of the people from Alpine simply packed up and moved on to the newer town. For years afterwards, the town held only memories and a couple of hermits. Lady Zabriskie and Napoleon Jones were the two inhabitants. Mrs. Zabriskie is alleged to have been a Polish princess and highly intelligent. She once wrote a scholarly treatise on minerology in which she said that Colorado was full of uranium and molybdenum. In it she predicted that these resources would become extremely valuable. Alpine was not her only home. At one period in her life she lived in a house beside the railroad depot in St. Elmo.

Mrs. Zabriskie seems to have been one of the most singularly migratory of recluses, moving in or out of empty cabins here, at Romley, and up at Hancock. In the latter town, one of the few remaining buildings, which was at one time the town saloon, is sometimes referred to as Mrs. Zabriskie's cabin. As time passed, both these people became more and more reluctant to give up their memories of the past.

Quite apart from any sociological reasons or considerations for their actions, Jones and Zabriskie continued to wander about the empty townsites of Chalk Creek for many years after all of the other residents had gone. It would be pleasant if a happy ending to this story could be reported but outside of fiction this rarely happens to those who have been so hurt by the world that they feel impelled to live apart from the rest of society. In 1930 the county commissioners brought out their frozen bodies for burial.

From then on, Alpine gradually became the property of Bird Fuqua who began acquiring land in Chalk Creek Gulch in connection with Hortense Hot Springs. When a good road was bladed up the valley, her efforts to preserve Alpine were frustrated. Sheep and cattlemen took refuge at will in the old buildings. Those who cared were unable to cope with the vandalism that good roads tend to bring. Thus, in an incredibly short time, Alpine was systematically stripped of most of the few remaining cabins that still stood in the old town.

Our second Alpine was really known as Alpine Tunnel and was only a few miles away and can be reached from a point near the other Alpine by taking either Hancock or Williams Pass. Both are Jeep roads that start up from the old ghost town of Hancock. A third trail follows the railroad grade out of Hancock to the east portal of the Alpine Tunnel. From there, a short hike across twelve-thousand-foot Altman's Pass will put you in the second Alpine. A simpler approach became a reality during the summer of 1964 when Gunnison County bridged Quartz Creek just a mile from Pitkin. It is now possible to drive all the way to Alpine Tunnel over what was formerly a hair-raising Jeep road.

The town is 167.7 miles west of Denver, built at an altitude of 11,546 feet. At the eastern end of the redwood-lined, 1,805-foot-long Alpine Tunnel was a settlement called Atlantic. Immediately adjacent to its western terminus stood the town of Alpine Tunnel. Its story is inextricably tied up with that of the pioneer railroad bore. Since 1879, ex-Governor John Evans had been putting money into the project. His goal was to allow the Denver, South Park and Pacific to extend its rails into Gunnison.

Bids for construction of the tunnel were let in November of 1879. Actual work was started in 1880. Serving as engineer for the project was another Evans, James A., who had cut his railroading eyeteeth on General Grenville Dodge's Union Pacific. Construction began at 11,600 feet, almost directly beneath Altman's Pass. Here the trouble began.

Construction workers were offered free transportation by the Union Pacific Railroad if they would agree to work on the tunnel. Before the job was completed in 1881, some ten thousand workers had come and gone. Most averaged two to three days before the altitude got them down. In the beginning, the laborers were housed in a series of six crude log cabins which stood above the tunnel's west portal. By the time the job was finished, it had cost a staggering sum in excess of $242,000. Three problems account for the cost— loose stone, underground water, and decomposed granite. Costly twelve-by-twelve beams of California redwood timbering were brought in to shore up the whole shaky proposition.

From the west portal, the Alpine station was just a half mile south. Although winter snow and cold had enveloped the site, a huge stone enginehouse was built during the worst part of 1881. That same season saw the completion of the telegraph shack and the installation of an "Armstrong" turntable and a switch. Later, a 29x56-foot stone section house was put up beside the enginehouse. A tent city appeared at the site and sheltered the laborers during construction.

Work on the Alpine Tunnel ended just a few days before Christmas of 1881. The bore was completed and the job was done. Historical events apart, bad luck continued to dog the project with heavy winter snows that required construction of 150 feet of protective snowsheds at Atlantic and another 650 feet of this costly construction a third of a mile away at Alpine Tunnel. Unlike most railroad tunnels, this one had no ventilation problems. Harsh winds whipped across Tomichi Pass, through Brittle Silver Basin, and kept the bore clear of smoke every hour of the day and night.

But bad luck was still at hand when the first narrow-gauge train whistled into Gunnison in September of 1882. The Denver and Rio Grande had beaten them with rail connections into town over a year before.

By January 1, 1886, the structures at Alpine Tunnel consisted of a stone section house, 29x56 feet, a 54x153-foot enginehouse, a 14x16½-foot bunkhouse, a 10x16-foot storehouse and a 10x18-foot washhouse. Inside the enginehouse stood a 4x14-foot coal bin and a water tank that held 9,516 gallons. All of these structures were built of stone and were located on the east side of the tracks. On the west side there was a wooden telegraph office, first used as a section house.

In the strictest sense of the word, Alpine Tunnel probably would not qualify as a town since it was never incorporated. What its actual status was is a question still being debated. It was listed as a station stop where meals were served. For many years it was a passing stop for trains and their crews often slept there. A siding of 1,350 feet was installed along with a fifty-foot turntable and a turntable siding that stretched out for 212 feet.

Beyond the town, two huge rock palisades were constructed in 1881. Both were built above Brittle Silver Basin to keep the tracks from sliding down the steep, rocky mountainside into Quartz Creek. They held the tracks up but didn't keep the tremendous snowpacks in place. In March of 1884 one of the trains whistled while approaching Alpine Tunnel, starting a snowslide that came roaring down the almost vertical mountainside. Before reaching the bottom of the valley, it had swept away the town of Woodstock which, for a short time, had been clinging precariously to life in a tiny meadow below the tracks.

In 1906 Alpine still had a few buildings and the stage
still ran along the road above Chalk Creek.

At the west end of the railroad tunnel, the town of Alpine Tunnel may be seen in this
old picture made from atop Alpine Pass. This was, of course, actually Altman's Pass.

When a fire swept Alpine Tunnel in 1906, all of the buildings were destroyed. Since no mortar had been used, heat from the blaze caused the stone structures to collapse. By September of that year a new boardinghouse had been built at a cost of $1,701.58. It saw little use. Suddenly, in 1910, the tunnel caved in. A work crew inside it was overcome by coal smoke gas and four or five (the accounts vary) lost their lives. Without a clear passage for the air, natural ventilation meant nothing. These were the only casualties ever to occur at the Alpine Tunnel. Miraculously, no life was lost at any time during the construction period.

From then on, the tunnel was never reopened. Although the cave-in was disastrous, other reasons compelled the management to close out this phase of their operation. For one thing, heavy snow removal during a large part of the year had far exceeded all cost expectations. Quite apart from any physical difficulties, the tunnel route simply had not paid off as anticipated. Contributing to this was the fact that both the Colorado Midland and the Rio Grande now had lines running across Colorado. Beyond this, a rockslide came down across the tracks that same year just below Alpine Tunnel, between it and the first palisade.

Shortly afterwards the tracks were torn out and Alpine Tunnel was dead. The caved-in boardinghouse, the telegraph office and remains of one stone building may still be seen. Historical events apart, the rest of the town is little more than a memory.*

---

* In the same general area, see also Pitkin.

Collection of Fred and Jo Mazzulla
The historic palisade of the Denver, South Park and Pacific Railway

Collection of Robert L. Brown
The abandoned right-of-way still offers a thrilling Jeep ride

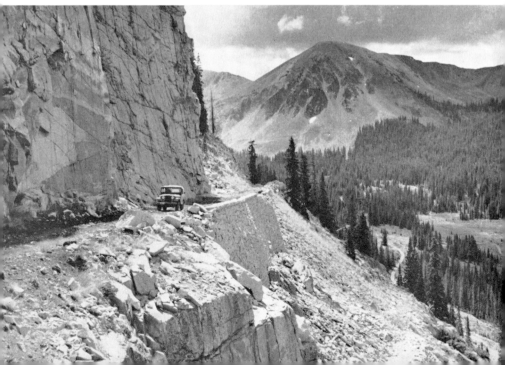

3.

BONANZA

Bonanza is nestled among the Cochetopa Hills, which vary in altitude from nine to twelve thousand feet. The general topography of the section is comprised of a main gulch running north and south. Through it flows a small stream known as Kerber Creek. From the center of town, Copper Gulch runs to the east. Nearby are Squirrel and Rawley gulches which formerly held some of the heaviest producing mines.

The history of Bonanza is much the same as that of a score of other camps created as a result of the Leadville excitement. Claims were worked as early as the 1870's. Following this, a continuous round of individual miners and prospectors passed through the valley on the way to the Gunnison gold rush. After discovering surface croppings of silver-bearing lead ore many of the gold seekers became silver miners.

In the spring of 1880, Pete McCardo and John Stansbury were making their way up the San Luis Valley, looking for a shorter route across Marshall Pass to the Gunnison country. Along Kerber Creek they found oxidized quartz in such quantities that it became comparatively easy to find the original vein in the hillside. They checked off a claim which they named Exchecquer. As the ore was quite heavy in sulphides, the refining process became extremely expensive. At that time the cost was thirty dollars a ton. A report of this rich discovery resulted in a stampede to Kerber Creek. Within two years five thousand people were scattered throughout the hills.

Four towns, named Exchecquerville, Sedgwick, Kerber City, and Bonanza were quarreling for preference. Inevitably only one of these could survive in such close proximity. As time passed, the growing and expanding Bonanza gradually absorbed the other three.

For a time Exchecquerville held out against all odds, thinking that it might continue to exist as a separate entity since it was built up around one of the very best and oldest mineral properties.

The Exchecquer Mine was still one of the finest in the camp. It was being vigorously worked by Rathvon and Co. Three tons of rich ore were shipped almost daily to the smelters. A large crew of men was employed and only limited housing held up the company in hiring more. The ore was a free smelting type of good quality that was often able to be shipped without sorting. Work on the Exchecquer began early and continued until late in the life of the camp.

In 1900 the Exchecquer Mine became the realization of a long-deferred hope. The owners had then been working the mine for many years on a sporadic basis until they came into a body of high-grade ore that promised to make it a good producer once more. That same year there were nearly two hundred men working in the immediate vicinity of Bonanza.

The settlement was officially incorporated as Bonanza City in 1881. New prospectors climbed the hills, explored the gulches, sunk shafts and drove tunnels, hoping to find rich, gold-bearing veins. In many shafts the prospectors passed over low grade silver ores that were to await treatment under modern, cheaper methods at a later period in time.

At the turn of the century, Bonanza had two principal streets, both of which were lined with creaky boardwalks. Twenty thousand inhabitants, according to one source, quenched their thirst in forty saloons. Such numbers made the town wild and wooly enough to require a United States deputy marshall, in addition to the efforts of a large police force, to maintain law and order.

During this entire period, Bonanza had no formal religious institutions. The late Dr. S. E. Kortright, pioneer physician and assayer at Bonanza, once recorded the answer he gave to a question about churches in Bonanza. The doctor replied that they never had one and then quoted the following:

> We have no churches there to confine
> The God that's with us all the time
> The mystery of these hills you see
> Are evidence of divinity.

To this day the town has never had a church.

Bonanza had its own fire department, bank, and a smelter built to reduce ores that did not carry lead. It was, consequently, a failure. The town enjoyed about all of the usual conditions of life that went to make up a typical mining community, including the enevitable visit by ex-President Ulysses Simpson Grant, whose itinerary included a seemingly endless number of Colorado's booming mining camps.

Bonanza endured its share of claim jumping, lynching parties, riots, and murders. An Irishman named John O'Hara was killed by a Negro musician named Forbush. "Bush," as he was more familiarly known, was a former Arkansas man who could pop off the head of a squirrel with the greatest of ease. During Reconstruction days he had been a member of the Arkansas Carpetbagger Legislature.

After a quarrel developed with O'Hara over some unknown offense, he met the Irishman on the street one day and deliberately shot him. Properly aroused, the Irish element in the camp organized and hastily prepared for a lynching. One man, later prominent in Denver business circles, agreed to go after the murderer. "Bush," meanwhile, had barricaded himself in a log cabin. The volunteer lawman left his team at the foot of the gulch, waiting to transport the culprit to the jail at Saguache. Shortly the Irish lynchers also assembled near the team and waited patiently for the arrival of the two men.

When the one-man vigilante party approached the cabin, he found the long barrel of a revolver protruding from between the logs. "Bush, I want you! Hand me that gun," ordered the gentleman. Being astonished at such audacity, the killer meekly complied. Descending the trail, "Bush" heard sounds on the path below and both men suspected the worst. His captor promised the Negro safety if he would obey orders.

Forbush was told to go up Kerber Creek, over the hills, and then to Saguache as fast as he could travel. A few moments later the mob saw only one man descending the hill to calmly inform them that the prisoner was safely on the way to town and that there would be no lynching. At the trial a verdict for acquittal was returned and Forbush disappeared. In later years he led a delegation of colored men from Arkansas to Washington, D.C., to assure Grover Cleveland of their support in the campaign, which resulted in President Harrison's election.

Bonanza was no single-mine camp. A complex labyrinth of mineral properties was scattered up and down the sides of most of the nearby gulches. The Empress Josephine was the most important mine of the camp. In the early days its production ran high in tellurides and one carload yielded twenty thousand dollars. The first owners sunk a shaft and burrowed in the vein without method, order, or system. With depth, the cost of operation grew too heavy and disaster came when the extravagant management spent its profits as fast as they were realized.

The Empress Josephine yielded minerals worth something like $200,000 during the Bonanza boom. It consisted of a shaft 300 feet deep, with several drifts along the vein. A new shaft was driven to a depth of 420 feet where further developments were stopped by a flow of water encountered at that point. No existing pumps could contend with its volume. Explorations with a drill at the bottom of the shaft revealed the ores lying in a true fissure vein close to the shaft. The existence of a larger body of ore below seemed likely.

In later years the new owners of the Empress Josephine had their own way in Bonanza. The company purchased scores of cottages at twenty-five dollars each, only to tear them down for the lumber. Having its pick of the best property in the district, the company often made its own prices on anything it cared to purchase. The old ranchmen in the district hauled quantities of building stone, supplies, lumber, and coke. They later worked in the mines which the company was putting in condition for operation. It cost the company sixty thousand dollars to repair the damage done to the Empress Josephine by the reckless and extravagant operations of the original owners.

Another of the prosperous mining properties was the great Bonanza Mine itself, owned by the Hon. Irving Howbert. Howbert later pioneered in the history of the Cripple Creek district. In January of 1900 he raised $3,500,000 for construction of the narrow-gauge Short Line from Colorado City up around Pikes Peak to Cripple Creek. At its peak the line carried fifty-four trains a day. At Bonanza, however, he built no railroad.

One of the richest strikes was made by James Downman and James Kenney who found the Rawley lode. Since it first went into production in 1880, this single mine has shipped more than six million dollars' worth of ore. Production was retarded somewhat by the closing of the American Smelting and Refining Company. The Rawley Tunnel was started in 1911 and was completed a year later. In size, it was an eight foot wide bore, seven feet high and six thousand six hundred feet long. In later years the Rawley was sold to Mr. W. P. Lynn, of Denver. When it was sold in 1881 it brought a record price of $100,000 to its original owners.

The Eagle Mine was owned and operated by the Lucrative Mining Company of Colorado Springs. A test carload, just as it was extracted from the vein without sorting, was sent to the smelter. Returns showed nearly $1,000 for this ten-ton lot.

Capt. W. B. McKinney was the founder of the first newspaper at Bonanza, the *Enterprise*. Its type all arrived at camp in January of 1882 and the press itself came along shortly thereafter. The town then had a daily paper that was greeted with pleasure and no little anticipation by all Bonanzaites. One early item from the new chronicle said that:

> W. C. Knowles, the Silver Creek murderer will surely be hung. This will be the first legal hanging in Saguache County and no doubt will be looked forward to with the usual interest.

All of the following items were gleaned from the pages of the *Enterprise* during the single month of June in the year 1882. They reveal not only some intimate glimpses into the life of people in a mining camp, but something of the intricate gyrations of a highly individualistic six-months-old newspaper as well.

> The only lady-like way for a woman to ride in Bonanza is side saddle.

> Everything that is now transpiring in our district inspires all our hopes as bright as the Star of Bethlehem, making each resident think that Bonanza is the new Eldorado on which the light of Aladdin's magic lamp has fallen, turning rocks into diamonds and mountains into gold.

> The smelter started up on the fourth of January and the results have since been most satisfactory indeed. Each five days three carloads of bullion have been turned out and the energy and perseverance of its owners is deserving of the highest praise. The reverses that were met were very grave but the determination of Mr. O. W. Kelly overcame every obstacle and his ultimate success is shared by every man, woman and child in the Kerber district.

> It has commenced snowing here lately which looks a little odd to us as we have had a perfect springtime up to the first. We now expect a little snow, however, intermingled with a little cool weather. This is considered the worst month of the year.

Rumor says that Dewey Dorn will soon take unto himself one that will share his joys and sorrows alike.

A party of Bonanza gallants went down to Sedgwick a few nights ago for the purpose of serenading their "ladie loves." All managed to get back safely but two have since been confined to their beds, one with frozen feet and another from too free an indulgence in his "ardent." Phil O'Rourke says they should remember the fate of the three little flies and never indulge in luxuries, especially on a winter night in the mountains.

Bonanza has more pretty girls than any other town in the state to its age.

Billiards and ten pins are the chief sources of amusement to our young men.

A rather novel wedding took place at the Cannon House a few mornings ago at Bonanza. The groom was Mr. Ike Doffelmeyer and the bride was Miss Henrietta Loy. The novelty was that the nuptial was celebrated at six in the morning which is indeed an early hour for a native of Bonanza to rise.

A second newspaper, the *Bonanza News,* flourished for a time but it was neither as colorful nor was it as successful as the *Enterprise.*

As the years passed by, rich discoveries around Ashcroft and Aspen drew the attention of capitalists away from Bonanza. The town began to dwindle in size until only a few families remained, still loyal to their faith in the future of the camp.

Miners who remained at Bonanza turned ranchmen to support their families while occasionally getting out a little ore which yielded them small profit. Among the seventy once-prosperous mines, only a few continued active in later years.

Gen. W. S. Rosencrans had learned of this near-deserted camp from a friend. After investing a small sum, he gained control of the Empress Josephine and eight other properties. After he interested a number of his wealthy New York friends in his enterprise, a company was formed. Engineers were sent out to Bonanza to reopen the mines and to get out the rich ores still believed to exist there. The New York syndicate spent money for three years in an attempt to reverse the trend of history in this district which was all but forgotten by the rest of the world. Their holdings amounted to two hundred acres of ground with a clear title.

An examination of a mineral map of Colorado will show that the Bonanza district is located on a mineral belt that is thought to extend all the way from Cripple Creek to Creede. Mining men still hold a theory that the gold belt is continuous throughout that entire area. This idea came in for considerable attention when reports of the operations of the New York syndicate were made public.

The possibility of the wealth of another Cripple Creek or a second Aspen seemed just around the corner. Old mine-owners began receiving letters from people who wanted to lease properties in the Bonanza district. County records at Saguache were searched to prove titles on property that had been neglected for more than ten years. During this last excitement over two thousand filings were recorded. Many of the old claims had been allowed to go by default during the previous decade.

Eventually, the rising costs of producing low-grade ores depleted the town. In 1900 there were only one hundred people still there. To further complicate matters, large numbers of beavers had invaded the idle mines, crawling down the shafts. In some cases they penetrated as far as two miles underground, gnawing the timbering and endangering anyone who ventured down that far. Three decades later their number had swelled to the point where trappers were brought in to rid the shafts of the unwelcome rodents.

In 1937 a fire destroyed almost the entire business section and damaged a number of houses and cabins. None of the structures has been rebuilt. In recent years lessors have continued to work the Rawley property. The decline in copper, lead, silver, zinc, and gold mining has contributed to depletion of the town. In 1950 nearly $240,000 in precious metals was produced as compared with $21,859 in 1953. Children from Bonanza now use the Saguache school. The 9,465-foot-high town now has an assessed valuation of $16,490 with one of the very lowest municipal mill levies in the state.

In 1955 the Whale Mine showed outstanding assays of uranium and was reopened for production of this and other ores. The Warwick was also reopened the first week of May and the few remaining residents were optimistic that these two properties would bring back the good old days.

Today, mining is still going on at Bonanza. This, along with the large number of summer people who have converted the old structures to fine summer cabins, now make up the main basis of Bonanza's seasonal economy.*

---

* In this same general area, see also Crestone and Turret.

Collection of Fred and Jo Mazzulla
An early photograph of Bonanza on Kerber Creek

Collection of Robert L. Brown
Bonanza still has many of its original buidings

4.

BOREAS

AT VARIOUS TIMES during our history, quite a large number of Colorado communities have claimed the distinction of being the highest in the United States and, in some cases, the world. For many years Waldorf, at 11,666 feet above sea level, claimed to have the highest post office in the country. During the Cripple Creek boom in the 1890's, Altman often boasted that it was the highest incorporated city in the civilized world, a distinction that actually belongs to La Paz, Bolivia. Currently, Leadville claims to be the highest municipality in the United States and calls itself the "cloud city." Although the foregoing by no means constitutes an exhaustive list, it will show some fairly typical examples of this highly elevated classification of civic pride.

One other member of this exclusive fraternity was Boreas, the subject of this chapter. Boreas was one of the claimants within the post office category. Actually, its claim was a relatively valid one, during its short life, since its elevation was 11,498 feet above sea level. Although the climb to Boreas seems like a comparatively short one, it is well to remember that you are already well above nine thousand feet when crossing South Park prior to beginning the gradual ascent of Boreas Pass.

Throughout its history the town that was constructed on its top was inextricably tied up with the pass itself. In the beginning it was alternately known as both Hamilton and as Tarryall Pass. Quite commonly many important roads took their names from those nearby settlements which they might serve. Both of these names came from very early mining camps in South Park, each of which is now gone. Shortly after Breckinridge (the original spelling) grew to prominence, the pass assumed its name, switching its allegiance to the western side of the divide.

It should be made clear that in this early phase, the pass was hardly more that a footpath. To supply the miners' wants, burro packtrains and foot travelers carried supplies over the range in 1859 and early 1860. Many records exist which describe how men skied over the range during these first two winters. Each new discovery made the need for improvement of the road more apparent.

Instead of waiting for a benevolent bureaucracy to do their job, men from both sides rolled up their sleeves and hacked out a crude miners' road by August of 1860, enabling wagons to get their supplies across the ridge. From that time on, it was widely used for a variety of purposes, including regular stagecoach travel for more than a decade.

When faced by the need to gets its rails into the fabulous silver camp of Leadville before its competitors, the Union Pacific Railroad pulled James Evans off his job as supervisor at the Alpine Tunnel. Evans and his crew of track layers began work in the spring of 1882. Construction was started from the Como side with rails being put down over a 3½ percent grade which did not follow the old stage road in every instance.

Perhaps, at this point, it might be well to note that this was not a standard-size railroad. Instead, it was a narrow-gauge branch of the Denver, South Park and Pacific, designed to connect the towns in South Park with the gold-producing facilities around Breckenridge (the later spelling), before going on to Leadville.

By June, construction crews had completed an amazing twelve miles of rails and ties from Como across the top. Building the last ten miles to Breckenridge involved an incredible drop of 1,925 feet in that short distance. Their task was a difficult one and the job was not completed until late in 1882. All too frequently, work and maintenance gangs were driven back by timberline blizzards and the biting, marrow-chilling cold. Since few obstacles can successfully buck the march of progress, the time finally arrived when the last tie and iron were carefully fitted into place and the job was done.

Nevertheless it soon became clear that their problems had just begun. Before reaching the top, sturdy little narrow-gauge locomotives were often called upon to plow their way through mountain-size drifts while on their way from South Park to Breckenridge. At other times the mountains of snow grew too large, swept high by the raging velocity of fierce timberline winds. Before trains could run, the slides and drifts menacing the road had to be shot down. The latter part of January was often the most difficult time. On one occasion operations had to be suspended for most of the latter part of the winter, and the first train did not reach Leadville until the following May.

In the course of attempting to operate and maintain a railroad across this particular section of windswept tundra, both workers and passengers endured biting cold, penetrating winds, and often real physical hardship. Because of the awful winter blasts, it seemed appropriate to rename the pass once more, this time in honor of Boreas, the ancient deity of the North Wind.

It was now absolutely clear that winter operations would be a problem. Often it was next to impossible for crews to keep the line open for more than a few miles beyond Grant. At such times nearly all commercial ventures were shut down at Como, with the notable exception of its five saloons where stalled train crews fell avidly under the influence of the grape and the grain. Under these circumstances, few trainmen complained of the inclement weather.

The tiny hamlet of Boreas was constructed exactly on the top of the pass, 11,498 feet above sea level. Its purpose was to serve the railroad and to provide shelter for crews and visitors to this remote part of Colorado. Through its fortunate geographical location, the town became the most important stop on this singularly most important route, capable of carrying people from Como to booming Breckenridge and Leadville.

Inevitably, a large number of log cabins were built at the site along with a few of the usual commercial structures. During its peak years, Boreas was a fair-sized town, although population estimates vary from the believable "few hundred" to the ridiculous.

Facilities for the Denver, South Park and Pacific included a stone enginehouse which also contained company office space and a two-room telegraph facility. Outside, one might see the very necessary turntable; necessary because it would have been next to impossible to turn a locomotive around on the apex of an alpine mountain pass. Nearby stood the inevitable above-ground water tank and a six-hundred-foot-long snowshed. The snowshed had doors only on the Breckenridge end. Old accounts reveal that they were very difficult to open when snowdrifts had piled up against them. Inside this latter structure was a depot where Mr. M. J. Trotter, an early-day agent, held forth and performed the usual functions indigenous to such an establishment.

Letters that went out of this "highest post office" told with almost monotonous repetition of the full terror of being marooned in horrible snowstorms, and of temperatures that went down to sixty degrees below zero. On one occasion the people at Boreas were snowed in for an incredible ninety days during which no trains were able to reach the station from either side. When supplies dwindled below the danger point, two men made a frantic effort to reach Como. Shortly after noon they started out over the awesome white wasteland on snowshoes. Nearly everything they attempted was futile and their frozen bodies were found along the trail during a search which was attempted the next day. Food was finally brought in from Grant by using horse-drawn sleighs after a semblance of a trail had been broken through the drifts.

Once, during the winter of 1898, a Boreas resident attempted a winter walk from the snowbound town on the top to Como. His mission was made all the more urgent by the fact that his wife was ill and medical help from Denver was deemed essential to her recovery. Regrettably, no trace was found of him until the following summer when the drifts melted. His body was on the eastern slope, between Halfway and Tarryall. When the remains were excavated, it was noted that his suitcase was opened and a number of his papers had been scattered about. It was thought that he had been preparing to build a fire to ward off the freezing cold. The fate of his ailing wife was not recorded in any of the sources utilized in researching this chapter.

Without a doubt the most bizarre happening in the history of Boreas involved the Phineas T. Barnum Circus train. The story has all the elements for a delightful musical comedy except the music.

Shortly after it had played at Denver, the circus train crossed Kenosha Pass and huffed its way across South Park to Como. In the course of trying to reach Leadville, it became stalled about three miles below the town of Boreas. Seemingly no amount of steam was capable of carrying the ponderous cargo of wild animals over the crest. Since the line, at this point, consisted of only a single track, all other traffic from both sides was effectively blocked as the sun went down and darkness began to descend.

To add chaos to confusion, the lions grew hungry and started roaring. In desperation the elephant keeper offered to remove his huge animals from their car, allowing them to push against the rear of the train. Frantically, the engineer is said to have replied, "Anything to get to Leadville." Carefully the pachyderms were arrayed behind the last coach.

*A part of old Boreas is visible at the left while a snowshed
dominates the foreground of this early picture.*

Very little of old Boreas can still be seen at this high, lonesome, and windy location

Impatient little knots of people gathered to watch hopefully as the strange hookup was arranged.

Almost simultaneously, the brakeman released his iron shoes while the caretaker uttered an impressive string of Arabic oaths. Up front, the shrill whistle split the darkening sky. From the rear of the train, a powerful snort was heard as the strange procession actually began to move.

When the top was reached, a few Boreas residents are said to have taken a hasty pledge of alcoholic abstinence, but Leadville got its circus anyway.

For today's visitor the ride to Boreas is a beautiful little jaunt. From either Como or Breckenridge, take the good graded road and simply drive to the top of the range. In autumn, this is one of the few places in Colorado where red aspens may be seen. In an incredibly short time, most of the original structures have fallen down or have been carried away. Only a few of the masonry buildings are still there, sitting bleakly above timberline on the cold and inhospitable tundra. The rest of Boreas has slipped away into the shadows of time.*

---

* In this same general area, see also Como, Dyersville, King City, Tarryall, and Hamilton.

5.

BROWNSVILLE

DURING MY RESEARCH for this chapter, two different spellings for the town's name were encountered with amazing frequency. Brownville or Brownsville, take your choice, since both forms seem to be accepted. When a miner named Brown found a paying lode here in the late 1860's, a mountain and a gulch were named for him, but the development of the town came about more slowly. It seems to have been started in the 1870's as a construction town for workers on the Atlantic and Pacific Tunnel.

Although regarded sometimes as a suburb of Silver Plume, Brownsville boasted a population of about six hundred people who gradually began to work in the nearby mines during the day, returning to the town that housed, fed, and entertained them at night. Prominent among the residents were large numbers of Cornish miners and their wives, often called Cousin Jacks and Cousin Jennies.

This was a happy town, built along a single main street. It had the usual saloon, a restaurant called the Fox and Hounds, about a dozen houses, a large boardinghouse, an Odd Fellows Hall, a smelter, and a slag dump that consisted of a huge pile of ground-up bones, purchased from the nearby slaughterhouse, which was used to flux the ores. The village was located at the foot of Brown Mountain, in a direct line with Brown Gulch. High above it at an elevation of 10,451 feet was the great Seven-Thirty property.

In many ways the history of Brownsville is tied up with that of the Seven-Thirty Mine. Facts concerning its beginnings are nebulous. Most sources credit its discovery to Clifford Griffin, an Englishman allegedly of noble ancestry, whose past in the old country was shrouded in mystery. Another version tells us that Clifford was not the discoverer. Instead, his brother Heneage is said to have purchased an interest in the Seven-Thirty from Jack McDonnel, who is also credited with being the original discoverer. Seemingly, Heneage, in an attempt to rehabilitate his younger brother, arranged to bring him West.

Although little was actually known about the background of the Griffin brothers, rumors, of course, were most plentiful. Many shared several points in common, and the story went something like this. Clifford Griffin had been engaged to an extremely beautiful girl, also of royal lineage. True to the melodramatic nineteenth-century tradition, his fiancée just naturally had to be a most attractive physical specimen. In all such stories, plain-appearing girls were as scarce as hiccoughs at a prayer meeting. At any rate, her dead body was found in his room on the night before their wedding. There are already many embellishments upon this story and newer ones will doubtless appear with time.

There have been some extraordinary blind spots within British justice when it comes to malfeasances among the nobility. Thus, in an incredibly short time, Clifford was on his way west. Shortly after his arrival in Colorado, he either discovered the Seven-Thirty lode or was taken under the protective wing of his older brother. Heneage planned to exercise his moral guidance but the press of duties in a new mining camp afforded him little time.

In the course of events, Heneage made Clifford superintendent of the Seven-Thirty, in an effort to keep him interested and occupied. He seemed to like the new job well enough but never lost his air of sadness. Although he built himself a cabin on the side of lonely Columbia Mountain, he was unable to wipe out the memory of the tragedy he had left behind in England.

For many years the mines on Sherman and Brown mountains had followed the practice of blowing their starting whistles in chorus at 6:30 in the morning. Shortly after the Griffin brothers acquired their mine, by whatever means, they decided that the earlier hour was a completely uncivilized time for going to work. From then on their whistle blew an hour later. In the course of time, their mine became known as the Seven-Thirty from this consequence.

The Seven-Thirty was rich in both gold and silver and seemingly the veins grew wider as the shafts went deeper into the earth. From then on, the Griffin brothers became the wealthiest mineowners in the camp. Clifford spent most of his time at the mine but there were times when he came down to the saloon at Brownsville, sang songs, and beat upon the bar with the miners.

But regardless of his personal popularity and the money that had come his way, the emotional burden that he bore became too much for him. People at the mine noticed that he had started to dig what appeared to be a grave, hewn out from the tough granite. This type of rock was often quarried at Brownsville and was frequently labeled as the world's toughest. Suddenly Griffin began to share his melancholy feelings with the camp. Being an accomplished musician, he emerged from his lofty cabin each evening at dusk to render haunting and sad melodies on his violin. Such performances continued far into the night to the cheers and applause of his appreciative audience far below in the town. Workmen and their families would gather each night in the fold of the gulch, listening to the music. At the end of the strange concerts, their cheers could be heard rolling through the canyon.

One summer night, following a pause in the usual concert, listeners in the valley heard the unmistakable sound of a shot. Rushing up the mountain, they found Griffin face down, stretched out in the grave he had dug. The bullet had apparently gone through his heart. Inside his cabin they found a note requesting that he be buried in the tomb he had dug. Since he was already in it, this seemed like a reasonable request under the circumstances. His older brother saw to it that the last wish was carried out. Just a year later, a monument was placed over the body as a lasting memorial. It can still be seen high on the mountainside but it takes a hike to reach it. Before leaving for England, Heneage left a sum of money to provide flowers for the site on special occasions.

For many years the huge dump of the Seven-Thirty grew until it completely filled Brown Gulch at its elevation. A small culvert was installed to carry the annual flow of water under the dump and on down toward the South Fork of Clear Creek. In the spring when the snows melted and the rains came, this culvert was sometimes not large enough to carry all of the flow. Surplus water came up to the top of the dump, cascaded over the edge, and slowly saturated the whole mess. As all of these thousands of tons of mountain became thoroughly soaked, they began to move.

Sometime in the 1880's a heavy rain swept the area for days and loosened the great tailings piles of the Seven-Thirty, the Brown, and the Dundenberg. A small segment slithered down the gulch toward Brownsville. All was quiet for a while until the next segment came down in June of 1892. This slide buried a few homes, part of the old Brownsville Hall, and the town saloon, which was occupied at the time by relaxing miners.

A still larger mass moved down three years later, on June 15, 1895. This time the huge Seven-Thirty dump completely gave way, squished down the mountainside, and demolished the Lampshire Boarding House in the town. Again things seemed to calm down for a while and most people appeared to have forgotten the dangers of living where they did. Later that year, the largest of all the slides struck Brownsville. This time, in addition to the Seven-Thirty dump, several of the mine buildings also went. The Griffin cabin, blacksmith shop, and ore house were carried away. More serious than before, this was a rockslide. Grumbling down Brown Gulch, the boulders devolved upon the town. Luckily, the roaring mass lost its momentum before reaching the mill.

Although the town was now pretty thoroughly inundated under tons of debris and slush, the elements seemed not to be content merely to let it go at that. There was still more to come. In June of 1912, the air was suddenly filled with a sound like muttering thunder. It was the same warning that had evacuated Brownsville and the adjoining village of Silver Plume seventeen years before. After a look up the mountain at the mass of moving rock, most women, men, and children lost no time in leaving.

Suddenly the muttering became a deafening roar as a gigantic river of stone came tumbling down Brown Gulch. Rapidly it spread over the town, burying everything that had escaped before. Down went the beautiful hotel with its grand piano. Miners' cottages, with all the worldly possessions of the occupants, were torn asunder. Two railroad cars, loaded with quarrying granite, were tossed about like children's toys. In the course of total destruction, the mud came again.

People came from miles around to watch the mud flow slowly down the mountainside. Most eyewitness accounts reveal that none of these slides was an instantaneous event. Some of the more imaginative have stated that they could hear the piano tinkling under the slide as the mud and rocks slithered slowly over the keys. This, of course, gave rise to the myriad rumors that men had been imprisoned by the slide. Both stories are almost equally unlikely. First of all, the tumult and noise would have obscured any sounds from a piano. Second, only a rare mental type ("The captain must go down with his ship") would remain at his instrument while being slowly drowned in a muddy ooze. Historical events apart, this is the stuff of folklore. Due to the slowness of a mud flow, it is difficult to believe that anyone could have been accidentally caught there. Likewise, the rumor that an entire train, filled with people, was caught by the slide, is also unfounded.

Gradually a rounded mound took the place of the village. It still stands today, a great rock pile about a mile and a half west of Silver Plume along the course of Highway 40, seemingly as out of place as a saloon in a new church district. On the opposite side of the road is a deep pit. These are the only remains of what was once the town of Brownsville.*

---

* In this same general area, see also Silver Plume, Fall River, North Empire, Gilson Gulch, and Freeland.

Collection of Fred and Jo Mazzulla
Brownsville, on both sides of Clear Creek, as shown in half of a stereo pair

Collection of Robert L. Brown
Brownsville today, as taken from atop the old mud slide

6.

BUCKSKIN JOE

THE TINY COMMUNITY of Laurette, which later became known as Buckskin Joe, has no connection whatever with the reconstructed pioneer village on Highway 50 which now bears its name. The two should not be associated in the mind of the serious student of history. As an attempt to duplicate a pioneer Colorado settlement, the recently established Buckskin Joe is now very much alive, is lots of fun, and has a picturesque name which offers a wide degree of appeal. The original town today is a very dead place indeed. Only a few dilapidated buildings, scattered foundations, and a very extensive cemetery remain to mark its location or spot in the sun.

Facts and legends have become so entwined here that it is already difficult, if not impossible, to determine what is the truth. Many stories still exist and their number is growing, but few authentic records are now extant. That the community first was called Laurette is disputed by no one. How the town got its name is something else again. In one version, Laurette appears to have been a contraction of the first names of Laura and Jeanette Dodge, members of the family of Horace Dodge, part owner of the nearby Phillips Lode. Another story identifies Laurette as the sweetheart of Joseph Higginbottom whose preference for aboriginal wearing apparel caused him to be known in the mountains as Buckskin Joe. The man himself is also something of an enigma. One source says that he was a mulatto. With this as a starter, he was subsequently identified as a Negro. Some other sources insist he was neither. Even his family name has come in for a share of confusion. To date, I have encountered spellings ranging from "Higginbottom" through "Higgenbottom" to "Higginbothan."

The chronology of Buckskin Joe ranks it among the very earliest of Colorado mining camps. Most, though by no means all, accounts credit Higginbottom with the initial discovery of lode gold along the banks of what is now called Buckskin Creek. Just how he did it and under what circumstances is anybody's guess. Without doubt the most theatrical version tells of Joe being on a winter hunting expedition in the valley. Different accounts tell how he sighted a bear (unlikely in winter), a herd of deer, or a large elk, and prepared to shoot. At the moment of discharge, or just before, he is said to have slipped on the snow, causing the shot to go wild. The game animal was promptly forgotten since the errant bullet grazed the side of a nearby hill, laying bare a surface vein or lode of rich gold deposits. Since this same story has shown up on at least four separate occasions in other Western states with names and places changed, its authenticity is certainly open to question. In still another version the hunting episode is credited to a pioneer named Harrison.

Some other accounts have Higginbottom making the discovery, but by more conventional means, while a few fail to mention him at all, or merely identify him as an early trapper and resident of South Park. At any rate, the Phillips Lode, a tremendously rich producer, became the mainstay of the town's economic life and a population of about one thousand eventually formed the nucleus which became a new town. As Laurette grew and prospered, more and more of the "Pikes Peakers" gravitated into South Park until a peak population of five thousand souls was reported to have settled there. Considering the size of this valley, the latter statistic is certainly open to question. For the entire district, including Montgomery and Mosquito, it may have been realistic.

All too frequently the census taker got carried away with his own importance and counted the same highly migratory people on more than one occasion. This circumstance was not always intentional.

The miners never completely adjusted to calling their town Laurette and from the earliest times insisted on Buckskin Joe. The change was seemingly made official in the early 1860's, when a post office was opened there by Horace and Augusta Tabor. At this time the Tabors were still casting about from camp to camp. The great wealth that later made the name of H. A. W. Tabor synonomous with the Silver Dollar was still a long way off. The Tabors were not newcomers but had arrived in Buckskin Joe early in 1861 from either Oro City or Montgomery—the accounts differ. Having operated a general store in their previous location, the Tabors lost little time in conforming to their previous calling. At this time the Henry Webber family, good friends of Horace and Augusta, also lived at Buckskin Joe. Here young Henry Webber and Maxcy Tabor attended school. The original Tabor store, or a reasonable facsimile thereof, was moved down to Fairplay some years ago and now stands in their restored pioneer village called South Park City.

The way of life in Buckskin Joe differed but little from that in other contemporary mining camps. People from a wide variety of backgrounds gravitated to the town: conspicuous among them were gamblers and others of their fraternity, including fifty women from "all walks of life." A fairly extensive red-light district flourished on the outskirts at one end of the camp. A variety of saloons, billiard halls, three dance halls and a brass band that played on the street corners helped the argonauts to pass their off hours. Two men, named Stansell and Harris, seem to have been responsible for having set up the first stamp mill in the narrow valley. In partnership with a man named Bond, Stansell and Harris also had a bank at Buckskin Joe. About a dozen mills were operating at the peak of the boom. In addition to the more conventional and efficient means of ore extraction, several crude arrastras were also in use. One of these, quite well preserved, may be seen in the edge of the creek just west of the townsite. While there are those in South Park who feel that this particular device dates from the period of Spanish exploration in the 1600's, I feel that its state of generally good preservation would date it more logically with the boom at Buckskin Joe.

During the winter, flights of stairs were cut in the banks of deep snow to assist the residents in entering and leaving their buried cabins. By 1861, there were two hotels, fourteen stores, and a bank building where most transactions were handled in gold dust. A large log building, erected in 1861, became the first courthouse in Park County and was distinguished by its huge stone fireplace and chimney. Soon thereafter, this structure became the seat of Park County. As the town grew, a terminal stagecoach station was built at Buckskin Joe and the Dan McLaughlin Stage Line carried passengers, freight, and gold to Denver. The student of history may recall an 1863 invasion by the Confederate guerrilla Reynolds gang which sought Colorado gold to further the Rebel cause. Loaded with gold from the Phillips Lode, the Buckskin coach was robbed at McLaughlin's station just east of Fairplay. Since the raid failed when the Rebels were scattered by a crossfire of pursuing posses, many legends have grown up around the $40,000 in gold the gang is alleged to have buried high in Handcart Gulch. Quantities of spurious maps now exist to guide the gullible who want to dig up a fortune from old Buckskin Joe.

No accounting of the early life at Buckskin Joe would be complete without at least a superficial retelling of the story of Silver Heels, a "dance hall girl" who was easy on the eyes and of easier virtue. So many versions of this story have been bandied about that truth, again, will probably never be extracted from fiction. An opera which attempted the story moved the locale from Buckskin Joe to Central City.

In two other versions the Silver Heels family name was given as Keller and as Josie Dillon, respectively. Actually, her identification was never established.

Most versions, however, agree on the following aspects of the story. First of all, the name Silver Heels was derived from her preference for wearing silver-heeled slippers when she plied her trade as an entertainer in the dance halls. Having a pleasant, cheery, personality, the girl soon became a great favorite among the miners.

Prior to the introduction of widespread public health vaccination programs, smallpox regularly took a frightening toll of human life in the mountain mining camps. These epidemics are easily documented by the prevalence of headstones for small children found in overgrown ghost town cemeteries where large numbers died in the same year. Buckskin Joe was a victim of one such epidemic.

Some say that Spanish herders from the San Luis Valley brought the disease into the camp with their herds of sheep, driven up for sale to the miners in the spring of 1861. Large numbers of the Buckskin residents were affected and flat on their backs. Mining nearly came to a standstill and business houses generally closed their doors. In one story it has been reported that only two nurses from Denver heeded the tragic cry for assistance. One of the first to die was Silver Heels' lover. Since hospitals in this era were little more than pesthouses, it is probably fortunate that no such institution was ever established at Buckskin Joe. The afflicted miners had no choice except to ride out the storm in their cabins.

Silver Heels, temporarily out of a job since the dance halls were closed, rose superbly to the challenge in the finest tradition of a slightly tarnished Florence Nightingale. For months on end she tirelessly nursed both miners and their families. She washed their clothing, cooked their meals and tidied up their cabins. This deliberate exposure through such a massive frontal attack once more proved the futility of defying the law of averages. Silver Heels, too, became a victim of smallpox. Following her recovery, a pockmarked complexion ruled out the possibility of a return to her former profession.

To show their gratitude for all she had done, the miners took up a collection which amounted to about four thousand dollars. Senator Edward O. Wolcott, when he heard about it, added another thousand of his own. Silver Heels, however, could not be found. In the best tradition of the theater, she took her few possessions and quietly left the camp for parts unknown. Not even a forwarding address was left behind.

In subsequent years there were periodic reports of a heavily veiled woman who appeared from time to time in the cemetery, placing flowers on the graves of the 1,861 smallpox victims. Sentimentalists chose to believe the veil hid smallpox scars and that these were nostalgic visits by Silver Heels. Today, one of the nearby mountains behind Alma bears the name of Mount Silverheels.

Late in 1865 the rich lodes began to show signs of exhaustion. Huge granite walls were found on all sides of the deposits and for a time tragedy was forestalled by operating the mines as stone quarries. By late 1866 the town was empty and the county seat was moved to Fairplay that year. One source makes the statement that Buckskin Joe was emptied in a single day and a night. Statements of this sort make superb copy but are hardly likely.

Visiting Buckskin Joe involves a very short and quite pleasant drive on a well maintained dirt road. From Fairplay, drive northwest on State Highway 9 to Alma. Near the center of town, turn west or left off the pavement onto the dirt road that follows Buckskin Gulch and drive two miles. Since so few authentic landmarks remain I would suggest that you refer to the photographs accompanying this chapter and merely drive until the peaks line up in proper sequence above the valley. As you approach the townsite a smaller dirt road leads off to the right into the trees and terminates at the cemetery. When last seen there was a "cemetery" sign at the fork. The actual location of the town was in the meadow to the right of the main road and about fifty yards beyond the road to the cemetery. Nearby is a road leading off to the left and ending at an old mine, possibly the Phillips. Along this road, on the right side is a badly dilapidated building which was pointed out to me as being the old Silver Heels Dance Hall. This structure is not visible from the main road. Although I feel that both these latter identifications are open to question, they were made by a person with long residence tenure in the district. The arrastra is on the left side of the main road, about a mile beyond the townsite.

Buckskin Joe was one of the earliest "Pikes Peak" boom towns to mushroom into existence in the early sixties as hordes of prospectors explored the hills in ever-expanding waves. Gold was the object of their search, and when the rich lodes were exhausted they moved on, leaving little behind to mark their brief stay.*

---

* In this same general area, see also Alma, Fairplay, Puma City, Quartzville, Montgomery, Leavick, and Sacramento.

Buckskin Joe, as it was photographed by George Wakely in the 1860's

The site of Buckskin Joe a century later

7.

CAMP BIRD

BY SOME HISTORICAL ALCHEMY of fate, the territory around the Camp Bird Mine was rather thoroughly explored during the late 1870's, but the greatest discovery of all was overlooked until 1895. George Barber and Bill Weston located the Una and Gertrude, two good silver claims, a full two decades prior to the gold discoveries by Andy Richardson and Tom Walsh. Weston and Barber sold their mines to the Reed brothers, of Ouray, in 1880. That next year, the Reeds resold both properties for fifty thousand dollars. Although the claims were good, the upper reaches of Canyon Creek had such a formidable reputation for snowslides that most prospectors shied away from the area. After the silver crash of 1893, the region declined on its own. Neither the Gertrude nor the Una was worth working under the circumstances.

Then, in 1895, Andrew Richardson, a scout for Thomas F. Walsh, uncovered the Camp Bird Lode. In another version, Walsh himself explored the old Gertrude property and made the discovery unaided. Most accounts, however, favor the Richardson location story. In any event, Walsh bought up the old claims for twenty thousand dollars. By 1900 he had spent close to a half million dollars both in buying up other nearby tracts as they came onto the market and in making improvements upon the properties. As a result of the silver crash, the price was down. Few people other than Walsh and Richardson suspected the presence of gold in the Imogene Basin. Incidentally, both this basin and the high Imogene Pass that went over to the Tomboy and Telluride were named for Richardson's wife. The Camp Bird name came from the thieving Canada jays that allegedly pilfered Tom Walsh's lunch one day while he was prospecting.

Walsh was a native of Ireland. He migrated to this country at the age of nineteen and worked as a carpenter. Near Golden he helped to build the Colordo Central Railroad, working as a member of a construction gang. At heart he was a frustrated prospector. During his career he mined at Del Norte, at Deadwood, South Dakota, in Central City, at Rico, and he also took part in the great silver rush to Leadville. For a time, principally after 1896, he operated a smelter at Silverton. He first entered the Imogene Basin in 1895.

After buying up the neighboring claims, Walsh first re-worked the old dumps. When he dug into the Camp Bird, his first samples ran $3,000 to the ton in gold. Over the years, the Camp Bird placed among the top three gold mines in Colorado. It produced from $3,000,000 to $4,000,000 annually during its peak years. Total production figures that have been given out place the Camp Bird's overall production at between $30,000,000 and $50,000,000.

At the head of Canyon Creek, but below the Imogene Basin, a settlement grew up and assumed the name of Camp Bird. All things considered, the town covered about nine hundred acres. There were many small white frame homes with gabled green roofs. A fine little school was built and used well into the present century. The post office was served from Ouray, six miles down Canyon Creek. After a very brief period, a general store also went into business at the site. By far the largest structure in town was the huge red mill with a sloping roof to prevent having to lift the ores. Packtrains and ore wagons plied their way up and down the narrow shelf road between Ouray and Camp Bird. In winter, horse-drawn freight sleds took over the hauling of supplies and ores.

Two or three miles above the town, at the end of an aerial tram, was the actual mine itself. One story tells us that there was a second red mill up there by the mine. To shelter the three hundred or so men who labored in the deep shafts, a huge three-storied boardinghouse was built. In his superbly written book, *One Man's West,* David Lavender gives a vivid and fascinating firsthand account of life in the Camp Bird boardinghouse. Despite the precarious location, it had electric lights, steam heat, modern plumbing, marble-topped lavatories, and a reading room. In one room, a highly individualized general store was run. In winter, the men tunneled in and out of their quarters and to and from the mine proper. Later, this boardinghouse burned and a new one, equally ornate, replaced it. It even had hot showers. Unfortunately, the second one was nearly destroyed by a snowslide. As the crow flies, the Tomboy Mine was only five to six miles away from the Camp Bird. Both properties were linked by under-the-range tunnels.

By 1902, Walsh had personally taken out something in the neighborhood of $2,500,000. That same year he sold out to a British syndicate, called the Camp Bird, Ltd., for $5,200,000. By 1902 he was already a millionaire. His daughter, Evalyn Walsh McLean, acquired the fabulous Hope Diamond and most of the ill fortunes that are alleged to have accompanied it. In better times, she became the leading social hostess in our nation's capital while Warren Gamaliel Harding was living at 1600 Pennsylvania Avenue.

Meanwhile, back at Camp Bird, life went on after a fashion. The nearly vertical walls of Canyon Creek had made this one of the most dangerous spots in Colorado. Over the years, many deaths have resulted from snowslides. Most of the slides run on the same courses, year after year, and are known. Many have even been named. Among these the Water Hole has been consistently regarded as one of the most treacherous. When it ran in 1909, four men and sixteen horses were killed. Another time it roared down onto the road to Camp Bird and snuffed out the lives of five men and twenty-three horses. Most frequently, the slides run in the spring after warm weather has promoted a certain amount of melting and shifting of the great masses of snow and ice on the peaks above. Generally the drivers cut new trails over the tops of the slides and transportation went on. Hardly a winter has passed without mishaps of some sort on this vital but dangerous road.

When costs rose in 1916, the Camp Bird closed down for a while. After reopening, it declined again during the great depression of the 1930's. In a search for paper profits, President Franklin D. Roosevelt boosted the price of gold to thirty-five dollars an ounce. With this shot in the arm, operations were resumed once more and have been pursued, with varying intensities, ever since.

Your tour to Camp Bird begins inevitably at Ouray. Near the south edge of town, U.S. 550, the Million Dollar Highway, begins its switchbacked climb out of the amphitheater. Barely beyond the town, a dirt road branches off to the right. This is State Highway 361. Two forks, barely fifty yards or so apart, confront you almost at once. At the first, go right and cross the bridge over the Uncompahgre River. At the second you should turn left. The right turn here, incidentally, goes into Box Canyon, an area well worth seeing if time permits. As your car grinds its way upward, visualize, if you can, the pioneer drivers and stagecoach passengers desperately clinging to a swaying and creaking wagon. Covered with dust, they gazed vertically downward into the awesome depths of the canyon. Six miles later, you will arrive at Camp Bird, situated slightly to your left where the vertical walls widen out into a circular basin. Here, in sight of the town, another road forks off to the right and goes on up to Mount Sneffels and Yankee Boy Basin.

From Camp Bird, permission must be secured if you want

to go on for the last two miles to the site of the original mine. On this last stretch, a Jeep or a horse or a pair of sturdy hiking boots is required. Since people often behave unpredictably and because liability laws are written as they are, the management has been understandably reluctant to permit access to the Imogene Basin. Nevertheless, this is a magnificent area, a fine place to come and enjoy the unmatched scenic beauty and historical significance of a bygone era.*

---

* In this same general area, see also Dallas City, Ouray, and Silverton.

In 1912 George Beam photographed Camp Bird and its reduction mill

   Vastly changed but still operating, the Camp Bird is an interesting place

8.

CAMP FRANCES

FOR AN ENGLISH TEACHER, life at Camp Frances would have been frustrating indeed for this was a community of a rather confused gender. In researching the chapter, I found nearly as many references to "Camp Francis" as there were references to "Camp Frances." I shall use the latter form since it seems to predominate, but we will probably never be sure whether the namesake of the town was masculine or feminine. However, one story has it that the community was named for the youngest daughter of William P. Daniels, founder of the town and president of the Ni-Wot Mining Company.

Camp Frances was started in the early 1890's and was operated by a syndicate that developed a series of well-paying mining properties in the vicinity. The Big 5 Mines Company employed about one hundred men and had control of some eight hundred acres of land. Under this single management, such mines as the Adit, Ni-Wot, Columbia, and the big Dew Drop at the head of the gulch, were operated. All of their combined ores came down to the town by way of the Adit Tunnel. Processing was carried on in the huge Dew Drop Milling Company plant or the even larger Big 5 Mill on the side of the gulch below the town. From the stream bed, the huge mill extended for some distance up the hill. The Big 5 powerhouse, with its huge black smokestack, stood nearby. Beside it there was a stone powder house, a portion of which still stands. Just up the hill, almost in the edge of the trees, was the red-pointed mining office building with a huge Arabic numeral "5" painted on the outside wall.

A close friend of mine recently excavated a spot near the door of this building and recovered quite a number of well preserved and rather attractive crucibles.

Throughout most of the 1890's there were about two hundred people in residence here. Most of them were employed at the Big 5 or Dew Drop mills. Before long it had a post office and a few business structures. The *Colorado and Southern Railroad Guide* for 1901-2 lists the T. J. Cox General Merchandise Store at Camp Frances. Before the turn of the century about fifty cabins had been built there. Despite the nearness of Ward and its excellent educational facility, Camp Frances decided to have its own school.

At the head of the gulch, near the Dew Drop Mine, the Colorado and Northwestern Railway built a station house. This line is more frequently remembered as the Switzerland Trail. On this particular branch, the tracks ended at Ward. In winter the train crews were always hard pressed to keep the tracks clear of snow all the way to Ward. After each storm, workmen shoveled out the snow-filled cuts. On April 24, 1901, a tragedy occurred. A double hookup was pulling a string of cars up the valley toward Camp Frances. As they gained altitude, the snows grew deeper until they were confronted with huge drifts blocking their track. Several times the engineer backed off and bucked into the big piles of snow. When they seemingly could go no farther, the coaches were uncoupled and left on the track. Both engines now went on ahead, bucking the drifts.

Some doubt exists about what happened next. Whether the snowslide started accidentally or whether it was precipitated by the concussion and noise from the two locomotives is uncertain. In any event a slide was started which carried both engines—and the men on them—down the gulch. Two firemen, the brakeman, and the conductor were killed. Several others were injured in the fall but recovered to tell the tale.

The location of Camp Frances is fourteen miles west and

three miles north of Boulder. From the other direction it is just a mile south of Ward. Several dilapidated cabins and a greater number of foundations still mark the site. On down the hill toward the stream are the mill foundations and a stone wall from the powder house. Slightly apart and up the hill is the Big 5 office building. Across the gully from the remaining cabins is an old bathtub, standing alone on the barren hillside. An open pipe protrudes from the earth nearby and keeps this fixture filled with cold running water. Surely nobody in Camp Frances was enough of an exhibitionist to have used this as a very public community bath; but what else could it have been? A watering trough, perhaps?

To see what remains of Camp Frances drive southwest out of Ward on State Highway 160, a fine paved thoroughfare that is known locally as the "peak to peak highway." At a point about one mile out of Ward, look for a rather large gravel pile on the left side of the road which now blocks the old trail down the side of the hill into the valley containing Camp Frances. Although there is one spot a bit farther on where it is possible to put a Jeep down over the bank, it is smarter to park by the gravel and walk from there.

Just follow the valley down until you see the scar that was once the old trail. It winds down past the bathtub on your left, the cabins to your right, and on down over the bank to the mills by the stream. Going back out, the distance to the highway is less than a mile but the grades look steeper than when you came down. At this altitude, several stops to rest and catch your breath will make your trip to Camp Frances a more pleasant one.*

---

* In this same general area, see also Eldora, Salina, and Tungsten.

Here, at the lower end of Camp Frances, we see a Colorado and
Northwestern train and some of the Big 5 mine buildings.

Just the old grade of the railroad, the large mine dump, and the Big 5 office
building serve as points of comparison with the above photograph.

9.

COMO

LIFE AT COMO began during the summer of 1879 when it became the newest in a series of end-of-the-tracks tent cities, put up to shelter construction crews that were busily laying tracks for the Denver, South Park and Pacific Railway across South Park. This was the era of the great silver rush to Leadville. Before the railroad was completed, migrants from Denver rode the trains to Como, then transferred to stagecoaches for the ride across South Park and over Mosquito Pass to the silver bonanza. Traffic headed for Leadville also included heavily loaded packtrains, big freight wagons, and people with packs on their backs. At one time Como was piled so high with provisions and freight that shipments had to be stopped until the town could be cleared. The population is said to have risen to six thousand during that first summer. This total was swelled somewhat when the last remaining residents from the old gold-mining town of Hamilton also moved down into Como.

This original Como was actually down in the meadow at the later site of King Park. When the railroad built a station three miles away in 1879, the people moved there and the town that grew up around this new facility became the present Como. Beginning in 1880, the original tent city site became King Park or King City. George W. Lechner laid out the second town after he had discovered a rich vein of lignite coal nearby. The first Lechner coal discovery dates back to 1871. Taken as a whole, the vein averaged from seven to ten feet thick. For several months he hauled loads

of coal to Fairplay where it brought ten dollars per ton.
Later, he sold his mine to the railroad. Several coal properties were found within the radius of a few miles. In addition, there were gold mines to the west. It will be recalled
that the early gold camps of Tarryall and Hamilton were
only a mile or two west of the present town. Off in this
same direction, the unmistakable signs of dredging may
still be seen with tremendous elongated ridges following the
riverbed.

As business from the railroad grew, so did Como. Daily
trains, some of them four-engined freights, huffed their way
up over the eighty-eight miles from Denver. The town became known as a division point, with one branch carrying
trains over Boreas Pass to Breckenridge while the other
went to Gunnison by way of the Alpine Tunnel. A lunch-
room was built and operated by the railroad at Como. By
far the most prominent feature among the railroad facilities
here was a huge roundhouse, built with partly frame and
partly masonry construction. Within a few years, between
fifty and one hundred men were employed in this facility.
To assure smooth operation, repair shops were also located at
Como.

For many years, starting in April of 1879, the South Park
Coal Company, which also operated the King Mines, furnished the railroad with a ready supply of fuel. Their King
Coal Mine was located about a mile and a half north of the
railroad station. As with most coal mines, underground
gases caused explosions, sometimes with fatal results. Worst
of all was an explosion in the King Coal that snuffed out
the lives of sixteen miners. The peak year for coal production was 1884.

Quite apart from the initial rush that brought thousands to
live and work at Como, the average population hovered
around five hundred to six hundred people. Most of them
were of Italian extraction. In fact, their nostalgia for the
northern Italian region around Lake Como resulted in the

selection of the town's name. Labor troubles once erupted late in 1879 when Chinese miners were brought in from Fairplay. Infuriated, the Italians banded together, girded their loins for battle, and ran the Chinese out of town. Having been deprived of a good fight, they then proceeded to beat up the man who had brought the celestials to Como.

Over the years four hotels flourished at Como. They were the Kelly Hotel, the Como House, the Gilman Hotel and the Montag House. During the early days three newspapers were published at Como, through the simple expedient of a name change. First came the *Como Headlight*, a weekly that became a permanent fixture between 1883 and 1904. Later, its name was changed to the *Record*. Beginning in 1879, Como also had a school. It continued to operate until 1948. Children from the town are now bussed to Fairplay. Three churches, a Methodist, a Community, and a Catholic, also served the residents.

Streetlights, illuminated with gasoline-fired lamps, were used after 1900. No electricity reached Como until the REA extended lines into the town in 1963. Among the commercial enterprises serving Como were several saloons and gambling houses, many restaurants, and a number of meat markets and grocery stores. Como's heyday extended through the 1880's and 1890's. At one point the residents underwent delusions of grandeur and the name was kited to Como City, but it failed to catch on and was soon dropped. Several professions were represented among the residents of Como. There was a resident physician, a dentist, several attorneys, and one busy and prosperous undertaker. The cemetery was just beyond the town, on a windswept hillside above the road to Boreas Pass.

For many years Como had an extensive business district. There were several clothing stores, candy shops, a tobacconist, at least one drugstore, a lumber yard, two Chinese laundries, a dairy, some barbershops that offered fifteen-cent haircuts, a dry-goods store and a couple of stables. Many of these succeeded abundantly until after the turn of the cen-

Looking across South Park. The town of Como reposes in the foreground while a narrow-gauge train of the D.S.P. & P. passes in the middle distance.

From the same vantage point, many of Como's original structures are visible

tury. Then in 1909 a series of disastrous events began, forecasting the decline of Como.

First came a fire that destroyed the railroad shops. Although some parts were saved, many jobs were eliminated and the fire-damaged sections were not replaced. When the railroad abandoned all attempts to maintain their winter schedule through the Alpine Tunnel in the fall of 1910, it cut the population of Como by nearly two thirds as additional jobs were eliminated. Shortly after that the roundhouse was closed. In the course of 1911, the rest of the railroad shops were also closed. No less of a contribution to the decline of Como was a fire in the roundhouse during 1935, started by sparks from the stack of a locomotive. Once again the damaged part was not replaced. Two years later, in April of 1937, the Denver, South Park and Pacific, which by now through a series of reorganizations was the Colorado and Southern, abandoned its line across the entire high alpine park. With support from the railroad withdrawn, the exodus began in earnest.

To see Como today, drive southwest out of Denver on U.S. 285 across beautiful Kenosha Pass to South Park. A few miles past Jefferson, you will see a black and white sign pointing to Como, barely a mile north of the paved highway. U.S. 285 may be followed with equal facility to South Park from other parts of the state.

Fortunately, Como has been spared the final indignity of becoming a ghost town. Here, at an altitude of 9,796 feet above sea level, this alpine-ringed community now has a second lease on life. Gradually activities other than mining and railroading have taken over. Many of the fine, tight little houses have now become pretty summer homes. The old cemetery, now enveloped in sun-dappled groves of green and yellow quaking aspens, affords a strikingly beautiful final resting place for the pioneers who lived the history of Como.*

---

* In this same general area, see also Boreas, Dyersville, King City, Tarryall, and Hamilton.

10.

CRESTED BUTTE

FOR SEVERAL YEARS prior to the existence of Crested Butte, mineral prospecting forays had been carried out in the immediate vicinity. A few paying placers had been worked from time to time in nearby valleys. In the spring of 1879, the settlement that was to become Crested Butte was laid out by Howard Smith, who brought in the first sawmill. His chosen location was the broad, open valley at the confluence of Slate and Coal creeks. Although hard metal production was the primary attraction, large coal deposits were also found in this early period.

By the end of the year, population figures had grown to encompass a total of almost 250 people. During 1880, the settlement expanded and included some fifty houses and a number of tents which sheltered around two thousand souls by the end of the year. Most Crested Butte residents were of Austrian, Italian, and German extraction, people who had come to the valley directly from their native Europe. Since we humans characteristically transfer elements from our former culture to any new environment, these people recreated familiar conditions in their new home. Being strangers in a new country, they sought happiness and security by sharing their problems and by raising their families in an Old World atmosphere.

To a degree Crested Butte became a supply center for other mining endeavors in the vicinity. Prospectors, experienced miners and their supplies, passed through here on the way to other nearby camps. A total of thirty-three businesses, including three saloons and at least that many livery stables, flourished to cater to the needs of incoming migrants who sought the gold, silver, iron, zinc, and copper lodes. Formal incorporation became a reality in 1881.

Despite the fact that it was almost completely surrounded by mountains, the altitude of Crested Butte was still 8,888 feet above sea level. Inevitably, this meant long and difficult winters. For about six months of the year, heavy snows still blanket the townsite. Residents, then as now, use skis and snowshoes. Old records are replete with stories about going cross-country over the fence tops. Even the mail was carried on skis.

In the early days many Crested Butte residents found it necessary to get out at night and push the snow off their roofs to keep their houses from buckling. As time passed, the later structures were built with sharply pitched roofs, often surfaced with metal, so that deep winter snows might slide off without crushing the structures. Even the clotheslines were strung considerably higher than average, often being attached to pulleys from second-floor porches out to poles in the yard that might be as much as twenty feet tall. Because of the snow depth, a housewife might not be able to get into her backyard for months at a time.

Since indoor plumbing was still far off in the future, the more necessary sanitary facilities at the Butte were constructed with two stories. In summer, the lower levels were used. During winter's icy blasts, people snowshoed out to the second story. Regrettably, no examples of these most original innovations still exist.

Miners who spent the winter in the valley carried dynamite sticks wrapped around their legs under their trousers. This kept the explosives from freezing while the man was on his way to work. One additional condition of life justifies this practice. When a miner had to cross a potential snowslide area, a few sticks could be placed on a long pole for detonation. The resulting concussion was sure to loosen the snow, causing the slide to run and thereby avoiding the avalanche.

To provide better access to the district, men from Aspen, Ashcroft, and Crested Butte hacked out a difficult wagon road over Pearl Pass in 1882. In this way they could facilitate the movement of equipment and supplies from the end of the railroad at Crested Butte to the Aspen district across the range. Prior to that time most supplies were packed in on the backs of burros. In this town, as in so many mining camps, a herd in excess of two hundred of these animals could be seen standing in the street, waiting to be loaded with supplies for the nearby mines. Such sights were extremely common in the days when Crested Butte was the commercial center for this entire region. On mules and in wagons, supplies were carried up to the Esta Mine at Pittsburg, to the Painter Boy and Silver Jewel in Washington Gulch, to the Silver Knight at Gothic, and to the tremendous Forest Queen at Ruby-Irwin.

Three hostelries served the needs of the transients. These were the Forest Queen, the Crested Butte House, and Mrs. Sanger's Hotel. Even with their combined facilities, there were never enough rooms to accommodate the many outsiders in addition to the regular people of the town. By February of 1882, the Elk Mountain Hotel had been completed and was widely advertised as being the best in the country. Notable among its claims to fame were an indoor system of hot and cold running water, three indoor "water closets" and three bathtubs. The latter accommodations were made possible by a pressurized water system which had to be hand pumped by the kitchen help.

The fourth estate arrived in town very early in the game. In 1880 the first of two newspapers, the *Crested Butte Republican,* began publication. A second paper, the *Elk Mountain Pilot,* started life elsewhere. It was conceived at Rosita, in Custer County, during the summer of 1879. J. E. Phillips was the publisher. When he heard that George and Harry

Cornwall had reserved a free lot to be given to the first newspaper at their new town of Ruby-Irwin, Phillips decided to move. Since town lots at that location were bringing anywhere from $100 to $5,000, he had little to lose.

His paper was a "first" and continued to be published until it was discovered by some presumptuous clerk that the townsite was actually seven miles inside the Ute Reservation. Under these conditions there could be no legal rights or titles to any of the town lots. Although Ruby-Irwin went right along its merry way, Phillips grew apprehensive and began casting about for a wider, deeper, and safer rut.

Crested Butte, only a few miles to the south, seemed to be a growing town—and legal, too. Its central location had the advantage of being able to provide circulation for his paper to a variety of the surrounding camps. Prospects were further improved by the fact that rail connections had already reached the camp. In the face of all of these compelling reasons, the editor decided to pack up his type and presses for one more move. On May 2, 1884, the *Pilot* was moved by bobsled over the entire distance of eight miles and Crested Butte found itself with two newspapers.

During 1883, Crested Butte really boomed. In October the city hall was completed. That same year saw their school buildings and a church added to the mushrooming village. On December 7, 1881, Crested Butte watched breathlessly as the first hand-cranked telephone was installed in their town. After a very brief period, several more "talkies" were in service there to speed up communication to the nearby mining camps.

Gaslights fascinated everybody when they were first installed. Some residents admit setting their alarm clocks so they could get up at night, turn on the light, and just sit there watching it burn. At first, the local plant suspended operations after 10:00 P.M. From then until 5:00 A.M., the consumers were forced to use candles or kerosene lamps.

When the community water system was completed in 1883, everyone rested more easily.

Nearly all of the larger mining camps set up elaborate protection organizations against the threat of fire. The Crested Butte Hose Company No. 1 consisted of several nimbled-footed men who boasted that they never gave a fire an even break. They once chalked up a record of thirty-five seconds for the regulation contest. On July 4, 1901, an eleven-man team from Crested Butte defeated a team from Gunnison by a single second. Although the team of "Fire Laddies" from the Butte was made up of men who could individually sprint a hundred yards in ten seconds the competition was frequently so close that seconds and even fractions of seconds became all-important.

The years 1882 and 1883 were the town's best. Although gold and silver production began to drop off, the void was more than filled by stock raising and by a coal-mining company which began developing coal mines close to the town. Properties in the valley produced not only a high grade of bituminous, but had the only large source of anthracite west of the Pennsylvania fields. From this series of mines, coal was shipped to the steel mills of the Colorado Fuel & Iron Company in Pueblo. Just outside the town limits of Crested Butte, a battery of fifty ovens was put into operation to burn the coke needed in the production of steel.

Coal became the greatest economic strength of the town. Well within the corporate limits, there were several producing mines. Equally promising outcroppings existed in the surrounding region and along the hillsides above Anthracite Creek. Among the best-known mines were the C. F. & I., the Peanut, and the Bulkley.

Without a doubt the worst single catastrophe in the region's history was the gas explosion in a mine up Coal Creek during February of 1884. Shortly after the morning work crew had entered its shaft, an explosion snuffed out the lives of fifty-nine men. Only eleven of the workers who were in the mine at the time managed to escape. Since most miners in most camps of this period were young and just starting out in life, only six of those who were killed were married. Most were Civil War veterans. The mine in which the disaster occurred had a shaft which penetrated the hill to a depth of 1,300 feet.

When they had been recovered, more than half of the bodies were buried in a special, isolated plot in the Gunnison cemetery. When faced by the need to transport the remains to their final resting places, a path was cleared through six feet of snow on the flats between Crested Butte and Gunnison. In one case, a mother attempted to keep the bodies of her two sons by packing snow around their caskets. Her desire to preserve them was prompted by several attempts to get word to her husband who was mining in the White River country near Meeker. For about a month she sent frantic messages. When her husband could not be found, she took the bodies East for burial. Quite apart from the tragedy, mining at Crested Butte went on. The town was booming then and it continued to do so for many years.

The evolution of transportation here followed along in the usual pattern. Use of burro packtrains, mentioned earlier, constituted the crude beginnings. At a later time, the Sanderson Stage Line came into the valley and even made an overnight stop at Crested Butte. In 1882, the Gunnison and Crested Butte branch of the Denver and Rio Grande Railway was extended twenty-seven miles into the town. Winter conditions were hardly conducive to a routine kind of operation. In the cold months of 1888, trains were snowbound in Slate Cut for seventeen days. Sometimes they were able to get through by using an engine with a rotary plow in the lead, followed by a wedge plow on the front of the regular passenger train.

During February of 1900, a snowslide in Slate Creek Canyon caught the noon train at a point about four miles below the town. Several cars were nearly reduced to matchsticks and mail delivery was delayed for several hours. Railroad operations on this run were interrupted with methodical frequency by accidents of this type during most winter seasons.

After enduring these conditions for what must have been a truly frustrating sequence of winters, the good people of Crested Butte held a mass meeting on February 22, 1909. For the previous seventeen-day period, no trains had reached their town. A resolution was drawn up condemning the Rio Grande Railway for failing to cope with the long blockade of snow which had cut them off from the outside world.

In this document the citizens not only condemned the railroad—they pledged themselves to a work program designed to open the road. Footing the bill became the forte of the Bank of Crested Butte which offered a sum of one thousand dollars upon completion of the work. The offer was conditional upon the company's willingness to give the assistance of its local crews and engines without charge.

At the turn of the century, the Colorado Fuel & Iron Company was shipping almost 1,200 carloads of coal and coke from Crested Butte each month. On many of these runs, the narrow-gauge Denver & Rio Grande freight lines had passenger coaches attached to serve travelers commuting to the several nearby towns. Earlier, the Denver, South Park & Pacific had tried to reach Crested Butte ahead of the Rio Grande by building through South Park, across the Arkansas Valley to Buena Vista before going through the mountains at the Alpine Tunnel. Having encountered 1,806 feet of loose material instead of the expected granite, a million feet of California redwood timbering was used to reinforce this section. In the chapter which deals with Alpine, this story is recounted in more detail. Tragically, it lost the race to Gunnison and Crested Butte by a year.

At some point in its history, almost every mining town was burned out totally or in part. Prior to 1890, Crested Butte had only the discomforts of the usual epidemics to worry about. At various times the town was swept by pneumonia, smallpox, scarlet fever, and diphtheria. Due to a lack of community funds, regular fire hydrants were not installed until 1889-90. Here it was a case of too little and too late. In any case, the hoped-for protection was not available when the first big fire broke out on the night of January 25, 1890.

A family, living in the second story of the Edwards building, had gone away. Their children were left behind with an overheated stove. Although the children were saved, a total of sixteen buildings went up in flames before the fire ended its rampage. Most homes in Crested Butte were built close together. Wet blankets were hastily applied to the tinder-dry roofs and nailed up against the exposed walls to curb the flames.

Curiously, the hydrant system was completed in the spring, just as many of the burned buildings were being replaced. Eventually, three fire companies were organized. Being volunteer groups, they kept pace with the times and often appeared in public demonstrations. Three years later, almost to the day, another fire was discovered. The date was January 8, 1893, and temperatures had dropped to forty degrees below zero. As fires go, this one was about par for the course but it did not destroy the town.

In this, as in so many mining camps, disease and fire were not the only sources of peril. For about a week prior to June 12, 1899, swollen streams threatened to spill over their levies on the edge of town. The banks of the creek along the western edge of Crested Butte gave way. Before the people realized what had happened, nearly the whole town was swept by water and had been reduced to a state of chaos.

In the business district, the first store to be flooded was the large and prosperous Colorado Supply Company. It was completely swamped, as were several other business houses. Down at the end of the block, the Glick Brothers store suffered a similar fate and was left virtually standing in a lake.

Across the street, the Axtell Lumber Company caught its share of the flood when the crest came pouring in against the post office next door.

Early that evening, those residents who lived along First Street, the thoroughfare nearest to the creek, moved out with everything they could carry. Shortly after dark, several onlookers noticed that a tremendous pile of driftwood had become lodged on the First Street bridge. To prevent loss of the bridge from the growing accumulation, dynamite was used to dislodge the mess. In the meantime several men had been detailed to watch and to work along the bank in an effort to contain the water and avoid any further spreading. All odds, however, were against them that night.

When the bank gave way, the surging torrent literally poured out of the breaks. Although relays of men worked in the water until the wee hours of the morning, it was touch and go at best. They ripped out culverts and bridges to assure the greatest possible flow of water, thereby preventing any further flooding of nearby homes.

When morning came, the streets everywhere presented a scene of wreckage. In the flooded business section, where water had slopped over from the swollen creek, sidewalks had to be elevated several feet above street level so that customers could walk "high and dry." Despite this, the regular street crossings everywhere were flooded. Even after the water had receded, there was deep mud to be contended with over much of the town.

At four o'clock on the morning of May 9, 1901, flames broke out from an overheated stove in the back room of Bruces' Saloon. Joining the "hooch emporium" on the west and sharing a common wall, the Colorado Supply Company's big store, now dried out from the flood, covered a space in excess of five thousand square feet. Quickly the fire spread to the roofs of both buildings. Despite efforts of the fire companies to contain the blaze at these points, it was soon a raging inferno. Nearby, Mrs. Lovelace's Notion and Confectionary store was wiped out. The Lovelace family, still asleep inside, had a narrow escape and saved only a few items of clothing, hurriedly grabbed up in their flight.

At this point the hardest fight of the day was made against further encroachments by the flames. A vacant lot allowed room for a determined effort by the fire laddies. Close to the vacant site was Otto Matsekey's jewelry store and beside it stood a large dry-goods house. Despite all efforts to save them, it began to appear that both of these buildings would go.

From then on, things started looking up. Fortunately for all concerned, a slight change of direction in a gentle breeze saved some of the structures and allowed the men to attend to the fire raging on the west side of town. Here it had already spread to the large Schainer Building, then occupied by the owner of a highly combustible hay and grain store. It was not until this structure had been entirely gutted and Young's Confectionary Store, next to it, had been badly damaged, that the flames were finally brought under control.

In the overall picture, the greatest loss was suffered during destruction of the Colorado Supply Company. Just a month earlier, this same store had experienced a nighttime fire which was, fortunately, discovered in time. The blaze was extinguished with only a slight loss. Since oil-saturated gunnysacks were found, there was little doubt as to the fire's origin. Since the second fire had originated in the same building and since oiled sacks were also found in several places to assure success, the overheated stove theory became somewhat suspect. In this as in so many other instances, the loss was only partially covered by insurance. Damage to stocks in this business alone exceeded thirty thousand dollars.

Beyond this, events on that incendiary front lay dormant until February 8, 1963. That night, the mercury dipped to forty degrees below zero and another fire was discovered. Summoned by the town alarm, firemen assembled to combat this latest threat to their town. Tragically, when they attached their hoses to a series of new fire hydrants, it was discovered that the whole system was frozen tight. Failure of the town's water system was nothing new. On December 28, 1939, it was shut down by a particularly bitter freeze, leaving the people dependent on Coal Creek and a few small wells.

In the 1963 fire, an entire block of business buildings tumbled in flames before volunteers brought in explosives and blew up Al Miller's furniture store with 150 pounds of black powder. Although the concussion definitely snuffed out the fire, it also shattered nearly every window in town. Without windows at forty degrees below, some folks playfully changed the town's name from "Crested" to "Frosted" and dropped the *e* from the second name.

So, gradually, activities other than mining have altered the economic base of Crested Butte. Coal mining was reduced to a trickle when the Colorado Fuel & Iron Company shut down its big operation on May 29, 1952. Directly as a result of the mining slump, the Denver & Rio Grande branch line was discontinued. Quite commonly, a town dies for less important causes than these. Miraculously, Crested Butte began to gain in popularity as a winter sports center. Some optimistic people think it is well on the way to becoming a favorite stop for summer tourists as well.

With ski resorts, a major revolution has transpired in what was once on the way to becoming a depressed mining area. Old Crested Butte, with its tin roofs, gingerbread-trimmed homes, and false-fronted business houses, stands in striking contrast to the ornate new lodges with red carpets, plush swimming pools, and vast panoramic picture windows.

By January of 1965, all ideas of becoming a ghost town were forgotten when the population more than doubled in the winter season. During the past winter, about 650 people filled 20 chalets and 5 lodges, not counting weekend people. About a dozen new businesses have started up in the past

few years. In summer, saddle horses and pack animals may
be rented by those who like to ride or fish in the nearby Elk
Mountains and adjacent canyons.

For the visitor who would like to view a town in process
of transition from the old to the new, Crested Butte is simple
to find. Drive to Gunnison on U.S. Highway 50, turning
north at the traffic light in the center of town. From this
point a fine paved road goes all the way through Almont to
Crested Butte, a wonderful spot to relax and unwind from
the tensions imposed by city life.*

---

* In this same general area, see also Crystal City, Marble, and Scofield City.

Rio Grande Archives
An early photograph of Crested Butte when it was still a thriving coal camp

Collection of Robert L. Brown
Crested Butte is now an exciting ski resort

11.

CRESTONE

THIS VERY ACCESSIBLE and beautifully located town experienced not just one but two separate booms. Life at Crestone was further complicated by conflict over ownership of the mines, brought on by arguments over title to one of the original Spanish land grants.

During the 1870's the first settlers began to move into this area while searching for precious metals. In 1879 fairly good prospects were unearthed and a small migration converged upon the lower slopes of the Sangre de Cristo Range. Since people need to have places in which to live, construction of the town began almost at once. Unfortunately, the early hopes for rich mineral returns failed to materialize as the diggings grew deeper and the booming prosperity of Crestone slowed to a grinding halt.

Economic affairs in the town hobbled along on a day-to-day basis until a promising quantity of free-milling gold was found in 1890, bringing on a second boom. During the 1890 prosperity the town was built. The usual variety of saloons, general stores and one hotel soon appeared. A railroad spur which reached the camp from Moffat provided better access and improved transportation facilities for the ores, mining supplies, and for the people. By 1900 the population of Crestone had reached a total of two thousand before the free gold pinched out when deep working was attempted.

One of the other factors affecting the destiny of Crestone dates back in European history. In 1823, King Ferdinand of Spain granted a very large land tract to some of his subjects in the New World. After winning its independence from Spain, Mexico recognized the rights of the family of Don Luis Maria Cabeza de Vaca to the original grant. As first conceived, the land included even the city of Las Vegas, New Mexico. In exchange for this latter region, the family accepted four new ranch sites. One of these consisted of 100,000 acres of prime rangeland in what is now Saguache County. When this whole region changed hands again following our war with Mexico, the United States also recognized the legality of the cessions as constituted.

Trouble developed when gold was found within the grant. Five towns grew up along the twenty-five-mile-long mineral vein which extended from the lower slopes of the Sangre de Cristo Range. Exercising their prerogatives, the owners threw out the miners and took over the rich mines themselves. Since Crestone was situated within the northeastern edge of the Luis Maria Baca Grant, the only alternative was for the community to pack up and move. The town of Liberty, once called Duncan, also got its orders to relocate at this time. Incidentally, to resolve any confusion, the name Vaca became Baca somewhere along the line and, despite the discrepancy in spelling, both names refer to the same family.

On March 21, 1901, W. J. Keim, the badman of Crestone, was placed in jail after building a dam across a high creek, cutting off the water supply of all six hundred of the people who lived in the town. Crestone derived its water supply from the mouth of North Crestone Creek. In November of 1900, Keim built his dam in the creek two miles above the town to secure a supply of ice. The ground near the dam was porous and the water soaked into the earth instead of going over the crest of the dam. As a result, the creek went dry. All residents of Crestone who had no wells were in trouble. Wails of protest from the townspeople fell on deaf ears. Keim defied the entire thirsty community for a total of four long, dry months.

Since laws governing such actions were rather inadequate at the time, the better legal minds of Crestone began investigating loopholes that might offer them some legal recourse. One suggestion that was made advocated prosecuting him for causing the deaths of thousands of fish. As the stream was state property the case was clear and Keim was arrested.

Deputy Game Warden Henry Moss and his deputy district attorney arrived from Denver to prosecute the culprit for the cruel mass murder of great quantities of innocent denizens of the deep in a watery concentration camp. The case was tried before Justice Lawrence at Crestone. A guilty verdict was almost a foregone conclusion. Keim was fined twenty-five dollars and costs and put under two hundred fifty dollars bail. Ten days were allowed for him to tear out the dam.

Keim swore at the judge before leaving the courtroom, and promptly found his bail raised and himself in jail. Residents of Crestone put their shoulders to the wheel and decided to tear out the dam themselves. Moss and his deputy were wined and dined by the grateful people of Crestone. In recognition of their services, both Denver men were made honorary members of the town's board of trade.

The experiences of Walter E. Perkins, of Crestone, read like a panorama of life in the several mining camps located along the rich mineral vein that paralleled the mighty Sangre de Cristo Range. Perkins was the town postmaster from 1900 to 1940. His memories of the area spanned some of the district's greatest years. His first work with the mail service found him in the capacity of postmaster at Liberty, another nearby ghost town. One man still lived at Liberty in 1940. Perkins was at Liberty during the forceful eviction of unhappy miners by U.S. marshals. He remained there until most of the other residents had left the town.

At another time in his career, there was an appointment as postmaster at Duncan, still another name for the same near-extinct ghost camp. John Duncan, originally from Indiana, was the source of the town's name. An extremely hospitable man, Duncan was both the first and the last townsman of that settlement. Any guests in the Duncan home were liberally supplied with hot biscuits, bacon, eggs, and other substantial foods.

John Duncan's most amusing characteristic was his enthusiasm for big words, most of which he used incorrectly. He once told a visitor, "I intend to build an addition on here for the hostility of my guests." When a friend called on Duncan, he noticed a fine new dictionary and inquired if he could borrow it. "Oh, take it," said Duncan, "I've already read it."

Life in the little town of Duncan saw both good and bad times. The killing of several persons, however, shook the townspeople. Once a man named Jim Stuart was killed by a mild-mannered prospector named Charles Thompson. Two women, a Mrs. Boyd and a Mrs. McFadden, were also killed at Duncan but details surrounding their cases seem to be conspicuous by their absence.

Today, Crestone is the only surviving town located along the once-rich mineral belt. A small permanent population swells in the summer and shrinks when deep snows begin to blanket the San Luis Valley. The drive to Crestone is a particularly easy and rather pleasant one over a fine highway. Drive north from Alamosa on Highway 17 or south from Salida on U.S. 285 to Mineral Hot Springs where Highway 17 begins. From either direction, drive to Moffat where, at the south edge of town, the road to Crestone branches west. Although narrow, the grade is good and it's an easy jaunt into the town.

Along the way, you will pass the entrance to the Baca Grant. Several old ghost town sites are found within its boundaries but permission is required before entrance. A short distance farther along will bring you into Crestone, a particularly beautiful location. Behind it, the horizon is dominated by Crestone Peak, 14,291 feet high, Humboldt Peak, and the Crestone Needle. Both the hiker and the photographer will find much to recommend this region.*

---

* In this same general area, see also Bonanza and Turret.

Collection of Francis B. Rizzari
This old photograph of Crestone shows the town at its peak as a mining camp

Collection of Robert L. Brown
Today Crestone still has a small resident population

12.

CRYSTAL CITY

ROUGHLY TEN BUILDINGS still stand in the town that once boasted a population of five hundred in 1880. The town's name was allegedly derived from the consequence of its location on the upper reaches of the Crystal River nestled in the heart of the Elk Mountains. Although there are references to the Crystal River in the early 1880's, it was officially known as Rock Creek until the early 1900's. In its heyday Crystal supported two hotels, a barbershop, general store, saloon, and pool hall. Its residents made up the working force for about seven nearby mines. Crystal had its own post office, plus a very popular and quite exclusive male retreat known as the Crystal Club. Crystal City was formally founded sometime in 1880. During most years the average population at the town still hovered around five hundred. The fourth estate made its presence known with two newspapers, the *Crystal River Current* and the *Silver Lance,* which were published in the town at various times.

The first prospectors entered the Crystal Valley in the 1860's, but development of its mineral resources waited nearly two decades. Curiously, the exploration of this beautiful area did not follow the logical route north from Glenwood Springs and Carbondale. Instead, the first road in, which was hardly more than a trail, came south from Crested Butte through Gothic and across Scofield Pass. This is by far the most difficult means of access and it is still a Jeep road.

When John K. Hallowell, a geologist, published his findings in 1883, he described veins of zinc, iron, galena, and copper sulphides among the hillsides above the river. His report contributed to the small rush that converged on Crystal City. Throughout the years the camp remained primarily a silver-lead-zinc producer. Gold was never a prime factor in its economy.

The winding road to Crystal twists narrowly up the canyon over the old grade of the Kirk and Shaw Stagecoach Road from Marble. It followed the grade for six miles, past Lizard Lake, to the town. Nearby are some of Colorado's most beautiful summits: Sheep Mountain, Hagerman, Mineral, and Crystal peaks, Beam, Treasury, and Whitehouse mountains. In the course of its travels through the valley, the Crystal River crosses three counties. From the point where it is first seen near Carbondale, it lies in Garfield County. Farther up, it flows through Placita and Redstone in Pitkin County. In the high country around Scofield, Crystal City, and Marble, its upper reaches lie in Gunnison County.

On May 17, 1889, the *Denver Illustrated Sentinel* reported that Crystal City lay in the heart of the most heavily mineralized belt ever looked upon by prospectors or developed by miners.

Crystal may be reached by way of McClure Pass, just east of Paonia, or by Highway 133 just south of Glenwood Springs, by way of Redstone and Marble. From Crested Butte, hikers, horseback riders, or those who own Jeeps, will enjoy the trip through Gothic, over Scofield Pass, and then steeply down to Crystal.

Roads leading to and from the camps were hardly more than wide trails twisting around and over the mountains. Being ledge roads, they were subject to frequent rock- and snowslides. Those miners who chose to stay through the winter were snowbound for many weeks at a time.

By 1899 the only businesses listed in the directory were a general merchandise store and one newspaper. At the turn of the century the *Denver Post* maintained a correspondent at Crystal City. In February of 1900 a dispatch was carried out on snowshoes. Crystal was snowbound again. The stage road through the canyon between it and Marble was under from ten to fifty feet of snow. Using snowshoes, the mail carrier, Fred Johnson, had been able to get through only once during the previous week. Supplies would be exhausted within another week, according to the dispatch, unless the road could be opened up. In addition, several of the mines would probably be forced to close down and send the workers outside on snowshoes.

Usually, when a severe storm hit, the residents had little choice except to wait it out. At its conclusion, a force of fifty men took to the drifts to shovel out the road wide enough to allow a train of packhorses to bring in supplies. Sometimes snow tunnels were dug. They usually lasted long enough to bring in supplies from the terminal station at Redstone.

Serving the valley in this and in many other ways was the Crystal River and San Juan Railway. All communications between Crystal City and the mines were carried out on snowshoes. Drifts around the various buildings in camp often reached as high as the eaves. The 1900 storm was regarded as the worst ever to hit the Elk Mountains. Despite heavy suffering, no lives were lost. Few among the people who had lived there took any chances. They knew only too well that weather can change and that warm days bring snowslides roaring down nearby mountainsides.

Crystal City was a rich producer of silver, lead, and zinc until well past the turn of the century. The panic of 1893 killed Crystal City. Although the Lead King property continued a schedule of limited production well into the twentieth century, it was not enough. At the Chicago World's Fair of 1893, ironically the same year the Sherman Silver Purchase Act was repealed, Crystal was represented with a fine display of rich silver ore from the nearby Black Queen Mine. In 1913 its last ores were shipped. Transportation difficulties, as much as anything else, contributed to Crystal's

Collection of Fred and Jo Mazzulla

*In this early picture of Crystal City, the town's main street
is visible in the center background.*

Collection of Robert L. Brown

*An unusually lush growth of trees now precludes an exact match of the above picture.
Note the same mountain above the roof of the powerhouse building
on the Sheep Mountain Tunnel.*

decline. By 1915 the town's population was down to eight. From then on it has had its ups and downs. For example, in 1916 it was back up to seventy-five, with two hotels, a store and billiard hall (why that combination?) in operation.

Getting to Crystal City today is comparatively easy when compared with conditions that were prevalent only a decade ago. State Highway 133 now has been paved nearly all the way from Carbondale to Marble. In recent years the old stage road from Marble to Crystal City has been improved enough to allow it to be used by conventional cars.

Summer residents of Crystal have restored many of the once-empty cabins, making them into fine houses. Nearby, the Outward Bound School brings additional people into the valley. Between June and October, there are still signs of life in this remote but beautifully located hamlet.*

---

* In this same general area, see also Marble, Scofield City and Crested Butte.

13.

CUSTER CITY

WHEN GEORGE ARMSTRONG CUSTER was massacred in eastern Montana in June of 1876, the United States took his memory to heart and American folklore acquired a new hero-martyr. All over the country streets were renamed and statues were dedicated. New communities like Custer, South Dakota, and an infinite number of schools adopted the vastly appealing name of the "Boy General" (actually a lieutenant colonel at the time of his death). Here in Colorado, the legislature, with a remarkable show of restraint, waited nearly a year after his death before vaulting onto the bandwagon.

From November of 1861 until 1877, the Wet Mountain Valley had been the southern portion of Fremont County. Then, on March 9, 1877, political surgery took place among the legislators in Denver, creating the new Custer County from this most handsome 720 square mile piece of real estate. Before this political subdivision took place, the Wet Mountain Valley had enjoyed a most distinguished series of rendezvous with history. It was first occupied by the Ute Indians. In 1806 Lieutenant Zebulon Montgomery Pike led his far-famed expedition across the valley and over the Sangre de Cristo Mountains. Among Colorado's earliest settlers was a group of trappers who moved within Hardscrabble Park in 1843, a circumstance frequently singled out with considerable pride by a later generation of Colorado historians. John W. Gunnison is known to have scouted the Wet Mountain Valley during his ill-fated search for an acceptable railroad route across the Rockies in 1853. Ranchers, the first of a hardy breed, found their way into this area in 1869. It was this land, rich in tradition, that became Custer County.

For the next quarter of a century, things were quiet on the General Custer front, and his memory was allowed to lie dormant. Then, in 1902, it started all over again. Near Querida, well within Custer County, a new town named Custer City was founded. Viewed in retrospect, the whole enterprise seems to have been started on speculation of the most spurious sort. Although two mine shafts were dug, no ore was ever shipped from Custer City. The entire setup was a stock deal and came dangerously close to being a hoax. Nevertheless, a fairly ambitious town plat was laid out and public relations were undertaken to attract people.

A community water system, with three-quarter-inch pipes laid under the ground, was installed. At strategic spots in the meadow, fire hydrants protruded along the streets-to-be. At the east end of town there was a ball diamond for interested parties. The Custer Mining and Realty Company opened an office in town. They were also responsible for the two mines that, hopefully, would justify the town's existence. As names for their mines, the company chose "Toledo" and "First Colorado." As a crowning touch, a fine statue of General Custer, with sword in hand, was installed in the fenced town park.

According to the *Rocky Mountain News* of June 10, 1902, quite an impressive ceremony was held in connection with the unveiling of the statue. Governor Orman, Colorado's chief executive, and ex-Governor Adams came to Custer City to attend the memorial services held later that month. On June 25, the exact anniversary of Custer's death, the memorial service was observed. There are rumors that Custer's widow visited the town a year later but no evidence exists to substantiate or disprove the story.

From a location standpoint, Custer City was in a good spot. The original road from Rosita to Querida passed through the eastern end of the town. Although a newer but

Custer City, showing the statue of General Custer in the center background

By 1966, Custer City was no more. The statue base has been moved and is visible at the extreme right of the picture.

poor dirt road now connects these towns, the ruts of the original trail are still to be seen where they crossed the high meadow. Nearby, in an eroded cut, a section of the pipe from the water system is visible. Down the hill toward Querida to the north, one of the old hydrants, now rusty from disuse, reposes on the ground. Originally, the statue itself sat on a three-stage base. Two stages of this foundation are still up there. A hole in its top and the outline of the metal base of the statue are still exposed to view.

The actual location of Custer City was on the hilltop just a mile south from Querida. To get there, take State Highway 115 south from Colorado Springs to Florence. Then drive south on State Highway 67 to Wetmore. From there turn southwest on State Highway 96 to either the Rosita or Querida signs. Both towns are south of the paved road a few miles and are connected by a passable dirt road. Assuming that you go to Rosita first, then turn north toward Querida. On top of the hill south of Querida, the last hill you drive down in order to enter Querida, look for a gate on your left with a trail turning off to the west. Follow the ruts, preferably on foot, through a gate to Custer City, a half mile away. An alternate route may be taken from Texas Creek, on U.S. Highway 50, east of Salida. Turn South at this point and take State Highway 69 to Westcliffe, Silver Cliff, and Querida to Custer City. The townsite is now on land owned by Mr. Joe Tomsick, of Querida. Common courtesy dictates that you get his permission and close his gate if you choose to see the relics of Custer City.*

---

* In this same general area, see also Silver Cliff.

14.

DALLAS CITY

FOR MANY YEARS the beautiful Unaweep Valley had been passing the time as a peaceful, pastoral, cattle-raising area. Shortly after the 1879 spring thaw, a small prospecting party made its way into the valley and put up a camp at the place where Dallas Creek flows into the Uncompahgre River. Within a few days they had discovered some rich gold placers along the riverbanks. From then on life was never quite the same for those who had settled there.

Once again, as with so many other new mineral discoveries, grossly exaggerated reports were spread and an impatient crowd came surging up from the south. Before it was over, the rush had depleted the populations of both Ouray and Silverton. Since no preparations had been made to accommodate this local nineteenth-century counterpart of the population explosion, those who had come got busy at once and threw up a hastily erected assortment of tents and ramshackle log and brush huts.

Someone recently called attention to a peculiarly American behavior characteristic by stating that whenever a group of Americans get together, they inevitably do three things. First of all they form a committee, the purpose of which can be determined later. Second, they choose a name for themselves or their group. Third and last, they try to elect someone as a member of Congress. Almost immediately these gold seekers faithfully carried out the first two of these steps. The name chosen for their disorganized slum was Unaweep. But regardless of the squalid condition of their surroundings, it was soon decided that Unaweep wasn't grand enough. True to form, another committee of the unqualified was appointed by the unwilling to do the unnecessary and Unaweep took on the grand sounding designation of Gold City. Someone should have told this group that a camel is nothing more than a horse that was designed by a committee. In any event, they ought to have spent more time placering and less time meeting because the deposits played out and Gold City was already dead by August.

When 1880 rolled around, some people had gone back again and had resettled beside the old gold placers. As more people came, a new town was platted that same year and it was to be known as Dallas. In this case the name was chosen to honor George M. Dallas who had served as Vice-President of the United States in the administration of President James K. Polk. A new firm called the Dallas Mining Company was formed to pursue further mineral investigations. Quite apart from any earlier reasons for the founding of a settlement at this point, its fortunate geographical location made it a logical spot for a major stage and wagon station on the new road to the West.

An eighteen-mile toll road had been built, running north along the San Miguel River to Placerville. This was another project of the incredible Otto Mears. From that point the grades were cut steeply up Leopard Creek to and over the divide, then through the Paradise Valley to the new station at Dallas. In some instances, maps of the period showed this location as Dallas Station, a designation that also persisted into its railroad period. Corrals were built to hold the large numbers of oxen, horses, and mules that were being used to pull the heavy freight loads along this road. Scarcely less significant were the several Concord coaches which hauled both passengers and mail over the same route. The trip took all day.

In the 1880's, population figures fluctuated between one hundred and two hundred people. To care for the needs of these early settlers, there were two general stores, two hotels (called the Placer and the Dallas), a saloon, a meat market and various other commercial enterprises. In 1884, Dallas kited a bit of status and became Dallas City. A private telegraph line was strung all the way over to Telluride. Once during a bank robbery it was cut in order to facilitate the escape of the miscreants.

When Dallas City acquired its own post office in the 1880's, mail came in directly instead of being hauled in from other communities by stagecoach. However, no postal service is any better than the personnel who operate it and the spoils system apparently dumped a couple of real gems at Dallas City. On May 13, 1899, the newspapers reported that Mrs. Carmichael, postmistress for the past ten years, had been arrested by United States authorities when her accounts were found to be four thousand dollars short, due to embezzlement. Also caught in the same net was Mrs. Emma J. Smith who carried the strange title of "Postmistress of the Dallas City Bank." Apparently Mrs. Smith was not as adroit as Mrs. Carmichael since her accounts were short only three thousand dollars, accomplished through the ingenious device of false cancellations. Although the firm members of Smith and Carmichael were arrested, subsequent issues of the local papers failed to report on the disposition of their cases. For some reason, Dallas City lost its post office on October 31, 1899.

When the Denver and Rio Grande Railway built through the valley in 1887, the hopes of Dallas City were high for a while, then word leaked out that the railroad planned to bypass construction in the town and build a city of their own a couple of miles or so to the south. This became Ridgway, established in 1888, and named for Superintendent Robert M. Ridgway of the D. & R. G. heirarchy. Although the Rio Grande also had high hopes for their operation at Dallas City, the people who owned the land in question put an exhorbitant price on it. As a result, only the right-of-way was used and a small station was put up. Their main installation was built at the much more receptive Ridgway.

From the west, Otto Mears was extending his Rio Grande Southern Railroad into the Unaweep Valley. In many instances his tracks were laid over the grades of his earlier toll road. The Rio Grande Southern was incorporated in October of 1889 and work was started the next year. By December of 1891 the job was finished and the tracks had reached Ridgway. From there passengers could transfer to the Denver and Rio Grande for Ouray or Montrose. Mears, too, had planned to build through Dallas City, but once again the asking price for land seemed too high and Otto built across the valley to the south. Two years later the Sherman Silver Purchase Act was repealed, the Rio Grande Southern went broke, and the Denver and Rio Grande was appointed as the receiver. In its earlier days the town had served as a stage station. Later it was a mining camp. Now it had become a railroad town of sorts and the Rio Grande officials shortened its name to just plain Dallas in 1890.

As Ridgway boomed, Dallas declined. Most of its residents straggled down the valley to find steady work and to establish homes in the newer town. By 1899 there were some six hundred people at Ridgway while only sixty diehards still stuck it out at old Dallas. By 1900 Dallas was already a ghost town.

At this writing, only the old railroad grade remains to remind us that a town once existed here. South of Montrose, U.S. 550 runs down the valley to Ouray and points south. Just north of the cutoff to Ridgway, a county dirt road leads to the west through rich farmlands. Barely below the pavement, the dirt road crosses a bridge above the river and passes the railroad ties on its way up a hill. Roughly a half mile past the top of the rise, look off to the south. There in the midst of this tilled field was the site of Dallas City, a town that led three separate lives in its day. Now the clock has run full cycle and the land has been returned to agrarian uses, just the way it was before placer gold was found here in 1879.*

---

* In this same general area, see also Ouray, Silverton, and Camp Bird.

Collection of Richard A. Ronzio
Dallas City once stood on the flats north of Ridgway. This earlier photograph,
like most, does not record the background mountains.

Collection of Robert L. Brown
Note the line of cliffs and hills in the middle background. These formations correspond
with those shown in the photograph above, pinpointing the site of the former Dallas City.

15.

DYERSVILLE

THE STORY OF DYERSVILLE is tied up in many ways with the life of the Reverend John L. Dyer, most notable of the early-day circuit riders. Despite his avowed Methodist leanings, he was far better known as "Father" Dyer. For many years, during the early part of the mining period, his mountain circuit covered Park City, Buckskin Joe, Breckenridge, and Fairplay.

Dyer was born in Ohio in 1812. His inspiration to preach seems to have come from a revival or camp meeting. He attended no theological school and was, therefore, never formally ordained. Prior to his decision to migrate westward, he gained experience in his calling by serving as a circuit rider in rural Minnesota. During the initial Pikes Peak gold rush he joined the westward-bound migrants. Incredible as it may seem, he walked all the way from Omaha to Denver.

While on a trek into the mountains, he was invited to preach for the miners at Buckskin Joe. Somehow, this engagement became a regular part of his early obligations. Each week Dyer walked from Denver to Buckskin Joe to conduct services. Being without adequate funds, he spent two and a half days on the road each way in order to save the ten-dollar stagecoach fare.

Like so many early-day men of the cloth, Father Dyer was forced to augment his meager income from the offering plate with another job. As a mail carrier he regularly packed quantities of weekly letters on his back as he made the various stops along his preaching circuit. Although he later built churches at both Fairplay and Breckenridge, his early sermons were delivered wherever he found people who would listen. When faced by the need to bring his message to the Argonauts, Dyer preached in saloons, gambling houses, tents, and in the streets. In winter he carried the mail on snow-shoes as he faithfully made his appointed rounds. For many years he was a beloved and familiar figure in the mining camps of the high Rockies.

In 1879, when Dyer was sixty-seven years old, he was placed in charge of the Breckenridge district where he built the quaint little edifice which still stands and is known as "Father Dyer's Church." A variety of unsettled conditions indigenous to most mining camps created an environment which was largely unfavorable to keeping up a religious society.

By late 1879, Dyer had begun to feel the pressure of his long years of overwork. He requested and was granted a superannuate leave. With his wife, Dyer made arrangements to live permanently at Breckenridge. Another of the periodic Summit County mining booms had just started. Within a year the excitement had passed and not even speculation in town lots was profitable. Following a fire, the town actually went into a temporary decline.

Since the Colorado Conference of the Methodist Church was unable to render him any financial help, most of his time was spent in work for wages. Most residents of the mining camps were financially embarrassed much of the time. Father Dyer felt and often said that a preacher had the right to earn his living at outside work if he could not get it by preaching. He also felt strongly that no clergy-man had the right to leave his congregation, regardless of conditions that had to be endured. He often preached three and worked the other four days of the week. In actual fact, he earned far more from his "moonlighting" labors than as a clergyman.

Since he was very well acquainted with the Colorado

Rockies and no stranger to mining, John Dyer was in constant demand as a claim locator. When deep snows blanketed the valleys, he went out on snowshoes in search of promising mineral leads. According to accounts given in *The Snow-Shoe Itinerant*, his autobiography, he was paid rather well for his efforts.

During the year 1880, the Dyers took in two boarders named Candell and Thompson. Although Father Dyer's practical knowledge kept him in demand as a locator he often gave his services to deserving young men. The two boarders seemed to fit into this category. In the spring of 1880 they sought his counsel. Both men were nearly out of money and had barely enough to cover their board bills for a few more days.

After securing tools, all three men set out up the mountain in waist-deep snow. When the trail ended, they broke their own path through the drifts, carrying picks, shovels, tents, and blankets. Dyer, despite his years, seemed to thrive on this kind of activity but the two inexperienced boys found it a tough climb. Reaching a likely spot, Rev. Dyer showed them where to dig and all slept in a three-foot prospect hole that night. Next day several trees were cut and a log pen ten or twelve feet square was erected. The structure served as a stopping place and was just tall enough to stand up in.

From their first prospect holes the two men took about three dollars a day. Later, with Father Dyer, they lined up a claim on some nearby ground together. In addition they also continued to prospect for themselves throughout the summer. At one point Thompson located some promising float samples and followed them up to the grass level where he sunk a ten-foot hole. In a short time he threw out over a hundred pounds of rich gray copper, worth about five hundred dollars to the ton. He promptly staked a claim measuring 150 by 1,500 feet.

Not realizing its value at the time, Thompson sold a one-fourth interest in his find to a man named Parkinson for a mere one hundred dollars. It now appears that he would have sold the remainder for $250 but the prospect failed to show up with the money. When its true worth became known, Thompson became secretive about his location. Dyer suspected that the find was on one of his own earlier claims, staked out three years before. A shovel had been left to hold his tract.

When the two men compared notes, they left to check the locations at once. Both the shovel and the old corner stake were found. Although the claims did not overlap, Dyer was pleased to note that vacant ground existed on both sides of the new lode. Quickly he staked one claim to the south and four more to the north of Thompson's workings. Both men were very pleased with the initial showings of the lode.

Since he had never done his own assaying, Dyer took several pieces of the ore to Breckenridge with him. The assayer became quite excited and inquired where the samples had come from. Father Dyer, now no longer a young man, had little enthusiasm for the physical rigors of hard-rock mining. Futhermore, he felt that the church building project was more worthy of his efforts at this point. In exchange for an interest in the property, the agitated assayer agreed to do the work for him. Within the next week, on-the-spot tests were made and a contract was drawn up.

Ultimately the Dyer and Thompson claims were merged. One evening the Dyers sent for Thompson. When he came into their home they told him they had heard of his offer to sell out for $250. Their advice was that he ask for more. Mrs. Dyer quoted platitudes and told him that it is easier to fall than to rise. Her suggestion was that he should ask for one thousand dollars. Thompson left at once for a meeting with his prospective buyers. They accepted and gave him one hundred dollars on a "10% down and the rest in 60 days" deal. Looking reflectively at the hundred dollars, Thompson said this was the first time he had ever seen this much money all at once. Parkinson's fourth interest was purchased for five hundred dollars with 10 percent down.

The ore was not very rich, ranging from low grade to some that assayed a thousand dollars a ton. Several cabins were erected by the stream and the tiny settlement that grew up there soon took on the name of Dyersville. By far the best mining property became the Warrior's Mark Mine, approximately a half mile above the settlement. Father Dyer built a rough log cabin in the town for use by himself and his family. He began construction in January of 1881, cutting and hauling his own logs. The completed structure was seventeen by seventeen feet and stood a story and a half tall. There were two levels, two doors, and a shingled roof. By February 19 the Dyers had moved up the last of their goods from Breckenridge, six miles away. A slab for livestock was constructed later.

When summer came a superintendent and fifty men went to work on the Warrior's Mark. Between seventy-five and eighty thousand dollars were taken out in six months of work. Three million dollars' worth of stock in the mine was sold. It paid one dividend. Father Dyer took ten thousand in stock for his part interest. He had little faith in mining stock and once wrote that most of it was issued for three times its actual worth. He further stated that the average lode is beaten by directors, clerks, presidents, treasurers, bosses, and superintendents, all on pay. If this fails to cripple the venture, there are always mismanagement, wire-working, whiskey, cards, and fancy women. Dyer eventually realized a profit of two thousand dollars.

A lawsuit over fraudulent assays did little to inspire faith in the Warrior's Mark. Later the property was leased to an operator who had managed to secure more than half of the stock. Here, as elsewhere, the town was depopulated when the vein pinched out. John L. Dyer outlasted his town by some years and lived to a ripe old age of eighty-nine. His death occurred in 1901.

The ride to Dyersville is one of the prettiest and most rewarding trips in Colorado when the brush of autumn has
spread vivid colors across the mountains. From Como a good
dirt road leads northwest and follows the old railroad grade
up through a series of cuts and across filled and long-aban-
doned trestles. At the top of the range it becomes Boreas
Pass. On both sides of this crossing are patches of aspen that
turn red as well as yellow, making for some extraordinary
picture possibilities. When crossing from the Como side
go over the crest and start down the other slope toward
Breckenridge. Not far below the top one finds a huge mill
on the right side of the road. Almost directly across from this
structure is the beginning of a trail leading off down the hill
in a generally southwesterly direction. A Forest Service
sign placed at this intersection indicates that the road provides access to both Pennsylvania and Indiana creeks. Being
essentially a no-nonsense road, whoever built this one must
have assumed that its purpose was to reach the foot of the
hill with as little ceremony as possible. Consequently some
grades are quite steep and have naturally been eroded away,
leaving a V-shaped trough in the center. Although I have
never seen conventional cars down here, this does not mean
that those with good clearance and adequate power could not
get out again. My own preference has been to drive this
section in a Jeep. Before reaching the bottom of the gulch,
watch very carefully for an extremely dim trail leading off
to your left and angling back up around the hill you just
came down. The trail is somewhat more visible about
twenty-five yards from the road at the point where it enters
the trees. You are now very close to Dyersville. The trail
leads around and down to the creek bed and one cabin. On
the opposite side are a few more structures. This was Dyersville. At one time there was a bridge here but it has been
gone for a long while. The creek is shallow and has a good
rocky bottom. It may be easily driven in a Jeep or crossed
on foot by stepping from rock to rock.

The roofless log structure on the left was the Dyer cabin. Beginning once more on the town side of the creek, the old trail heads uphill again and terminates at a large dump. This was the Warrior's Mark Mine, in which Father Dyer had a financial interest. All surface buildings are gone now but there are some huge holes for the unwary. During the fall of 1964, a huge tree fell across this trail to the mine. With this out of the way, the ride up to the mine is a very easy one.*

---

* In this same general area, see also Boreas, Como, King City, Tarryall, and Hamilton.

This is the sheltered, wooded site of Dyersville

*Here is the likeness of Rev. John L. Dyer which appeared
in his autobiography, The Snow-Shoe Itinerant.*

16.

ECLIPSE

IN 1894 THE GREAT GOLD BOOM was in full swing in the Cripple Creek District. Before it was finished, production figures would make this the second greatest gold camp the world had ever known. In the midst of all this activity, a construction crew in the heart of Victor's business district went almost unnoticed. These workmen had been engaged to put down the foundation footings for the newest and finest hostelry in the district, the new Victor Hotel. Situated almost in the middle of the business district, it would be handy to the stores, and one railroad nearly passed its front door.

Day by day, the blasting and excavation continued. Then, quite suddenly, a most unexpected thing happened. One of the workmen drove his pick into what he had thought would be solid rock. Instead, he opened up a rich vein that paid out over a million dollars in dividends before it closed. Here was the beginning of the fabulous Gold Coin Mine. The fortunate owner was one J. R. McKinnie. Actually, this type of find was not unusual in Victor. The Strong Mine was right behind the railroad station. Many people put shafts down in their backyards and got rich without even leaving home. It was not without justification that Victor was often referred to as the city of mines. Victor was actually built right over the top of miles and miles of underground shafts and tunnels.

When development of the Gold Coin got underway, a monumental problem faced the owners. With a mine in the center of a major metropolitan area, what does one do with the tailings pile or dump? Their answer was not only unique, it resulted in the founding of the new town of Eclipse. First of all, a pioneer bore was cut straight through Squaw Mountain. Next, it was enlarged to become a tunnel of respectable proportions. One source calls it the United Mine Tunnel while another refers to it as the Columbine-Victor Tunnel. Both names could be correct and were possibly just used at different times. In any case, the bore was completed in 1899.

Around the opposite end of Squaw Mountain, at the point where the tunnel emerged, a huge mill was erected. H. E. and Frank M. Woods, Cripple Creek capitalists and owners of the Golden Crescent Water and Light Company at Gillett, had put up the money. The Warren Woods Company was also involved in the partnership. Called the Economic Gold Extraction Company, this huge mill was one of the earliest attempts to use the chlorination process to refine gold in the Cripple Creek District. Unrefined ores from the Gold Coin Mine were trammed from Victor, through the 3,700-foot-long tunnel that pierced Squaw Mountain, running directly into the mill. Inside, huge roasting furnaces were fed by crude oil that was being shuttled up on the Florence and Cripple Creek Railroad from the petroleum fields near Florence.

Boasting of a three-hundred-ton daily capacity, the huge Economic Mill covered a good part of the hillside. At the other end, the Gold Coin operated night and day, yielding thirty thousand tons of ore yearly. When Victor's fire destroyed its frame shaft house, little time was lost in replacing it with a similar one of brick construction. On one of his visits to Cripple Creek, Teddy Roosevelt looked aghast at the huge installations on both sides of Squaw Mountain and pronounced it "bully." The date was 1901 and everything was fresh and new. If any ugly thoughts about trust busting crossed his mind while viewing the huge plant, Teddy kept them to himself.

Below the mill a string of houses and business structures

grew up along the bottom of the gulch. Somehow the name of Eclipse became attached to the small settlement. It was a single-street community, stretching out in a generally up-hill direction from the mill. Many of the employees found it convenient to live near their work. Such people accounted for a majority of the population of Eclipse. Nearby, close to the head of the street, was the lower terminal of Dick Roelofs' aerial tram from the Cresson Mine. After passing through nearby Elkton, the cables terminated in the Midland Terminal Railway yard at Eclipse. In addition to the two railroads already mentioned, the town was also served by the Low Line Electric cars as they ran from Cripple Creek to Victor.

When the inevitable fire engulfed the mill in 1908, it spread to the town and much of it was destroyed. For some reason, or collection of reasons, neither the Eclipse nor the Economic Mill was ever rebuilt. The availability of other and more efficient processing plants may account for some of it. Its extremely close proximity to the larger community of Victor was no doubt a contributing factor. Curiously, in 1915, an operator secured a lease and reworked one of the old dumps below the mill. His efforts yielded ten thousand dollars in gold, left behind by wasteful processing methods.

There are many reasons why a town dies. Eclipse seems to have expired chiefly from the inefficient techniques employed by the industry that was its chief source of income.

State Highway 67 begins at Divide and terminates at Victor. Just a mile northwest of Victor one may see the huge foundation of the Economic Mill below the highway. To the right, running along the spine of the gulch, are a few rock foundations of the town. For a better view, go on another mile or so around the loop and look back at Squaw Mountain and the tremendous perforated foundation. Eclipse was a town that enjoyed a very brief priority in time. Its demise, or eclipse, was sudden, and its return to nature is nearly complete at this writing.*

---

* In this same general area, see also Elkton, Gillett, Goldfield, and Mound City.

An early view of the Economic Gold Extraction Company Mill at Eclipse

Today, the empty site of Eclipse lies below the highway between Victor and Cripple Creek

17.

ELDORA

LIKE SO MANY CAMPS that belong logically to the latter phases of Colorado's mineral mining boom, those events that paved the way for the establisment of Eldora go back to a far earlier chronology. There had been some small-scale prospecting activities in this neighborhood as early as 1860. Some limited successes led a few of the more fortunate to form the Grand Island Mining District in March of 1861.

At the beginning the district included a section of land about sixteen miles long by four miles wide. From Castle Rock in Boulder Canyon, it included everything westward to the crest of the Continental Divide. On the south, its limit was the northern boundary of Gilpin County. Due to the Civil War and a collapse of the speculative mining boom, little actual work was done for more than a decade.

A series of discoveries, beginning in May of 1875, heralded the prospect of better days for the district. While prospecting near the Arapahoe Peak, C. C. Alvord uncovered the great Fourth of July Lode. Barely three months later, the Alvord Placer was located. Their locations were about five miles west of what was to become the village of Eldora, on the north fork of Middle Boulder Creek. Not far away, as the crow flies, was the great Caribou Mine, located by Sam Conger in 1869. For many of the early years, the district realized considerable financial support from this source.

Curiously, the two Alvord placers were both potential gold producers but little actual work was done on either of them. Yet the Caribou, just two and a half miles away on the north side of Eldorado Mountain, became a rich silver camp. For nearly two decades life in the valley of Middle Boulder Creek remained almost static. But when the wheel of fortune finally stopped on its number, it was not silver but gold that made Eldora spring to life.

Although the Huron Lode was found in August of 1887 and the Clara Lode, on Spencer Mountain, became a reality just two years later, it remained the task of the Happy Valley Placer to begin the real boom. John H. Kemp and seven associates from Central City laid claim to a tract of about five hundred acres along Middle Boulder Creek on September 5, 1891. Since a few log cabins had already appeared in the valley, the Kemp party decided to go ahead with a survey for a townsite. In 1892, their task was completed and the area was divided into building lots. At that time the settlement was known only as Happy Placer.

With the increase of new arrivals, the little hamlet started to grow. Within a few months it began to assume some semblance of a budding town and the residents effected the first of several name changes. With pardonable civic pride, the name of Eldorado Camp was chosen. In this, as in so many other similar instances, there was a conflict. California already had a town of the same name. The job of dispatching the mails now became infinitely more complicated for the postal department. To facilitate better reception of their letters, the miners agreed to drop the word "Camp" and call their town Eldorado. When the town was incorporated on March 9, 1898, it was under this latter name.

In the meantime a minor revolt was brewing within the ranks, headed by one A. L. Tomblin. In April of 1897 a group of new arrivals, backed by Nebraska capital, organized themselves with the purpose of surveying a townsite of their own on ground already taken up by the Happy Valley Placer. They chose a tract of 320 acres which included the land already occupied by the new town. Since the ground was not valuable as a mineral location anyway, they argued, the original locators had no right to it. Actually, this was not entirely true since their proposed plot also extended up the side of the mountain for several hundred feet behind the town. Curiously, a number of lode claims were being actively worked on the slopes at that time. Also conveniently overlooked was the fact that the greater part of the land which they proposed to incorporate had been occupied for months by several miners' cabins.

Opinion in the town was divided into two rival factions and matters began to look serious as the dispute grew hot. When faced by the need to save his claim, Kemp took out a petition in opposition to the townsite scheme, reminding people that his was the earlier claim and that the new plot was actually covered by his placer claim. A large majority of the miners signed with Kemp.

In the midst of claims and counterclaims, the dispute was heard in May of 1897 before the Registrar of the General Land Office in Denver. After weighing the evidence, a decision was rendered in favor of the outsiders. Within a few days the (un) Happy Placer people appealed the case. In the course of time, the original decision was reversed and the Kemp group lost no time in completing their own town plot and embarking upon the sale of their lots. When the final two letters were dropped from Eldorado, the town assumed its present name.

With problems of legal ownership settled, Eldora began to enjoy a small boom. Early in 1898, a rich strike was made in a mine called the Enterprise. It had the distinction of igniting the fireworks that really set off Eldora's boom. A great stampede of new arrivals began to find its way up the valley and the town grew up almost overnight. Although one source reports that not a single saloon existed in 1897 many things were due for a change.

Quite suddenly, Eldora found that it had mushroomed from a sleepy little hamlet of prospectors to a fair-sized city with a population in excess of one thousand by the latter

1890's. Like most other new camps, the people here were poor. Living at an altitude of 8,600 feet was not easy. In winter, snow retarded their work. There was little money or influence available for interesting the right people in the outside world in what they had found or about its value. Most of the early residents were honest, hospitable, and industrious, barring consideration of the attempt by Nebraskans to jump the claim of the Happy Valley Placer.

Geologically, Eldora's mining properties were in a sulphide belt, although streaks of tellurium had been found in some of its outcroppings. There were also several large deposits of low-grade ore near the camp which could be treated profitably if mills were erected. Hundreds of new claims were located on almost any ground that was available, regardless of its mineral indications or lack of them. By far the greatest number of new locations filed were on Spencer Mountain. Among the better properties were such mines as the Virginia, Virginia Bell, and the Bird's Nest.

During 1897, the Mogul Tunnel was completed near the foot of Spencer Mountain. W. C. Andrews and N. B. Bailey constructed a fifty-ton-capacity mill at the foot of Ute Mountain, about a mile west of town. Although designed to take advantage of the chlorination process, it was never a success. Business from the huge tonnage that had been expected from the Mogul Tunnel failed to materialize.

Quite apart from the town itself, the great Eldora Mine was down the valley about four miles west of Nederland. Its deepest shaft reached a depth of only 110 feet. At the beginning, its owners took out a ton and a half of ore that assayed one hundred dollars to the ton. Fortunately for them, large and well-defined veins were found near the surface.

Along both sides of Middle Boulder Creek, from water level to the crest of the mountains, shafts and tunnels were being driven. Although the slopes were precipitous, footpaths provided access to some rather unbelievable locations. Most of the incurable optimists in the lower valley were filled with the belief that their own individual prospects were certain to become paying mines. One local assayer made the statement that the relative values obtained for these depths were unusually high. According to him fifteen to twenty-five dollars from a four-foot hole were common returns.

To supply the wants of the miners, new buildings were going up on all sides in the town which became not only a residence center but the principal source of supplies for most of the mines. Although commercial structures took on the dignity of false fronts and stylish windows, the log cabin remained as the favorite type of dwelling for most people.

Both the Goldminer and the Mines hotels were fine places to stay. In addition, there were several well-kept boarding-houses where prices were moderate. Despite the earlier boast, eleven saloons now flourished in Eldora. In time the inevitable newspaper and a bank also found their way up the valley. For the pioneers who sought entertainment and enlightenment, there was a photographic gallery, a free reading room, and in later years there were two ladies clubs. A Methodist church seems to have been the first to be built in the town but other denominations soon followed their example. A single public school employed two teachers and boasted an average daily attendance of one hundred children.

Considering the seamier side of life for a moment, most kinds of gambling were allowed in the appropriate establishments. For those who could or would not conform, Eldora had a sturdy little jail which originally stood at the rear of the Goldminer Hotel. Later it was moved to another location across the creek. In the course of time, a fair-sized red-light district also grew up. Inevitably, one of these took the name of "Bon Ton." In view of the existence of all these organized institutions of dissipation, it seems incredible that the town had no cemetery. Even today, there are no burial grounds at Eldora.

Other real or imagined needs of the townspeople were

Courtesy Library, State Historical Society of Colorado
A typical stagecoach, drawn by six horses, was a common
sight on the main street of Eldora.

Collection of Robert L. Brown
With the same mountain backdrop, Eldora today presents a far different picture

served by a number of stores. Particularly outstanding was the N. M. Mills General Store which was truly general. Here one could choose from an array of merchandise including clothing, butter, beef, dynamite, prunes, and rubber boots. Well before the close of the boom, a well-equipped drugstore, a hardware establishment, several bakeries, and an assay office found it profitable to set up shop here. Later, of course, a telephone exchange strung its wires across the valley to serve some of the more status-conscious settlers. Over the years, several physicians settled here to care for the sick, the injured, and the hypochrondriacs who lacked even the solace of a cemetery.

For many years, transportation into and out of the valley had been a hodgepodge. With the completion of a road from the Nederland end of the valley, a horse-drawn stagecoach was used. From the other direction, a twice-weekly stage crossed over from Central City. Four more lines came up from Boulder, using canopy-topped Concord coaches in summer. Four- or six-horse hitches were used to draw the load. Necessarily, passenger and mail service were erratic at best. When a post office was established in 1897, these facilities improved. By the turn of the century, daily mails came up from Boulder. Freight and lumber outfits also used the route, once described as one of the best mountain roads in the state.

Many of Eldora's mines had started to experience hard times around the turn of the century. Some people saw a railroad extension as the solution to their problems. Town officials encouraged the construction of tracks by the Colorado and Northwestern which had already built a line elsewhere in Boulder County. The company was assured that the mines here could furnish two hundred tons of ore per day for shipment over the rails if they were to reach Eldora.

At the Fourth of July property, in the northwestern part of the district, improved machinery was installed and a three-thousand-foot bore was completed. Management at the

Mogul, and at other mines, hoped that the railroad would provide a remedy for what had become their very sick industry. By late 1904, tracks had been laid from Sunset, around Sugar Loaf Mountain and Glacier Lake, to terminate at Eldora. Operations began on New Year's Day, 1905. The hoped-for millenium did not transpire. Mining troubles were far too serious for pump priming. Actually, the ores had played out at about the turn of the century.

On all sides the mines began to close down. Employees at the Bailey Mill staged a riot when the management missed a payday. Mr. Bailey was smoked out of his house and shot. Little time was lost in putting his mill to the torch. What remained went into receivership, to be torn down and sold for salvage in 1916. By that time Eldora was nearly a dead camp. Some people held out, but population for the whole district in the 1910 census had been reduced to about six hundred people. By 1917, all except a few individual operations had been shut down.

When the railroad reached town, it had practically ended the stagecoach business. One company attempted to recoup its losses by operating a fleet of Stanley Steamers to Eldora in 1914. Two receiverships, the last in March of 1909, nearly stopped the railroad. In the course of reorganization, the company reappeared as the Denver, Boulder, and Western Railway. Its operations continued in a sporadic manner until a severe flood destroyed the right-of-way in July of 1919.

Since fire seems to have been the greatest nemesis of all Western mining camps, the one that damaged Eldora should be mentioned here. It broke out at roughly nine o'clock on November 28, 1902. A defective flue in the second-story stove at the Miller residence was its source. Extinguishing the fire was made more difficult by a harsh wind that fanned the flames from structure to structure. Final loss was estimated at $15,000 and a slightly scorched school building. By comparison with fires such as the ones that destroyed Rosita and Cripple Creek, this was not a severe blaze since the whole town was not destroyed.

Gradually, as the years passed, activities other than mining came to be the basis for Eldora's economy. Today, a fine ski center flourishes at Lake Eldora. Within the town, many of the old cabins have been converted to use as picturesque summer homes. The handsome scenery and easy access to hiking, camping, and picnic facilities are likewise assets to the community.

Eldora is located twenty-two miles west of Boulder and just nine miles east of the Continental Divide. Sulphide Flats is an elevated plain, roughly a mile square. Just beyond its eastern edge is the town of Nederland. The old settlements of Cardinal and Caribou are situated short distances beyond its northern boundaries. Highway 119 will lead you into this country from either Boulder or Black Hawk, while Highway 160 comes down from Ward. An excellent dirt road leaves Highway 119 and turns west just a few miles south of Nederland. Following along its three-mile course, you will enter the rather wide U-shaped valley of Middle Boulder Creek in which Eldora will be found. If you spend some time here, you will likely agree that the original Happy Valley was a most appropriate name.*

* In this same general area, see also Salina, Tungsten, and Camp Frances.

18.

ELKTON

WHEN GROVER CLEVELAND instigated repeal of the Sherman Silver Purchase Act in 1893, Colorado's shattered finances nearly scraped the bottom of the barrel. Fortunately for most residents of the Silver State, gold was almost immediately discovered at Cripple Creek in the cone of an extinct volcano. In its entirety, this story has been superbly chronicled by Marshall Sprague in his magnificent book *Money Mountain*. This book also details life in the multiplicity of little towns, such as Elkton, that once flourished during the Cripple Creek excitement. Before it was over, total production figures had made this the second greatest gold-producing district the world has ever known. Over the long haul, it was surpassed only by the Witwatersrand in the Transvaal of South Africa.

Quite an amazing array of notable persons was associated with the Cripple Creek District in its heyday. Bernard Baruch, late advisor to many recent American Presidents, worked in the Bull Hill mines and once defeated the boxing champion of Altman in a wild bare-knuckle melee that should have made the Marquis of Queensberry spin in his tomb. Tom Mix once worked here as a cowboy and later as a bouncer for a Bennett Avenue saloon. Groucho Marx at one time drove a grocery wagon in Victor. Texas Guinan began her musical career by playing an organ at the Sunday school in Anaconda. Lowell Thomas was born in Victor and graduated from high school there. The late Ralph Carr, one of our ablest state chief executives, also grew up in Victor and worked on the newspaper there. Bill Dempsey and brother Jack worked as muckers in the Bull Hill mines. When Jack was killed in a mining accident, Bill took his name and went on to become World's Heavyweight Boxing Champion. Another heavyweight champion, Jack Johnson, also worked as a Cripple Creek mucker in the Portland Mine.

When William Shemwell made his way up the side of Raven Hill, the Cripple Creek boom was already well underway. Shemwell was a former blacksmith from Colorado Springs with no known previous mining experience. Since gold formations here defied every known theory of mining, it was not at all unusual for the inexperienced to show up to dig with hoes and pitchforks. In one instance two druggists from Colorado Springs threw a hat in the air and filed on the spot where it fell. The result was the Pharmacist Mine which sold for a half million dollars.

Shemwell dug a hole near the head of Arequa Gulch, part way up Raven Hill. Although some gold was found, he could not foresee that his property would become the second largest producer in the district. One set of figures places total production from the Elkton at $50,000,000 while another says it was $45,000,000. Either figure represents a tremendous quantity of gold.

Shemwell took in a couple of partners. One of these was a colored man who gave him a mule to cover his share.

When the time came to register his claim, the ex-blacksmith found that he needed a name for the property. Thinking back over his labors on Raven Hill, Shemwell recalled having seen a pair of bleached antlers lying on the ground a short distance from his shaft. This coincidence seemed to suggest as good a name as any other and the name Elkton Mine was born.

Arequa Gulch had seemed an unlikely spot for a mine but conventional rules were abandoned here in wholesale lots. In the early days this had been the site of the original Womack Homestead. It was "Cowboy Bob" Womack who had located the first claim in the old crater, giving initial impetus to the whole Cripple Creek rush. Later, Horace Bennett and Julius Myers, Denver real-estate men who owned the property, subdivided the land and sold lots for $320,000. Historical events apart, the gulch had originally been named for a prospector of Italian extraction named Requa. His verbal attempts to master the English pronunciation of his own name caused others to indulge in a good-humored mimicry and the valley where he put up a cabin became "Arequa" Gulch.

In the meantime William Shemwell had given a half interest in his discovery to a pair of Colorado Springs grocers who had grubstaked him to the tune of a $36.50 grocery bill. When mineral production went up, Sam and George Bernard lost interest in their groceries, bought out Shemwell and his partners, and assumed active management of the Elkton. Next they hired Ed De La Vergne, an important name in the Cripple Creek story, to take over the operation. De La Vergne was the man who helped out when the Post Office Department refused to accept Fremont as a name for the first camp in the crater. It was his suggestion that it be renamed Cripple Creek. Before production declined after 1916, the Elkton had produced $16,200,000 from the depths of its 1,700-foot shaft.

Within a comparatively short time, a cluster of cabins and a few homes of dressed lumber began to go up on the steep hillside above the mine. Transportation facilities were not particularly good as yet and it was far more convenient for the miners to live close to their work. By the time of the 1900 census, there were 200 people at Elkton. In 1904 the population had grown to 2,500 people and the peak was reached when 3,000 had settled there by 1905. Despite this, the town was never platted; it just grew up and spread out on its rocky hillside at an elevation of 9,692 feet above sea level. In general, the town grew up around the mine.

A large part of the population increase at Elkton can be

explained by the fact that as the community mushroomed, it gradually absorbed its smaller neighbors. Arequa (sometimes called Requa), Beacon Hill, and Eclipse were all taken in or annexed by Elkton. In addition a further growth stimulus was provided by another penetration into the depth of the unpromising Cresson shaft. The Cresson was located about a mile above the Elkton, in the gulch between Raven Hill and Bull Hill.

J. R. and Eugene Harbecks, of Chicago, owned the Cresson. In 1915 they hired Richard Roelofs, a mining engineer, to survey their property. What he found nearly blew the roof off! In a state of high apprehension he insisted on taking Hildreth Frost, company attorney, and Ed De La Vergne of the Elkton down with him as witnesses. Roelofs led them into a 1,200 foot underground vug or cave. Its dimensions have been given as being 20 feet high and 30 feet in diameter. From another source we find that it was 40 feet high, 20 feet long, and 15 feet wide. In either case it was fabulous since the walls were lined with gold crystals, refined by nature to such a point of purity that reduction or milling were not always required.

Forty thousand dollars' worth of gold was scraped off the walls during the first week. To prevent high-grading or other popular forms of robbery, vault doors were installed on the mine entrance and the miners changed clothes after work. Whenever an ore shipment was loaded onto the trains, armed guards rode along to assure its arrival at the destination. Sealed boxes were also used to facilitate safer local transportation of the gold. From the depths of the Cresson came one world record carload which was worth a milloin dollars. Before they were done, the Cresson shaft had been dug to a depth of 2,400 feet. Total production amounted to $49,000,000.

Dick Roelofs built an overhead tram from the Cresson vault doors to the railroad station at Elkton, a mile down the gulch. In 1914, Albert E. Carlton purchased the Cresson for $4,000,000. It was worked well into the present century.

In 1904, labor wars enveloped the entire Cripple Creek District. At issue were the usual questions of wages and hours. The Western Federation of Miners wheeled out their heavy artillery in the person of Harry Orchard, a professional assassin. Deep inside the Vindicator Mine, he set off a dynamite charge that took the lives of two supervisors. At Independence, he dynamited the railroad station, killing and injuring a number of nonunion men who arrived home on the late train. In an attempt to restore peace, the governor called out the state militia. One of the hastily improvised military camps was at Altman. Another one was in Elkton. Both of these towns were hotbeds of unionism. In the end the unions lost out and their members were herded out of the district at gunpoint. The mines reopened and the soldiers went home. In one of the accompanying photographs, the troops at Elkton posed in the business district.

When it came to public transportation, Elkton was remarkably well endowed. The Florence and Cripple Creek Railroad, The Midland Terminal Line, and the Colorado Springs and Cripple Creek District Railway all built through the community. In all three instances their tracks were on the same level as the town. The Low Line Interurban System built an overhead bridge to allow passage above the Midland Terminal tracks. In addition to the electrified passing track, the streetcar line, and regular road tracks, Elkton also boasted a station house below the Elkton mine and a nearby telegraph office. The station closed in 1919.

While the decline of many mining camps was abrupt, the abandonment of Elkton was gradual. On today's market, the price of gold is still fixed at thirty-five dollars an ounce. Although costs of mining equipment, labor costs, and other factors have gone up, the controlled price of gold has not kept pace. At present, gold mining is no longer profitable. Large quantities of the yellow metal still repose in the Elkton and in the Cresson. But most of the people moved away;

some went around the hill to Victor. Occasionally families still move into the old homes in the town, but most of them stand empty now. There were once twelve towns in the whole Cripple Creek District. Today, only three are still occupied and even their populations are small.

State Highway 67, between Cripple Creek and Victor, is a fine paved road that works its way around Raven Hill. Above the grade, a dirt road leads up the hillside to the sun-browned houses of Elkton. In summer, a herd of cattle grazes here under the watchful bloodshot eye of a noisy and ill-tempered old bull. His big horns and passion for raising clouds of dust make this a less than desirable picnic spot. There are no fences at Elkton. Neverthless, the view to the northwest is great on a clear day. Although the buildings of the mine and the railroad tracks are gone, much of the past remains to remind the visitor of the Elkton that was.*

---

* In this same general area, see also Gillett, Goldfield, Mound City, and Eclipse.

During the 1904 labor wars, troops of the state militia posed at Elkton

Elkton now. Note the same false-front building at the left in both pictures

19.

FAIRPLAY

SHORTLY AFTER THE Pikes Peak gold rush of 1859 had started, many of those who came met disappointment. At one point the "turn backs" actually outnumbered those who were headed for the Cherry Creek diggings. It was soon clear that the late arrivals would need to take second best. As a result, many drifted deeper into the mountains. Good placer gold beds were found on Tarryall Creek, north of present-day Como. Two towns, Tarryall and Hamilton, grew up there. Here, again, the first arrivals grabbed off all the best claims and guarded them jealously. In this case the late arrivals were literally driven out of the camps.

When faced by the need to survive, the émigrés who had been expelled from Tarryall started referring to that camp as "Grab-All," and moved across South Park to start a town of their own. As a slap at their oppressors, they named their location Fair Play Camp, and invited all who had suffered at the hands of those in the older settlements to come here and receive fair treatment. Actually, this location was not so new. Others before them had also found this spot to be a desirable place in which to live. Chief Tierra Blanca of the Utes had camped here regularly, on Sacramento Flats, through the 1840's. Even John C. Frémont (see Alma) once made camp in this vicinity.

On the north bank of the Middle Fork of the South Platte River, A. L. Doge (or Dodge) erected what has generally been credited as the first cabin in the town. Jim Reynolds, who later gained a measure of notoriety as a Confederate renegade leader, quickly established himself as boss of the camp. In 1864, when the town was still in its infancy, an Indian uprising stopped all mail service for three months. Finally, Rev. John L. Dyer (see Dyersville) set an example of bravery by driving the mail coach to Denver. The deadlock was broken and service was restored.

Fairplay also claims the oldest operating courthouse in Colorado, dating from 1874. When a second Indian scare developed in 1879, its stone walls sheltered all of the women and children in town. As things turned out, it was all a hoax. One of the town's most notorious drunks shot his own hat full of holes. As his alcoholic dilemma became more intense, he decided Indians had done it and staggered, wild-eyed and screaming, through the main streets of Fairplay. When someone yells, "fire," people act first and investigate later. The same rules must have applied for Indian scares.

Effective in 1866, Fairplay became the county seat, following the demise of Buckskin Joe. One newspaper, the *Fairplay Flume,* was published as a weekly. Adolph Giraud put a waterwheel into a stream that flowed close to his ranch in order to operate a butter churn, because he hated doing it by hand, and acquired one of Colorado's first water rights through the doctrine of prior use. Later, residents settled around his ranch and anglicized his name to "Garo." A small settlement by that name now occupies the site of his ranch.

Quite a large number of well-known religious leaders were active in early Fairplay. Rev. John L. Dyer moved his building down from Montgomery to establish the first Methodist church in the town. From Santa Fe, the Rev. Joseph Machebeuf, who later became a bishop, arrived and rode the circuit for Catholics in the South Park region. Sheldon Jackson built his beautiful little white Presbyterian church in 1874. It still stands and is now called the Sheldon Jackson Memorial Chapel.

Going from the sublime to the ridiculous, Fairplay also came in for its share of criminal activities. In an earlier day, the notorious Espinosa brothers committed six of their many murders in the area between Alma and Red Hill. When the United States acquired this portion of the Southwest from Mexico, the Espinosas lost some land and swore vengeance on all Anglo-Saxons. Tom Tobin, early-day mountain man and contract hunter at Fort Garland, finally ran them down and beheaded them to prove his claim to the reward.

Fairplay had a full-blown lynching in 1880. A murderer named Hoover was given only a life sentence following a particularly brutal crime. That night, a vigilante group broke down the jail door, got the sheriff out of bed, used the keys to extract Hoover from his cell, locked the sheriff up in his own jail, put a noose around Hoover's neck and dropped him out of a second story window of the courthouse.

When Judge Bowen arrived to hold court again the next morning, there was Hoover dangling above the courthouse door. To make matters worse, another noose was found beside the judge's gavel on his desk inside. Bowen took the hint and left at once for Denver.

A second version of this story also gets bandied about occasionally. In this case, Hoover's neck was broken but he did not die. Some of his friends cut him down and smuggled him out in a hay wagon. A physician in the Kenosha area tended a man with a broken neck who arrived in a load of hay the next evening. Somehow he managed to recover. When he was recaptured, the crowd felt it was "probably unconstitutional" to hang a man twice for the same crime, and let him go. Although the initial story has likely grown more lurid over the years, the second sounds like sheer folklore.

Once, during a jailbreak, the escaping man hired a fiddler to play loudly in order to cover the sound of sawing the bars (Music to Break Jail By). Later, allegedly, the fiddler decided that he knew something about crime and became a candidate for sheriff of Fairplay.

Most of the mining around this end of the park was of

the placer variety. Huge dredges sought and found gold among the coarse gravel of the bars along the South Platte. Many of the better placers were worked by hand. Large numbers of Chinese came into the area and built cabins along the south bank of the Platte, called "Chinaman's Gulch." The "celestials" were charged one dollar per day per man, whether they found any gold or not. Some deep mines existed in the nearby Mosquito and Horseshoe districts. Many of the workers lived at Fairplay. The far-famed silver rush to Leadville after 1878 brought hordes of people through Fairplay. Earlier, in 1872, there was a minor flurry of excitement over some silver discoveries in the South Park neighborhood. When George Crofutt visited Fairplay in the seventies, he recorded a population of 515.

To assure access to and from the outside settlements, a thrice-weekly stagecoach ran between Fairplay and Denver. A total of eighteen hours was required for the trip each way, with an overnight stop. From Denver the road came up Turkey Creek and crossed Crow Hill to the depths of Platte Canyon. For several miles it followed the river. From Webster, it crossed beautiful Kenosha Pass into South Park. Here the trail was an easy one until they got to Red Hill, the last obstacle before Fairplay. From the top of Red Hill, drivers often whipped up their horses for the last couple of miles and made a dramatic dash into Fairplay. Another wagon and staging road crossed the Mosquito Range from just north of Fairplay. This was the Mosquito Pass road to Leadville, one of the most spectacular cliff-hangers in North America. When the 112-mile-long narrow rails of the Denver, South Park, and Pacific Railway reached Fairplay, one could ride all the way in a single day for only $9.90. In general, the railroad followed the canyon of the Platte River. In many places its tracks paralleled the old stagecoach road. Today, U.S. Highway 285 follows this old road over many of the original grades between Denver and Fairplay. In many other places, old cuts and grades from the original railroad route may also be seen paralleling the highway.

Fairplay is one of Colorado's oldest mining centers, a place literally loaded with history. Mercifully, it survived the ghost town epidemic and a fire that destroyed much of its business district in 1873. In fact, the gutted structures had been rebuilt by 1879. In 1930, Prunes, the burro, a local fixture that became a local pet after outliving the mining era, was laid to rest in the town. The monument is unique, one of the few ever erected to an animal. The ashes of "Rupe" Sherwood, last owner of Prunes, were entombed behind the monument.

Two miles away, across the meadow, one may also see an original dredge sitting among its huge piles of boulders; also something of a rarity today. The whole Fairplay area is reached most easily by driving southwest from Denver on U.S. Highway 285, an excellent paved road that offers the traveler or the native a remarkable variety of scenic vistas. Incidentally, Fairplay is still the seat of Park County. In addition, it is a mecca for fishermen and hunters. It survives today as a center for people engaged in hay ranching, cattle raising, and agriculture. At the northern edge of town, South Park City may be seen. This is an authentic restored pioneer Western town, with original buildings and fixtures from Rosita, Alma, Buckskin Joe, Montgomery, and other locations from the long roster of Colorado's yesterdays.*

---

* In this same general area, see also Alma, Buckskin Joe, Puma City, Quartzville, Montgomery, Leavick, and Sacramento.

Courtesy Denver Public Library, Western History Collection
Fairplay, in South Park, as it appeared in 1879

Collection of Robert L. Brown
*When this picture was made in August, 1965, the old stagecoach
road could still be seen in the foreground.*

20.

FALL RIVER

BY THE FALL OF 1863 the great silver discovery near Georgetown found a wealth of new technical knowledge about
mining and refining that allowed for a far greater and more
prosperous mineral development. In the excitement connected with these discoveries of the white metal there, at
Saints John and elsewhere in Summit County, the earlier
rush to Fall River has often been overlooked. Most stock
Colorado histories attribute the initial silver finds in the state
to the Georgetown area and use the 1863 date. In actual fact,
silver was found, but not successfully refined, at Fall River
in 1860. In addition, the little town of Fall River survived
for many years after its silver excitement was over.

Quite apart from the error in chronological history, Fall
River is also interesting geographically. Its location was at
the point where Fall River flows into Clear Creek; the only
spot in the United States where a river flows into a creek.
Usually, it's the other way around, with literally thousands of
creeks that flow into rivers. Below, just a few miles, stood
an early placer gold camp called Paynes Bar which eventually
evolved into the modern city of Idaho Springs.

Fall River was just a small hamlet but in 1860 it boasted
an excellent hotel, several assorted stores, and a variety of
residences. In 1860 it also had its own post office. All around
the town the mountainsides were pockmarked with huge
numbers of prospect holes but no shafts were sunk to any
appreciable depths. Some gold was mined here but such
operations were of brief duration.

By mid-1860 most of the gold-panning ventures were proving to be worthless. On July 1, 1860, either William Ritter or a Mr. Weller (the accounts do not agree) wandered over the hill from Central City. Other sources credit the first discovery on Fall River to William White and his brother, although they didn't record their claim until August 30, 1860. Back then very few people bothered with who was first. It wasn't very important to them.

At any rate, instead of gold they found silver, which no one knew how to handle profitably, and these first silver discoveries were brushed off. Despite these problems, a strike is a strike and even the vaguest rumor or faintest of hopes will often send discouraged miners stampeding to new localities. Maybe, they reasoned, silver was the answer. Eight thousand would-be miners had swarmed into Fall River by autumn. There were far more people than there were paying claims.

Staking their claims proved to be only the beginning. These men knew little about silver mining. It proved to be expensive just getting the ore out of the earth and even more costly to mill it by then-known methods. All along the course of Fall River, all the way to its head, a visitor might see discoveries but little profitable mining. The silver excitement turned out to be mostly recording claims. Meanwhile, gold panning continued on a limited scale. In all, over seven thousand claims were filed along the course of Fall River from its source at St. Marys Glacier, some ten miles away, down to the townsite at Clear Creek. At Georgetown, the small leather-bound record books in the office of the county clerk contain hundreds of names of would-be miners from faraway places who chose their silver lodes along the canyon walls above the river.

Since the canyon is rather narrow, Fall River itself was unable to accommodate all of the people who came. Other towns were established farther up. The Upper Fall River Mining District had been founded in July of 1860 to provide for a measure of government among the migrants. Silver City was built near the head or source of Fall River. Almost overnight the place grew up into a town consisting of slightly over one thousand men who slept in tents, under trees, and in some instances on the bare hillside.

Today, a single log cabin on the shore of Silver Lake dates back to these early days. Although it is not far from the original site of Silver City, the nearby town of Alice was built at a later date than the 1860 excitement. Farther down the canyon the Lincoln Mining District was formed. Within it stood Glenard City with a small resident population of working miners.

Fall River itself was really the third settlement of the group. Being by far the largest, it became the actual seat of government for the Lower Fall River Mining District. To serve it and to tie this ramshackle series of settlements together, a stagecoach road came over from Central City to Georgetown. After climbing the steep grades across Yankee Hill, the road followed down the stream to Clear Creek before continuing on up to Georgetown. In fact the life of this road exceeded the life of the Fall River towns it served, and it was used extensively until the railroad was completed in 1877.

By the late autumn of 1860, Fall River had reached its peak. New refining processes would be required before either gold or silver discoveries could add up to much in this location. Smelting was still something new. Soon the silver excitement was forgotten. Gradually the eight thousand prospectors had to seek comfort in a different locality. Some, however, stayed on.

Today, Fall River still flows into Clear Creek but no trace of the early town remains. Some evidence of mining is still visible but it dates from a later time. U.S. Highway 6 became a four-lane throughfare during 1965 and now passes right over the bar where the town stood. The location is barely west of Idaho Springs, on the right side of the high-

Fall River, a very small town at the mouth of Fall River Canyon

The old site of Fall River, west of Idaho Springs

way as you drive toward Loveland and Berthoud passes. Only the sign which points the way to St. Marys Glacier marks the site now. The accompanying pair of pictures show the location from the other side of Clear Creek, looking up Fall River. The background mountains still retain their same contours but just about everything else has changed.

With disuse, the original stagecoach road over Yankee Hill is returning to nature. Tremendous rocks, long rough sections, and steep grades have relegated this once-important thoroughfare to the status of a wild Jeep road. In the overall chronology of Colorado mining developments, Fall River was a little before its own time. Given a later date, it might have made it. Now, however, it is little more than a memory.*

---

* In this same general area, see also North Empire, Gilson Gulch, Freeland, Brownsville, and Silver Plume.

21.

FORKS CREEK

THE EXISTENCE OF Forks Creek came about as a direct result
of a feud between the Kansas Pacific and Union Pacific railroads. In March of 1872 an organization was formed to construct a railroad across the mountains to Salt Lake City.
Named the Kansas Pacific, this group sought an independent
outlet to the coast. As a first goal, they planned to connect
Denver with the mining camps and to tap the coal, iron, and
precious mineral deposits in Middle and South Parks. Beginning at Denver, the route was to proceed west through Idaho
Springs and across the mountains. Another branch would
serve Black Hawk and Central City.

R. E. Carr was elected president and John D. Perry became a very busy vice-president. Almost at once, Perry
found himself thrust into the role of a commissioner to
negotiate with Clear Creek County for the issuance of sub-
scription railroad bonds. When the county commissioners
submitted their proposal to the electors, $200,000 in aid was
approved.

Meanwhile, the Colorado Central Railroad, backed by the
Union Pacific, also hoped to build west from Golden, by-
passing Denver and making Golden the greater rail metrop-
olis. This latter proposal was advanced as a foil to the other
plan with the hope that the Denver Pacific might be destroyed in the process. For months the news media brimmed
with arguments pro and con. Senator Henry M. Teller and
W. A. H. Loveland headed up the Colorado Central con-

tingent in opposition to Carr and former Governor Evans who led the Denver interests.

Teller and Loveland regarded the mountain counties as their exclusive property when it came to laying rails. Denver people, they felt, had no right there and should be kept out, even though the Colorado Central had no intention of building at that time.

When General T. E. Sickels, chief engineer of the Union Pacific, arrived on the scene in June of 1872, he brought a plan that would reduce the Colorado Central to some practical order. Also in the offing were additional plans to extend their rail connections to Black Hawk.

Meanwhile, the residents of Clear Creek and Gilpin counties were becoming restive over the many delays that had deprived them of their railroad. Most felt that if the Union Pacific delayed much longer, support should go to anyone who would construct the line. General Sickels put on his best public "airs" and went to work on a grass-roots campaign to curry public favor.

As a result, a new proposition was advanced by the county commissioners. In effect, this amounted to another bond issue of $250,000 which was to be submitted to the voters. If approved, the railroad promised to finish its line from Golden to a point near the North and South forks of Clear Creek by September 1, 1872. Scarcely less significant was their promise to build into Black Hawk by January of 1873 and on to Central City within the next year. Although the Denver interests had originally planned to extend the line on to Nevadaville, the more realistic Colorado Central eliminated this projection from their plans as being too difficult.

Fortune seems to have smiled on the Colorado Central and they succeeded where their opponents had failed. On September 1, 1872, their tracks had reached the site of Forks Creek and the first excursion was run on the line that same day. A total of 13.11 miles had been built up the canyon from Golden. By December 15, Black Hawk had its railroad at last.

Forks Creek was never actually a town in the sense of being a permanent community of persons. Instead, it consisted of a small cluster of buildings that grew up on a prominence of land where the North and South forks of Clear Creek combine their waters. Forks Creek, sometimes called the Forks of Clear Creek, existed primarily as a fueling station for the Colorado Central. Here also the tracks separated with a wye. The left, or south branch, went to Idaho Springs and Georgetown. The right, or North branch, carried the traveler to Black Hawk where the tracks ended until May 21, 1878. On that date the last rails and spikes were installed near the depot on up the hill at Central City. At the Forks Creek wye, a wooden bridge divided the tracks, routing the locomotives and their strings of cars in either of the two directions.

Here at Forks Creek, the altitude was 6,880 feet and it marked milepost 28.71 on the company's line. When a station was erected there it was designated as number 1346. Its depot was housed in a two-story frame structure measuring 14x24 feet. Inside, one could also find comfortable living quarters for the employees. An iron roof assured protection from the rigors of mountain winters.

Outside, above the rushing waters of the creek, stood an incredible 1,943 square feet of wooden platform. As shown in the accompanying photograph, there was also a two-story section house of frame construction. Curiously, no brick structures were ever put up at Forks Creek. To provide a ready supply of water for the locomotives, a tank of wood construction, with a capacity of 8,930 gallons, was kept filled from Clear Creek. Not far away, an 11x13 coal shed held the vital fuel. To assure a trouble-free passage of trains bound in opposite directions, 577 feet of siding were installed. During those years when the trains still ran up Clear Creek, Forks Creek functioned primarily as a coal and watering station for the wye going either to Black Hawk or to Georgetown.

Many years later, as passenger and mining loads decreased, abandonment was of course the inevitable fate. The last train passed through Forks Creek on May 4, 1941. Work crews were brought in and the tracks were removed in late May and in June of that same year. Forks Creek had been active for an impressive total of sixty-nine years. At several locations along the way, many sections of the original grades are still visible. A fine paved highway now leads from Denver out through Golden and enters Clear Creek Canyon at that point. Over much of its route, the pavement follows the original grade. This is U.S. Highway 6. Where the pavement divides beyond the three tunnels was the site of Forks Creek, ghostly reminder of a colorful period in Colorado's early mountain railroad era.*

---

* In the same general area, see also Russell Gulch, Mountain City, and Perigo.

Collection of Malcolm E. Collier
At Forks Creek, two locomotives headed downstream toward Denver

Collection of Robert L. Brown
Highways 6 and 40 now separate at the site of Forks Creek. Note the background rocks
and cliffs. Note also that part of the original abutment of the railroad bridge
is now being used as a part of the present highway bridge.

22.

FREELAND

SHORTLY AFTER THE first spring thaw in 1877, good silver ore was found near the head of Trail Creek, just a few miles from Idaho Springs. Generally speaking, the discoveries were made on the silver belt that crosses Clear Creek County. Here, at an elevation of 8,914 feet, where the Freeland Lode crosses Trail Run or Trail Creek, a town was built. In addition to being close to Idaho Springs, the community was only about eight miles from Georgetown, and Lamartine was on the mountainside a couple of miles above Freeland.

An issue of the *Georgetown Miner,* published in September of 1878, reported that there were seventeen houses at Freeland, all of which had been completed within the past twelve months. Many more, it was reported, were nearing completion. That next week another reporter visited the camp and noted that thirty-four homes were occupied. Quite a large number of business houses seem to have flourished at Freeland from its earliest days. J. D. Armstrong operated a general merchandise store. The village meat market was run by John T. Jones. In the corner room of an old stone mill, Edward Jones and Company had a grocery and variety store. The town's single assay office was manned by George Vivian.

After 1879 a public school was conducted by Miss Emma Hull who reported twenty-one pupils in daily attendance. In later years, Bernice D. Poppen, a veteran teacher from Dumont, came up to Freeland and reported that many of her pupils were older than herself. A Mr. Price organized the first church service, prayer meeting, and Sunday school to be held at Freeland. Although they met in whatever quarters were available in the beginning, a later newspaper reported that Price organized a Presbyterian Church at Freeland in March of 1879. Price also doubled as the village blacksmith, operating an iron works in the town. On Sundays he was described by one of his contemporaries as one who "points out the errors of their ways to perishing sinners on Sundays." Without a newspaper of their own, the *Georgetown Miner* was read avidly. Along with their mail from the outside, it was carried up to them from the post office at Dumont. Freeland got its own post office on February 1, 1879. J. D. Armstrong moved the facility into his general store and became the town's first postmaster. He apparently filled the position capably for many years. The post office was later moved to the Kramer General Store. There is also a record of a Mrs. C. Redding who became postmistress at Freeland in December of 1896.

Water for community uses was obtained from Trail Creek by the simple expedient of the old oaken bucket. Family life in the town seems to have been rather well developed even in the early days. One visitor reported that Freeland was a "severely moral town." In another story a statement appeared to the effect that there was "no enticing jingle of beer glasses at Freeland." A roving journalist from the *Georgetown Miner* noted in March of 1879 that there were twenty-nine "legally ordained" families in the town already and that the better half of a thirtieth was already on the way from Kansas. Among the single men who worked in the mines, the same reporter noted that "many of their houses rather suggested of celibacy." His articles then went on to state that there were only "six correspondingly lonesome bachelors in the camp." Since the published census figures for Freeland in 1879 showed two hundred people there, one might wonder at the matrimonial propensities of all those other people not accounted for among those six celibate bachelors and the twenty-nine "legally ordained" marriages. It's probably a good thing that Freeland was a severely moral town.

Politically speaking, the Trail Creek Camp seems to have been fairly typical of most Colorado communities in this period. In 1878 there were only fifty registered voters, most of whom were Republicans. One of the exceptions to this rule was J. K. Mills, a Greenbacker, whose minority ideas were particularly offensive to the Republicans. Mills spent considerable time working with the members of the majority party, trying to help correct the error of their ways. In reality, fifty registered voters was a pretty good average for a town of this size when we realize that as late as 1954, the national election was decided by only 43 percent of the eligible registered voters. Even the Kennedy-Nixon contest enticed only 64.5 percent of those who could have voted.

From a total population standpoint, Freeland was pretty typical. In 1878 there were 175 people prospecting along Trail Run. Figures for the years between 1893 and 1900 showed a consistent four hundred souls. The *Georgetown Miner* remarked that most of them were males. From 1901 to 1905 a head count of only one hundred was recorded. Curiously out of place in the midst of all this was a last paragraph that told how "Freelandites have a decided, profound and chronic weakness for pumpkin pie, serious enough to provoke an appetite in a marble statue." Facetiously, perhaps a massive loss of appetite accounts for those three hundred souls who left between 1900 and 1901.

In addition to silver, some quantities of both gold and copper were also produced at Freeland. The Lone Tree Mine was notable, owned by Buttingham-Jones and Company. The Freeland Mine, above the town, was larger and turned out somewhat greater quantities of ore. It also had its own sawmill, built right there at the mine. John M. Dumont was the proprietor. Ex-Governor, ex-Senator Herbert Lehman of New York once owned stock in the Freeland. Down in the town, the Bullion smelter employed a small work crew

A photograph of Freeland taken in the 1880's

A large dump, roads, and scattered cabins are all that remain of early Freeland

and maintained a busy schedule during the boom years. The *Colorado Business Directory* lists Freeland in its volumes from 1893 through 1905. It declined rapidly in the years that followed.

Although there is more than one way to reach Freeland, only one of them is easy. Drive west on U. S. Highway 6 and 40 out of Idaho Springs. At the first exit past West Chicago Creek, get off the four-lane divided highway and onto the service road that parallels Clear Creek on the south side. Go on past the Stanley Hotel on your left. After passing a group of cabins, take the next good dirt road that goes off to the south or left. This road climbs sharply up the hill for several miles. You will see many abandoned mining properties along the way. When you come to a large field-stone mill foundation on the left side of the road, Freeland is just around the corner. A few houses across the creek to your right are about all that remain of the town. A big dump beyond the houses on the way to Lamartine was probably the Freeland Mine. In the gulch directly behind the field-stone mill foundation, the remains of several more homes can be seen. Once upon a time a street led up this steep hill, bisecting the rows of homes. This was either a suburb or the very earliest beginning of Freeland.*

---

* In this same general area, see also Brownsville, Silver Plume, Fall River, North Empire, and Gilson Gulch.

23.

GILLETT

MANY AMERICAN COMMUNITIES have secured their place in the sun by capitalizing upon some unusual event that transpired there. Gillett registered its claim to fame by boasting that it was the only place in the United States where a genuine, bona fide Mexican bullfight was ever held. Although there are rumors that Dodge City, Kansas, also staged a bullfight in its early days, the Gillett "fiesta" is definitely out of the rumor category. It really happened.

Like Goldfield, Gillett was always a family town from the days of its inception. It all started back in December of 1893 when it was decided to erect a town in the huge, very level meadow known as West Beaver Park. In elevation, the site was barely four thousand feet below the nearby summit of Pikes Peak, best known of the visible landmarks that surrounded the town. On January 19, 1894, the town was formally plotted. When an identity was sought, it was decided to name it for W. K. Gillett, an official of the Midland Terminal Railway. Throughout its life, Gillett was always remembered as being the most remote or outermost of the several towns in the Cripple Creek District.

At its peak the population amounted to only seven hundred people. Nevertheless, it enjoyed good transportation facilities in the form of a fine wagon road that crossed the meadow and dropped in over the edge of the old crater to Cripple Creek. In addition, the Midland Terminal's wide-gauge tracks bisected the town. During the peak years, two daily trains ran to and from Gillett. A wooden station house and a telegraph office were put up almost immediately. For many years the community boasted of the existence of forty-one assay offices, a rather startling total when we consider that only a few mines were located around Gillett. Discovered in 1892, the Lincoln was the top mine. It paid $114 to the ton in its best years. Surprisingly, little outside capital was invested in the mines around the town. Most of the operators owned their own properties.

In the town, a barrel concentration works was in operation. According to a couple of different references, it processed either 50 or 100 tons of ore daily and employed about 100 men. Out of its population of 700, Gillett boasted that it had 91 practicing attorneys, a rather startling ratio of the whole, if true. Very early in its life, the community built and began the operation of a fine water system, fed by waters from the melting snows of Pikes Peak. They also had a good system of fire hydrants. To supply a variety of other community wants, a local electrical plant was organized. It was owned by the Golden Crescent Water and Light Company which, in turn, was owned by Warren, Frank M., and H. E. Woods. At Eclipse, on the other side of the crater, these same men also owned the huge Economic Gold Extraction Company mill.

Many churches seem to have flourished at Gillett. From one source we hear that the first church in the Cripple Creek area was erected here by Reverend T. Volpe. If true, this would be Father Volpe, early-day Catholic priest who first resided at Anaconda. First or not, Volpe did put up a church, doing the manual work with his own hands. It was constructed of a combination of brick and native field stone. Winfield Scott Stratton, who made millions from Cripple Creek mining, once gave Fr. Volpe a large sum of money to assist in this church building project. By contemporary standards, Stratton was a notoriously irreligious man who publicly proclaimed his disdain of preachers throughout most of his later life. In Stratton's estimation, Volpe was a notable exception who did good work and was, therefore, deserving of help.

In August of 1895 this tiny hamlet really broke into the news and found its place in the sun. Going from the sublime to the ridiculous, Gillett had the only available racetrack near Cripple Creek. Charles Tutt and Spencer Penrose, district capitalists, laid out the track and had circular stands erected in the big meadow. The track became the pride of the area and a valuable recreational asset. Here many of the Cripple Creek District people raced their horses and exchanged proceeds from a few side bets. In 1895 some unusual events at this racetrack really hit the headlines.

Arizona Charlie Meadows, an itinerant cowboy, stood nearly seven feet tall without his boots. Joe Wolfe was a gambler and sometimes confidence man. Together, they pooled enough talent to organize and carry off a bullfight. After two Cripple Creek merchants had agreed to back the venture with five thousand dollars, Meadows and Wolfe rented the racetrack for August 24, 25, and 26. Next, they laid plans to get the bulls from Mexico into the country under provisions of the recently relaxed embargo on Mexican cattle. Only a few problems were encountered in securing the services of the necessary assortment of matadors, toreadors, and other varied window dressing necessary to this scheme.

To tie things up in a cozy fashion, Wolfe appointed all of the elected officials of Gillett to the board of directors of the Joe Wolfe Grand National Bullfight Company. Twenty tiers of seats were erected around the 250-square-foot bull pit. Tickets were printed and a gala affair was promised. Then the Humane Society of Colorado Springs got wind of the doings and lodged protests with a variety of state and national agencies. They seem to have been successful in securing the government order that stopped the bulls at the Mexican border.

When the great day arrived, special trains were run to

bring spectators from Denver and Colorado Springs. Most estimates agree that about fifty thousand people came to Gillett for the occasion. To assure that everyone was properly cared for, Wolfe had invited his old friend Soapy Smith to come down from Denver. Widely heralded as the King of the Con Men, Smith had set up five banks or rows of assorted bunco and gambling concessions around the track entrance. No less of a contribution was the saloon which had been hastily installed. From one source we hear that Soapy fleeced so many people before the gates opened that it interfered with the volume of ticket sales. After playing Soapy's games, many lacked the price of admission.

Meanwhile, Joe Wolfe was busily engaged in recruiting substitute bulls to replace the missing animals from south of the border. From a nearby ranch he inveigled the necessary quota of untrained domestic pasture stock. Wolfe became so overwhelmed with his own importance and with the auspicious occasion that he donned a cape and flat-crowned Spanish hat to become José Wolfe, the great impressario.

During the festivities a few unenthusiastic bulls, which didn't want to fight anyway, were killed in a series of pretty sloppy exhibitions. At the beginning of the second day, nearly all of the remaining bulls refused to fight. By this time the S.P.C.A. from Colorado Springs had the bit in their teeth and were demanding that arrests be made and the killing stopped.

Law enforcement officials arrested Wolfe and Meadows and jailed them in Colorado Springs. Later they admitted that the men had been clapped behind bars to protect them from the angry crowd which had finally resented being taken. The only positive result of the entire fiasco occurred when the dead bulls were cut up and given to the poor.

When the fortunes of Cripple Creek began to wane, Gillett was carried along inevitably. By 1900 the population was down to 524 people. By 1911 the racetrack stands had been torn down and the land was plowed up for farming. One

Courtesy Denver Public Library, Western History Collection
In its heyday the principal business street of Gillett was
lined with many double-storied buildings.

Collection of Robert L. Brown
Today's paved highway passes through the old site of Gillett and
cuts obliquely across the former business district.

of the surest signs of decline was the closing of the chlorination mill. Father Volpe's old church was now used as a hay barn. The interior trappings were removed and now repose in St. Peter's church at Cripple Creek. A fire in 1949 destroyed most of the remaining shell. Today its rocky foundations stand alone, a forlorn symbol in the middle of a vast hayfield.

State Highway 67, a beautiful paved road, leads south from Divide and passes right through what is left of Gillett, just before you reach the crater rim and Cripple Creek. Father Volpe's church is on your right just before the road makes a curve. Beyond it are two buildings and an assortment of smaller farm-type structures. Behind them is a wind sock to guide light planes that occasionally land here in the flat meadow. These are the only reminders of the Gillett that was, once upon a time.*

---

* In this same general area, see also Goldfield, Mound City, Eclipse, and Elkton.

24.

GILSON GULCH

MANY SMALL COLORADO communities with far less to justify their existence than Gilson Gulch, frequently put on airs, incorporated themselves, and added the dubious distinction of "City" to their names. Professional windbags were often hired to trumpet the local civic virtues, real or imagined, to a gullible nineteenth-century society. Exorbitant claims were made for the richness of nearby mineral deposits and for the zestful climate which produced such longevity that the town undertaker was forced to move elsewhere. In terms of a stable population, extent of economic development, and of legitimate community activities, Gilson could have qualified but never took the trouble to do so.

The Gilson family first settled here in the late 1870's or early 1880's following the discovery of some very good gold-bearing lodes. Two conflicting sets of chronology are available to confuse attempts to establish a firm date when the settlement actually began. A small community soon grew up in close proximity to the several mines. The inhabitants were principally Italians with a few families of French and German extraction. It is doubtful if the total number of residents at one time ever exceeded 150 to 200 persons.

The Gem Consolidated Mines Company had the best paying properties in the gulch. So rich were their ores that it was found profitable to drill a tunnel connecting Gilson Gulch with the Newhouse or Argo Tunnel down below at Idaho Springs. A large number of other mines also dotted the surrounding hillsides. Among the better known were the Dove's

Nest, Freighter's Friend, Garden, Franklin, Silver Age, Gold Medal, and, high on the hill above the town, the Southern Moon. Large four-horse ore wagons plied their way up and down the narrow trails carrying the rich ores to and from the mines and the smelters far below.

In 1893 the Dumont family arrived to open a boarding-house since no hotel has ever been recorded as having existed in the gulch. The Dumonts also opened a new saloon along the principal street. In addition, brewery wagons constantly plied the Virginia Canyon road from Central City with a barrel of beer on each side for Gilson Gulch.

The town itself, if such it may be called, was built low down in the bottom of the gulch. One grocery store was the only such enterprise in the community. Actually, it functioned more in the nature of a general store. Twice during each week a wagon came up from an Idaho Springs meat market to supply the residents with fresh beef, pork, and poultry. A similar service was rendered by a bakery wagon which came over from Black Hawk. The closest post office was at Idaho Springs and there was no free, home delivery in those days. Most people alternated with their neighbors in order to cut down the number of mail trips that might otherwise be necessary.

In the beginning, children from Gilson Gulch rode or hiked down the steep grades to Idaho Springs. In later years the volume of school children increased, a schoolhouse was con- structed and a teacher was hired to ride up from Idaho Springs each day on horseback.

Since most communities seem to need a local mystery to keep things interesting, Gilson Gulch managed to fill the need with a real baffler. The man's name was Demi, possibly a contraction from Dimitri if local stories were true. Ru- mors were rife throughout the district that Demi was a turncoat member of the Russian royal family who had run away to make a new life for himself elsewhere. Why he chose to live in a mining camp is unknown since he was never known to have engaged in the extraction of precious metals. None of the residents who are still living is able, in fact, to recall any instance when Demi ever worked at anything. There seemed to be enough money at all times. His home was one of the larger structures and stood below the mines in the lower end of the gulch. Facts concerning his early life are very scarce. A large steamer trunk that belonged to Demi still exists in the possession of a former Gilson Gulch resident. Perusal of its contents may yet provide some clues to the enigma.

The present condition of Gilson Gulch is disappointing. A very few buildings, some empty foundations, many yellowing mine dumps and the old roads are all that remain. A comparatively easy route follows Virginia Canyon up out of Idaho Springs and winds its way steeply around the hills on the way to Russell Gulch and Central City. At one point the road divides. It matters little which branch you take since they both rejoin each other a few miles farther up. The right branch is longer but contains easier grades; that is the reason why it was built. The left fork is steeper, more direct, and therefore shorter. This was the original toll road. Beyond the point where these two branches come back together are several blind corners and the road seems to emerge on the crest of a small rise where it forks again. The left branch is still the Virginia Canyon road. Turning right will quickly take you to Gilson Gulch. Park your car at the turnout by the next fork in the road. Below you is Gilson Gulch. The right branch of the road now descends steeply to the townsite. It is usually passable for conventional cars but better have a quick look first. The distance is short. Turning left from the turnout will carry you along a delightful little single-lane road which permits several good vistas of the gulch before it climbs over the hill and eventually enters Russell Gulch from the back side. In autumn this is an extremely pretty ride and as of this writing is still passable for regular cars. Many small trails leave this road from one side or the other and most terminate at old mines in the surrounding valleys. Many of these latter are Jeep roads.

Despite the number of turns, the trip to Gilson Gulch is an easy one and all distances are comparatively short. It can be made effortlessly in a single day from Denver, leaving more than ample time for lunch, exploring, and other pursuits before embarking on a leisurely late afternoon ride home.*

---

* In this same general area, see also Freeland, Brownsville, Silver Plume, Fall River, and North Empire.

Collection of Francis B. Rizzari
In its heyday Gilson Gulch was a busy and prosperous place

Collection of Robert L. Brown
The site of Gilson Gulch now shows few signs of its former activity

25.

GOLDFIELD

ALTHOUGH MUCH OF THE Cripple Creek district was already booming in 1894, Goldfield was still a timberline cow pasture. During the next year the town was founded by the owners of the great Portland Mine, James Doyle and J. F. Burns. Doyle and Burns were a couple of inexperienced Irish prospectors from Portland, Maine, who had struck it rich on Battle Mountain above Victor. One of them had been a carpenter while the other was an ex-plumber. In secret, Winfield Scott Stratton had assisted the two men in developing their claims which eventually became two of the greatest producers in the district, the Portland No. 1 and the Portland No. 2.

Barely north and slightly east of Victor, just around the slope of Battle Mountain, Doyle and Burns found a large open meadow that seemed ideal for their purposes. Here their Gold Knob Mining and Townsite Company went to work on the business of starting a town. Jimmy Burns, who actually headed up the Gold Knob Company, put his men to work laying out streets and selling lots here in the valley that lay between Bull Hill on the northwest, Battle Mountain to the west, and Big Bull Mountain on the east.

Contrary to popular opinion, most Western mining towns of this era were surprisingly quiet and decorous places in which to live. Although the West had known such places as Dodge City, Leadville, Tombstone, and Abilene, these were not typical. If their overly-publicized bacchanals had been emblematic, the mortality rate would have precluded any "settling" of the frontier. Even the most lawless settlements calmed down within the first year or so of their existences.

From its beginning, Goldfield acquired the reputation of being a family town. Homes, schools, and churches were far more common here than were saloons and dance halls. In some records, Goldfield was referred to as the "City of Homes." It also had more sidewalks than any other town in the district. Over the years residents have also laid claim to having the oldest, continuously operating Sunday school in the Cripple Creek area. There is a very good chance that it was the highest Sunday school, too, since Goldfield was built at an elevation of 9,903 feet above sea level.

As the town developed, a fine business district grew up along the principal streets. Many of the best mines were only a stone's throw from the settlement. Consequently, many families elected to settle here in order to be closer to the husband's work. By the end of the first year, 2,191 people had already found homes at Goldfield. Not far away, the town of Independence had grown up around the Hull Placer deposit. Within an incredibly brief time the two communities grew toward each other and merged. By 1895 Independence had been taken in or annexed by Goldfield. In the process, the population for 1895 had grown to 3,000. By 1900, there were 3,500 people there and Goldfield had become the third largest town in the district.

Among the nearby mines that contributed to the influx of population were the Findley, the Independence, the Portland No. 1 and No. 2, the Golden Cycle, and the Vindicator. Together they shipped twenty thousand tons of ore per year. The previously mentioned Hull City Placer had furnished the initial impetus that resulted in the founding of the now absorbed town of Independence. To better serve this massive mining complex, all three of the major district railroads extended lines into or through Goldfield. Since the town had been fortuitously located in a huge open meadow, all three of the railroads took advantage of this precious space and built freight yards here. There were also wooden stations and a telegraph office. Ultimately, three fourths of all the ore mined in the Cripple Creek basin was shipped from Goldfield.

Although the labor wars of 1894 and 1903-4 have been mentioned in two other chapters, Goldfield was also affected and in a rather unusual way. It seems that all of the elected city officials were members of the Western Federation of Miners. To put it bluntly, Goldfield was a veritable hotbed of unionism. When Governor Peabody called out the state militia and placed troops in the district to maintain order, it was deemed prudent to station one of the garrisons at Goldfield. Less than a mile away, the Strong Mine had been captured by the strikers in the first clash. Ultimately the operators won their victory, the unions were broken and known members were loaded on flatcars for deportation out of the state. By the close of 1904, nearly half the homes at Goldfield were empty. All unionized city officials were ousted from office by a group of nonunion citizens in 1904 and control of the city was restored to the mineowners. Incidentally, the original city hall still stands. Although badly in need of repair, it is an architectural gem with weathered brown exterior walls. For more than two decades it has been unused. Upstairs one may see the old courtroom and a huge safe still emblazoned with "City of Goldfield" in gold-leaf lettering. Nearby is the ancient firehouse with its original hand-drawn pumper still inside.

With the coming of electricity, the La Bella Power Plant was erected here. For ten years or so it supplied power to a variety of communities including Cripple Creek, Victor, Anaconda, and of course Independence and Goldfield.

Currently Goldfield still has a small resident population. To find it, merely drive around the corner to the northeast from the edge of Victor where State Highway 67 stops. If time permits, the old Florence and Cripple Creek railroad grade is now a fine dirt road and you may enjoy driving over

Collection of Fred and Jo Mazzulla
Goldfield, the family town of the Cripple Creek Mining District

Collection of Robert L. Brown
With Pikes Peak on the horizon, a few families still carry on life in lofty Goldfield

it through Phantom Canyon, coming up from Florence. Another choice, and a very scenic one, allows you to drive over the abandoned grades of the Short Line from western Colorado Springs. This is the fabulous Gold Camp Road. Although longer, either of these two latter routes provides a most unforgettable approach to Goldfield.*

---

* In this same general area, see also Mound City, Eclipse, Elkton and Gillett.

26.

JASPER

ALMOST TWO DECADES had passed into history since the original Pikes Peak gold rush when a group of experienced miners from Cornwall, England, chose to seek the yellow metal within the virgin wilderness southwest of present-day Monte Vista, Colorado. Deep in Rio Grande County, where Bitter Creek empties into the Alamosa River, their efforts met with success and the Conejos Mining district was established.

There, in 1880, they started erecting a ramshackle assortment of tents and log cabins on the north side of the Alamosa River. They named their settlement Cornwall, after their former home. Another source tells us that the town was named for John Cornwall, the first postmaster. There is also a difference of opinion concerning the town's chronology. In her superb *Stampede to Timberline*, Muriel Sibell Wolle tells of finding information about Jasper having been established in 1874-75.

Within a few months the town had doubled both its population and its building construction. Early records described the settlement as being 18 miles south and 4 miles west of Del Norte. From another source we find it described as being 10 miles east of Summitville, at an altitude of 9,145 feet above sea level. In reality both directions were correct and would get you there.

To provide for the miners' welfare and to assure themselves a tidy profit, the Marion Gold Mining Company began its operations on April 4, 1880. For many years the Perry and Miser lodes were the two best producers at Cornwall. Ultimately, two separate but adjacent towns grew up at the site. For some reason the second community assumed the name of Jasper and few obstacles could check its growth, although the two locations existed for a time, side by side. In any case, Jasper gradually absorbed Cornwall and its separate identity was no more.

Within an incredibly short time weekly stagecoach and mail service from the outside world had reached the community. When George Crofutt visited the camp it was still named Cornwall and had apparently just acquired its mail service. On that occasion Crofutt remarked, "The mail to Cornwall is being transported on a broncho, straddled by a Fifteenth Amendment." Since this was the Negro Suffrage Amendment, passed in February of 1870, I assume that the rider must have been a colored man. Crofutt also described the town as being on an old wagon road that ran from Fort Garland to Pagosa Springs. He also wrote that it was impossible for wagons to go on for any distance west of the town. Actually, the legal plot for Cornwall was filed with James A. Shields, a county judge, on April 5, 1881, not long before Crofutt arrived in camp.

By 1886, there were two hundred people living and working there. Ten years later, the first post office was established and D. A. Wolfe was appointed to be the first postmaster on December 3, 1896. This account of a first post office and a first postmaster differs from the one given earlier in this chapter. Since both bits of information came from very reliable sources, I decided to include both accounts and let the chips fall where they will. Obviously, the first postmaster could not have been both John Cornwall and D. A. Wolfe.

All sources of information about Jasper seem to be in agreement concerning the beginning of its demise. Instead of being content with local conditions, the operators loaded up a ten-ton shipment of ore to be refined at Denver. An impatient crowd milled about at Jasper awaiting the results of the assay. From then on, things went from bad to worse.

Jasper, on the Alamosa River south of Del Norte, as photographed by George Beam

Many trees now obscure the terrain at what remains of Jasper

Word soon arrived that the smelter had burned down. To this day the results are unknown. In any case, the exodus began and the population of Jasper started to dwindle. Within a few years, the town was on the skids.

Then in 1902 a group of capitalists from Massachusetts appeared on the scene with $100,000 clutched in their hot little hands. Directly they opened up the Sanger Mining and Milling Company, a reduction plant capable of treating 125 tons of ore daily. Located about two and a half miles above the town toward Stunner Pass, the Sanger operation gave Jasper a second lease on life. Fortunately they located a good mine on the hillside directly above their mill. Ore was brought down the incline by wooden chutes.

Eventually the Sanger properties pinched out and Jasper resumed its slumbers until some years ago when many of the old residences were refurbished to become fine mountain cottages for the fortunate people who now return to Jasper each summer.

Like so many of the towns in this book, Jasper is an easy-to-reach location. Drive straight south on Highway 15 out of Monte Vista. After 12 miles the pavement stops. At this point turn right, or west, and follow the graded dirt road that gradually climbs into the hills. After you enter Rio Grande National Forest, a road to Capulin branches left; don't take it. Keep straight ahead past two campgrounds, to Jasper. If in doubt, follow the signs to Platoro Reservoir. This road goes through Jasper long before reaching the reservoir.

It is also possible to drive the somewhat longer route southwest from Del Norte to Summitville and beyond to the forks of an unnumbered road. Keep left at this point and follow the Alamosa River to Jasper, a gem of a town in a truly beautiful, wooded alpine setting.*

---

* In this same general area, see also Platoro and Stunner.

27.

KING CITY

BACK IN 1871, George Lechner discovered some rich semi-bituminous deposits of coal in South Park. Eight years later he sold some of his holdings to the South Park Coal Company. From April of 1879 until the area declined, this company operated the King mines. Among the workers who labored in the pits, Europeans predominated. In the beginning these people were mostly of Italian extraction. Their nostalgia for home resulted in a name for the community that grew up around the mines. They called it Como, for the beautiful lake in northern Italy. The name was retained until the Denver, South Park and Pacific Railway erected a station at the end of their tracks in June of 1879. At that time many of the residents moved over the three miles or so to the new location and took the name with them.

In a historical sense, the first or original site of Como ultimately became King Park or King City. Both names have survived. As a source of the new designation for their momentarily nameless settlement, they chose W. H. King, clerk of the South Park Coal Company. King also kept the general store, and when postal facilities became available, he was made the first postmaster.

In the accompanying photograph we see a typically unimaginative company town. Apparently no effort was made to harmonize with the surrounding ranges of tumbling peaks that encircle one of the most majestic high-altitude parks in all of North America. Within a few years about sixty two- and three-room company houses had been put up. Later, of course, the inevitable saloon also appeared. For those families that had the time and inclination to travel, there were four livery stables that stood ready to supply both wagons and horses. One busy blacksmith shop took care of keeping all of the animals well shod. Since most Europeans have a high regard for craftsmanship, King City soon boasted a fine carpenter shop. From earliest times the coal company had built and operated its own store here. Such facilities became a fixture in most of the company-owned towns during this period.

Although the average population of King City ranged between two hundred and four hundred people, it was an active and proud little place and for years the residents even insisted on having their own school. For the company-owned mines, there was a powder house for storage of all dangerous explosives. They also had a scale house for weighing the coal. To store water, there was a wooden-sided water tank. Near the edge of town, not far from one of the stables, stood a livestock pen. Although there are references to a cemetery, my research leads me to believe that most of the dead were interred at nearby Como.

Since there were no civil rights laws to twit men's consciences, segregation of the races at King City became an accepted pattern of life. Traditionally, the Germans, Italians, Austrians, Hungarians, and Swedes occupied the north side of the town. The southern portion was populated by Americans and persons of British descent. When the Chinese were brought in to work in the mines during 1880, they lived wherever they could find a place. In point of time, their tenure at King City was rather brief. The resentful Italians attacked in force and drove the Chinese out before peace could be restored. Scarcely less significant was the continuance of this segregation in the life of the only church in the town.

Taken as a whole, there were seven coal properties being worked at various times. When one was exhausted, another would be opened. A few, like the King No. 1, succeeded abundantly while others produced less well. All of the King Mines were slope rather than shaft mines. Allison Chandler, my source for much of the material in this chapter, says that the prime year was 1884. Accumulations of explosive gas in the several underground levels contributed to a perpetually dangerous situation. Many Chinese were killed in an explosion at the King No. 1 in 1885. Subsurface fires swept this same mine in 1886 and again in 1889.

Then, on January 10, 1893, came the most awful tragedy in the town's history. An underground explosion in King Mine No. 5 took the lives of something over twenty men; the totals vary. Among themselves, the survivors decided on a mass funeral for seventeen of the men, with subsequent interment across the way at the cemetery adjacent to Como. The rest of the bodies were shipped out for later burial at their own homes elsewhere. From the time of the tragedy until the day of the funeral, bad weather added to the general atmosphere of gloom. A sullen, lowering rack of storm clouds and driving, whirling snow had enveloped South Park. Dense white mists rose like smoke from Tarryall Creek, contributing an eerie quality to the entire saddening sequence of events.

The day of the funeral brought a change. It dawned clear and cold, filled with the icy breath of the great winds that swept down from the tumbled mountaintops and roared through the high pine forests. At the tiny church far below, the minute interior could not hold all of the bodies, let alone the mourners. A single coffin was selected and brought inside to symbolize all of those who had perished in the tragedy. Following the services, the coffins filled two railroad boxcars. Accompanied by sorrowing families, the train moved slowly across the meadow, through Como, and out to the cemetery. Two trenches, each about twenty feet long, had already been dug. Eight coffins were somehow placed in each of the two excavations. Andy Anderson was the seventeenth or odd-numbered body. Since he had been of a different faith, his remains were buried apart from the others.

In a historical sense, King City only lasted for about twenty years. After the coal deposits had been exhausted in all seven of the King Mines, the town was abandoned in the late 1890's. Some short-term leases were taken to rework a number of the properties in the 1930's but, except for these instances, the town has been dead for most of the present century. Gone now are the lawns and beds of flowers that once fringed the neat rows of little white houses. Nothing more than a string of depressions in the earth now marks the former sites of the workers' homes. Only the dumps of the several King Mines show that life once existed here.

From U.S. Highway 285, about halfway between Jefferson and Fairplay, a one-mile-long road leads north to Como. Almost directly across the highway is the start of the Elk Horn Road, a dirt trail that leads off across South Park to the south. Roughly a mile south of U.S. 285 you will come to an intersection. The main or best road keeps to the left. A much less desirable but passable pair of tire tracks turns off to the right and goes down for a half mile into the gulch that once held King City. When you park above the banks of the twisting creek, you are in King City.

All around you, the barren gulch is now deserted by everybody and the curious antelope and other animals have returned to drink from the little stream that once more flows nearly as clear and pure as it did when George Boyd first viewed it.*

---

* In this same general area, see also Boreas, Como, Dyersville, Tarryall, and Hamilton.

Collection of Francis B. Rizzari
King City, the old coal-mining town in South Park

Collection of Robert L. Brown
Apart from the mountains and the dump, King City is only a memory

28.

KOKOMO

SWEEPING DOWN from the icy pinnacles of the Ten Mile Range, the cold blasts of a high-altitude blizzard roared across the valley below, engulfing a small party of migrants who were defying the odds in an effort to reach Leadville. On nearby Fremont Pass, a ten-foot snowfall had blanketed the slopes. The biting cold had already taken its toll when one member of the party, a Scotsman, had died. Pausing temporarily, a burial party was dispatched to prepare a grave. While hacking away at the frozen earth, they discovered silver about four feet below the topsoil. "Scotty" was stashed in a convenient snowbank, the claim was named and became the productive Dead Man Mine, and that's one version of how Kokomo got started.

Still another story relates that it was founded by the Recen brothers. They, too, discovered subsoil deposits in December of 1878. One more version still favors the Recen brothers but moves the occasion ahead to early 1879. George Crofutt says the town was incorporated on June 3, 1879. All versions agree that the town's name came from Kokomo, Indiana, hometown of most of the first party that came into the valley. Although the first story is a little too perfect as a story and certainly makes for superb theater, there was, nevertheless, a Dead Man Mine and the time is about right.

Little doubt exists in regard to the role of the Recen brothers in getting things started. However, although I believe this spelling of Recen to be correct, there are also references which report the name as "Racene" and as "Racine."

Almost immediately, a second town grew up beside Kokomo. It assumed the name of Recen. Within an incredibly short time, the two communities grew toward each other and met. Most contemporaries were unsure just where the dividing line was located. One reference noted that Kokomo and Recen were separated by the little rill (stream) that flows from the mountains, running between them and bisecting the meadow at a right angle to the present paved highway. Another source says the two towns were divided only by a street. In any case, the rivalries between them were intense.

In this meadow where the town developed, the elevation is 10,618 feet above sea level. Population statistics from some sources stretch credulity to the breaking point. In a few cases the totals for Recen may have been combined with those of Kokomo. For example, in 1879 Kokomo supposedly had 1,500 people. Yet, in 1880 it is reported as being down to 808. By the end of 1880 it seems to have returned to the 1,500 figure. During its peak year, 1881, a figure of 10,000 has been given.

Mining developments here seem to have started with the previously mentioned subsoil deposits in the meadow where the town grew up. Nearby, George Crofutt reported that there were placer claims along the banks of Ten Mile Creek. In the mountains a wide variety of mines were worked. The aftermath yielded between $80 and $400 to the ton from carbonate of lead. The Crown Point and the Ruby Silver assayed out ore at $1,500 per ton. Other notable properties were the Hoodoo, Grand Union, Gilpin, Wheel of Fortune, Silver Blossom, Michigan, Reconstruction, Queen of the West, Snowbank, Forest Combination, Wilfley, Little Chicago, Eagle Mining Company and the White Quail on Elk Mountain. The Mayflower and Enterprise were on Jack Mountain, and there were also some gold mines on Fletcher Mountain. Two smelters, the White Quail and the Greer, maintained a heavy schedule.

In the combined townships there were several hostelries.

Among them was the Woods Hotel which had two large tents on the principal street and an annex in the form of an additional tent for boarders, pitched on the hillside. Some other hotels were the Pennsylvania House, the Summit House, and the Western Hotel. Early in 1882 a fine two-story Masonic hall was erected. It gave up its home in September of 1965. Furnishings from Kokomo's eighty-five-year-old lodge are now preserved in a special room at the museum in Leadville. Members of the lodge have currently joined with the one at Leadville and the two have formally merged. In its heyday, the Kokomo Lodge boasted that it was the highest in the nation, 10,618 feet above sea level. At the time of the merger with Leadville, there were still 137 members on the books. With Leadville at 10,200 feet, the newly consolidated lodge may still hold the altitude record.

A rather pretentious two-story school, complete with belfry, was also among the town's early achievements. Children frequently attended school on skis or snowshoes. In fairly recent years, a modern school was built to replace the ancient two-story frame structure. At least one church, a bank, four sawmills, and several general stores were also built. Three newspapers seem to have flourished in the early days. Earliest of all was the *Summit County Times,* published in September of 1879. Prices here at this location reflected the remoteness of Kokomo. Flour brought twelve dollars a sack. On the other hand, ham or sugar sold at only twenty cents a pound.

A disastrous winter fire in 1882 nearly cleaned out Ten Mile Avenue, the principal business street. Losses ranged between $300,000 and $500,000. The fire had several results. Actually, the blaze had been in the Kokomo end of the settlement. Recen offered free lots within its town limits to all survivors. Although Kokomo had been known for a short time as Kokomo City, the "City" was dropped from the name after the fire. Also, as a direct result of the conflagration, Kokomo moved its post office to Recen. Although

Collection of Francis B. Rizzari
Looking down Ten Mile Avenue in early Kokomo

Collection of Robert L. Brown
A contemporary view of Kokomo in the 1960's

much of Kokomo was later rebuilt, the two towns, nevertheless effected a permanent merger. While the post office retained its legal designation as the Kokomo Post Office, Recen became the legal name for the town. Incorporation papers with these changes were duly filed. Despite this, only one map (from an oil company) currently lists the town of Recen. To all others it is still Kokomo.

In the early days, Leadville served as the chief supply center for most of the satellite mining camps. Teams of horses and packtrains hauled freight over the twenty miles that separated Kokomo from Leadville. Freight was hauled for seven cents per pound. It cost twenty dollars to haul a barrel of vinegar over the road. From Georgetown, the Ten Mile Toll Road Company built a grade across the range to Recen and Kokomo. Stagecoaches operated over the road between 1879 and 1886.

Later, the Denver and Rio Grande extended their rails into the valley. Two railroads, the Denver, South Park and Pacific and the Rio Grande, served the town. At this writing, one of the old depots, which later became a store, is still standing. Fare on the Rio Grande line was $16.50 to ride one way from Denver to Kokomo. An alternate route could be arranged by riding the stagecoach from Denver to Georgetown for $7.00. Passengers might then switch to the Colorado Division of the Union Pacific and ride to Leadville for $10.30 more.

With such a well-developed system of transportation, food was more varied here than elsewhere. Upon his visit to the camp, George Crofutt remarked that the pioneer larder could be varied by the availability of wild game nearby. Deer, elk, bear, mountain lions, grouse, and quail abounded in the Ten Mile Range.

When winter snows covered the valley, the residents of Kokomo kept track of the miners who toiled high on the mountainsides, in an unusual way. Shortly after it got dark each night, at a prearranged hour, all miners placed kero-

*With the school as a backdrop, here was a D. & R.G. train
waiting at the station in Kokomo.*

*In April of 1966 only the school remained of the group of
buildings shown in the photograph above.*

sene lamps in their cabin windows that faced toward the town. Should a lamp fail to appear, people in the valley acted accordingly and a snowshoe rescue mission soon brought aid.

Even now the fate of Kokomo has not been entirely decided. It was formally abandoned in 1965, and the Climax Molybdenum Company purchased the site. Several years ago the settling pond of the Climax Company buried the town of Robinson, just up the valley. Presumably, Kokomo is destined to share the same fate. When last seen, the dump was already close to the edge of the old town. In October of 1965, the Kokomo Post Office closed its doors for the last time. Up until the very end, the town retained a vestige of its municipal government. Mrs. Helen Byron was the last mayor. With so few people in town, every other homeowning family was represented on the six-man town council. All early municipal records of Kokomo have been gathered up and now repose in the office of the Summit County Clerk. Approximately one hundred graves in the Kokomo Cemetery have been moved to higher ground. The Robinson graveyard had to be moved earlier.

To reach Kokomo, drive on U.S. Highway 6 over Loveland Pass to State Highway 91. An alternate route may be taken by driving on U.S. 24 through Leadville to the southern end of State 91. In November of 1966 a new section of highway was completed to replace this older portion that passed close to Kokomo. The new road is located somewhat higher on the mountain but both the old grade and the townsite are visible below you. Access to the original road, still paved, is from the north end, at a point three miles south of the intersection of Highway 6 and State 91. The town was below the old highway and west of it on the north side of Fremont Pass. Kokomo and Recen, once proud names on the roster of historic Colorado mining centers, have lived out their last days.*

---

* In this same general area, see also Oro City.

29.

LEAVICK

THE OLD TOWN OF Leavick was formerly one of Colorado's most picturesque ghost towns. Then, in 1948, operations were temporarily resumed at the Last Chance Mine. The name of the lode proved prophetic for what was to be the fate of the town. Arrangements were made by the mining firm to purchase the right-of-way of the old Denver and South Park rail line. Park County agreed to maintain a graveled road on the old grade from U.S. Highway 285 up to Leavick. Opening this road also opened up the valley to senseless vandalism and curio seekers at a later time. These elements, coupled with some particularly severe winters, have combined to leave the site in ruins.

Possibly the earliest prospecting activity in this valley dates from 1869 when the first traces of silver and lead were discovered. The ore deposits were exploited solely for their precious metals and little interest was manifested in building a town. At that time silver had a market value of fifty-three cents an ounce while lead sold at four cents a pound.

The actual beginnings of Leavick date from 1873 when the Last Chance lode was discovered. Its location was high up on the 12,600-foot saddle ridge between Mount Sherman and Mount Sheridan. Later, the Hilltop Mine was opened up only a short distance away, on the same saddle in the lofty, rich Mosquito Range. Both were silver properties. Eventually, two huge mills were placed at the base of the range in Horseshoe Gulch. Water was readily available from Four Mile Creek for their operations. In the beginning the ore was hauled down to the mills by teams of horses and by mule-drawn ore wagons. As the volume of their production increased, a three-mile-long tram line was installed, with tremendous steel cables, to connect the mills with the mines. Huge black iron buckets moved overhead, dumping tons of rich ore into bins at the mills. The momentum of full buckets coming down pulled the empty buckets back up the tram for another load.

The cluster of cabins and other structures that grew up around the mills was named for Felix Leavick, an early prospector in the district. The mills and mines gave the town its lifeblood. At the peak of its boom, Leavick housed slightly more than one thousand people who came to wrest a fortune from this rich, rocky, timberline basin in the shadow of Horseshoe Mountain, a glacial cirque that has long been a landmark at the western head of the valley. The town stood at an elevation of 11,294 feet, nestled in the bottom of a high gulch beneath the towering 14,000-foot peaks of the Mosquito Range. Although Leavick was actually closer to Leadville, a scant seven miles across the Mosquitos, the fifteen-mile approach from Fairplay was far easier. An approach from the Leadville side would make a wonderfully scenic ride but cutting such a road would be a dangerous and complex proposition.

One early and rather overoptimistic account said that Leavick had just one street which extended all the way up from Fairplay to the top of Horseshoe Mountain. Although such gross exaggerations were common among nineteenth century tub-thumpers for early mining towns, local people accepted these lies with tongue in cheek as necessary for attracting outside capitalists or to impress Eastern tourists.

During its boom Leavick was a busy and a happy place. There were two saloons, a community-sponsored baseball team, and a brothel on the edge of town. A dentist and a barber found community need sufficient to justify their full-time attention in the community. Further prosperity

seemed assured when the Denver and South Park built a narrow-gauge branch line up Four Mile Creek through Horseshoe and Mudsill to the Last Chance Mill. Ores and concen-
trates were hauled out in quantity during good times and,
in the 1920's, this same line took out zinc.

In terms of up-to-date communications, the town lagged
behind. No telegraph office existed in the camp and no telephone line connected the community with the outside world.
In order to find out what was going on, the mill superintendent drove down to Fairplay each day for his market letter,
which came by telegraph, and brought back the latest news.
I have never found any record of a newspaper being published at Leavick. Under such conditions gossip probably
flourished to a high degree.

As one entered the town along its principal street, the first
building was the Baker boardinghouse where many of the
unmarried teamsters and miners "batched." Farther along up
the hill stood the school. In winter the children climbed up
the hill on web snowshoes to attend classes. Back down the
street on the opposite side were some private residences with
barns which were used only occasionally. On the upper side
of the street stood the cookhouse. Behind it were two long,
low barns which house the fine big teams used to haul supplies up to the mines and to bring the ore back down. One
general store and the post office stood at the far end of the
settlement. Farther down the valley, about three miles below Leavick, the older town of Horseshoe was gradually
abandoned with the miners moving up the creek to be absorbed into the larger population.

July 4 was always a great occasion. The men came down
from the mines to participate in a big camp picnic. Huge
bales of hay were dragged in and spread all over the floor of
the old hotel until it was quite smooth. Close to one hundred pairs of feet spent the evening dancing quadrilles,
waltzes, and polkas.

With the repeal of the Sherman Silver Purchase Act in

1893 history repeated itself once more at Leavick. When word came by telegraph that the price of silver had fallen, a spectacular exodus that has few parallels began. One source says that the town was emptied of people in a single day and a night. Improbable as this may seem, there are many accounts which try to substantiate it. One story says that when word of the market crash reached the camp, miners were finishing their noon meal. Without waiting to clean up, the men just left the table, grabbed a few belongings, and departed for the gold camps. Years later, when Leavick was "rediscovered," the dirty dishes were still on the tables just as they had been left when the unwelcome news came.

In another account the superintendent reached the workings of the Hilltop Mine with his telegram, which read, "Blow your whistle and pack your diggers. We're through!" Apparently he did just that, but some limited operations were nevertheless pursued until the autumn of 1899, at which time all operation shut down and the town has never made a successful comeback. The attempt to reopen Leavick in 1920 was not successful and the last mill closed down again in 1923, never to turn a wheel again. This repeal of the Sherman Act was the same debacle that ruined Horace A. W. Tabor and others in Leadville and, in fact, sounded the death knell of the pure silver camps throughout the American West.

Leavick remained virtually isolated and almost untouched in its lonely valley, unnoticed until after World War II. Reaching Leavick today is simple. Drive south out of Fairplay on Highway 285 for about one mile. At this point a dirt road turns west beside a small white sign that says "Horseshoe." Follow this well-graded dirt road for about ten miles, through the empty meadow that once held the town of Horseshoe. From this point another two miles will carry you past the crumbling remains of Mudsill. One more mile and you are at your destination.

A few old snow-crushed buildings can still be seen. The

Collection of Fred and Jo Mazzulla
In this early photograph of Leavick the two mills are at the right and the town is at the left.

Collection of Robert L. Brown
Leavick as it looks today, photographed from the same angle

huge old tram house of the Hilltop operation is on a knoll above the road to your right. As of this writing the Last Chance Mill was still standing by the edge of the stream. Beyond it are the crumbling foundations of the Hilltop Mill. Above the road, leading up the mountainside, are a few of the tramway towers while piles of decaying timbers mark the sites of the others. A scar that was once the main street still has a few rock foundations on both sides. Now the last of the still-standing small buildings have been transported down to Fairplay where they currently repose as museum pieces and Leavick has been left in shreds.*

---

* In the same general area, see also Alma, Buckskin Joe, Fairplay, Puma City, Quartzville, Montgomery, and Sacramento.

30.

LULU CITY

NEARLY EVERY COMMUNITY has some unusual historical claim
to fame if one digs deeply enough in search of it. Lulu City
was no exception. It was founded on a hoax, perpetrated to
make people believe there was placer gold in the sands of
the upper reaches of the Colorado River. At that time the
river was known as the Grand and several locations still be-
lie its former identity. Such places as Grand Mesa, Granby,
Grand Junction, Grand County, and Grand Lake, among
others, are keys to its earlier name.

Lulu City was founded during 1879 near the headwaters
of the river's north fork, deep in the Never Summer Range.
Fortunately for all concerned, both gold and silver were
found nearby in limited quantities. In the spring of 1880, it
was rumored that the surface outcroppings "surpassed anything known in mining history" a completely ridiculous
claim. The actual fissures were quartz lodes, found lying
between the walls of granite, and containing more gold than
silver. The elevation here was 9,400 feet above sea level.

During the brief flurry that followed, sometimes called a
mining boom, several towns sprang to life in the area. In
addition to Lulu City there were three others, called Dutch-
town, a mile away, Gaskill, to the south, and Teller City.
Near the towns, several mines were opened up. Some were
good and others left something to be desired. Their names
displayed the usual touch of adventure and nostalgia so frequently encountered among lonely men so far from home.
Some of the names were fanciful ones like Southern Cross,

Wolverine, Tiger, Rustic and Friday Nite. From the start, they were beset with troubles, principally transportation. It was just too far to the railroads and the smelters. Shipping costs quickly ate up the profits and the last of the mines closed in the nineties.

When discussing this town, someone invariably wants to know, "Who was Lulu?" With such a name she should have been a dance-hall girl and that's how folklore gets started; but she wasn't. Lulu was the favorite daughter of Benjamin Franklin Burnett (or Barnett); the accounts vary. In the finest Victorian tradition she was described as being beautiful and popular in the community, so Daddy, who was the founder of the town, named it for her. Sandwiched away in an old document at the State Historical Society of Colorado is a notation that Lulu Burnett was a "raven-haired belle." She must have been very beautiful and very popular because the principal street soon became Lulu Avenue and the chief crossing of the range to the north became Lulu Pass. As time passed, she must have faded, though, because it's called Thunder Pass now. In researching information about mining camps, one is frequently struck by the sameness of the descriptions reserved for the feminine contingent. All are described as "beautiful, popular," etc. Didn't any plain girls ever settle in a mining camp? The term "plain girl" is a euphemism employed by older people to designate otherwise nice, wholesome girls who, being sound of wind, limb, and character, are somewhat deficient in pulchritude. In the predominantly male environment of a frontier town in the days of chivalry, all women looked beautiful. Even Calamity Jane was so described in one lonely narrative. The men got there first and opened the country. The women, as usual, took their time.

Meanwhile back at Lulu City, an ambitious town plot had been laid out with about one hundred blocks, divided up by nineteen streets and about four avenues. At first the anxious men lived in tents, but gradually the more substantial log cabins predominated. By 1881 there were about five hundred people here although one source kites population statistics to a highly unlikely one thousand. Before long, the customary array of stores and saloons had found their places on Lulu Avenue. Sandwiched in among them were one assay office, several restaurants, a land office and the inevitable hotel. No church ever got a foothold at Lulu City. In the June 5, 1882, issue of the *Rocky Mountain News* a report about Lulu City was carried. It said that thirteen business buildings had been put up in the previous month alone. Three lumber mills, the Hertel, the Tabor, and the Boyd and Harrington, all turned out green lumber for the booming town. To supply the miners' other wants, the Godsman and Company General Merchandise Store was opened. At times it seems to have doubled as a hotel. Other businesses included the William Dugnay Drug Store, the Holly Saloon, the Denver Saloon, the Howard Mountain and Galena Mining Company.

Above the bustling community, impatient prospectors staked their claims on the rocky hillsides, looking for the elusive deposits that would pour tons of gold into their laps. The dark blue-green forest world of leaf and needle gave way as the hills and gulches swarmed with men, burros, and machinery. By May of 1882, a crude road from Georgetown had been opened to a point only six miles from Lulu City. Another road came in over the pass from Fort Collins and was reported to be free of snow by June. Three times each week stagecoaches lumbered up from Fort Collins with more people for the growing community. Along the way, this same line also made stops at Teller City and Grand Lake. During 1884, a new mine, the Rabbit Ear, was discovered. Active lumbering filled an economic void for a while.

Within the short life span of Lulu City, the miners regrettably found very little gold and those silver deposits that were located proved to be of a low grade. Some sources place the beginning of decline late in 1884, while others prefer the following year. Without a mill or refinery at the site, costs of shipping the ore out of the district to Denver, 113 miles away, were staggering. With such a ready supply of water, it seems incredible that none of these enterprising souls saw fit to put up a mill. It was just too far from either railroads or the smelters at that time.

A few of the mines were worked into the 1890's but most of the people had pulled out long before that. With little idea of permanence, the families moved out, heeding the call of more promising strikes elsewhere. Behind them they left rows of stoutly chinked cabins, strung out along the river. At the edge of town a wagon petrifies, waiting for the last resident to depart. Most accounts speculate upon the speedy evacuation of Lulu City. Apparently the people were so anxious to get out that they left most of their accumulated belongings behind. Dishes remained on tables, clothing was not removed from closets, and one highly unlikely story tells us that dinners were left cooking on the stoves. By January of 1886 even the post office had been discontinued.

Instructions for going to Lulu City are a bit different than those for any other location in this book since the site is now within the boundaries of Rocky Mountain National Park. Without a doubt the simplest way to find it involves going into the park at the Grand Lake entrance. From that point drive north along the north fork of the Colorado River past Timber Creek toward Milner Pass. Just before you get to the switchbacks that climb the pass, watch for a small sign about Lulu City on your left. Follow the short dirt road beside the sign to a picnic ground where you can leave your car. From here on you must walk or rent a horse.

A fine trail begins here and goes generally up the valley, sometimes following the river. Since the National Park Service uses two sets of figures, the trail is either 2.6 or 3 miles long. The difference is of little significance, however, since it is one of the very easiest of walks as mountain trails go. Total distance will be about six easy miles for the round

Courtesy Denver Public Library, Western History Collection
Lulu City flourished briefly in the handsome valley near the
headwaters of the Colorado River.

Collection of Robert L. Brown
Lulu City is practically gone now, and the area is a part of
the Rocky Mountain National Park.

trip. In many places the trail follows the old grade which was originally used to reach Thunder Pass. In some instances the Park Service has cut fine new approaches to avoid swamps and assure a dry and easy walk. Almost no steep sections will be encountered and even the novice should make this one with ease and relish. Pretty mountain scenery and occasional glimpses of wildlife offer pleasant diversions along the way. There's even a sanitary facility just off the trail near Shipler's cabins.

As you will doubtless gather from the accompanying photographs, Lulu City is apt to be something of a disappointment to the purist in search of prime ghost towns. Although the remains of many cabins still dot the beautiful meadow, nothing approaching the one-hundred-block town plot was ever built and there are no whole buildings still intact.

Personally, I'm fond of Lulu City not only because of its unusual history but because I also like pretty mountains, abundant trees, and restful green valleys. A short hike with pleasant companions is also much to my liking. Potentially, this trail offers all of these. If you take this walk, I hope you will also take the time to enjoy nature in this handsome Rocky Mountain setting.

31.

MARBLE

IT WAS A RELENTLESS search for silver ores that brought the
first group of white men into the beautiful Crystal River
Valley. After pushing in across Scofield Pass, the small party
made its way down Rock Creek, now called the Crystal River.
At the point where Yule Creek flows in from the southwest,
they made a permanent camp and began to put up their shelters. Exact dates are difficult to prove in this case and most
people take the easy way out by placing the crossing in the
late 1870's. Their settlement was first called Yule Creek,
then Clarence, and finally Marble City.

Some silver was found, along with a lesser amount of
gold and lots of lead. Most of the mines were on Whitehouse
and Treasure mountains. Among the better producers
were the Lead King Mine and the Black Queen Mine which
was found in 1886. By 1890, the Hoffman Brothers Smelter
was working and in 1897 there was a second refinery in the
valley. From one other source we find dates of 1879-1900
for the Hoffman plant. Anyway, there was smelting being
done, even though the mines were not very good.

Despite admittedy slim mineral leads, the aforementioned
town of Clarence seems to have been located in 1880. John
Mobley and W. F. Mason, acting on behalf of the Clarence
Townsite Company, seem to have been the chief instigators.
Within a relatively short time, another town grew up beside
it, calling itself Marble City. William Woods and W. D.
Parry founded the latter town in the winter of 1882-83. Al-

most at once the two towns grew together and became one. Clarence ceased to exist as a separate entity and Marble City became just plain Marble.

With a nucleus of population already settled in the bottom of the canyon, it is indeed fortunate that a better economic base was found. The finest grade of quarrying marble in the world, a nearly solid mountain of it, was found at a point less than two miles from the town. In this, as in so many other discoveries, confusion exists about who got there first. As a result there are references which credit the find to George Yule in 1874, before the valley was even peopled by mineral seekers. Nevertheless, William Wood and W. D. Parry are also credited as first locators of the deposit in 1882. In any case, the site was Whitehouse Mountain. First among the several who eventually opened quarries on the slopes were the Kelly brothers in 1890. Two years later, J. C. Osgood opened up a second quarry nearby. Curiously, the White Quarry and the White Marble Company on nearby Treasure Mountain, were owned and operated by the Mormon Church.

Best known of all the companies was the Colorado Yule Marble Company which arrived on the scene a bit late and went into operation after 1900. Down in the town, they set up the world's largest marble finishing plant. It measured 1,700 feet in length by 150 feet wide. To assure a consistently high quality of work, expert stonecutters were imported from Italy. In a nearby mill the blocks were cut before being sent to the finishing plant for final shaping and fitting.

In the early days marble blocks were loaded on packtrains of forty burros for transportation to the outside world. During the winter of 1895-96, horse-drawn sleighs carried the huge blocks over the same route. As the quarried chunks increased in size, heavy-duty freight wagons came into general use. A wagon road was built up Yule Creek to the quarries in 1905. From Carbondale, the Denver and Rio Grande Railway began hauling the ponderous marble cubes to their varied destinations. To cut costs and improve service, the Colorado Yule Marble Company built the Crystal River and San Juan Railroad from Placita to Marble in 1906-7. It continued to run until it was torn out in 1942, during World War II.

In the town, population figures fluctuated according to the prosperity or decline of the marble business. Here as elsewhere, the head counts are open to doubt. In general the number varied between one and two thousand souls during the peak years of the early twentieth century. Most of the streets in town, and a majority of the houses, were illuminated by electricity. Good churches, an elementary and a high school, and a motion picture theater added diversion and enlightenment to life in Marble. There were also five general stores, two hotels, a drugstore, a dry-goods establishment, two pool halls, a Masonic hall, two barbershops, and six very busy saloons.

Civic improvements arrived in the form of a wagon road up the valley from Carbondale in 1907. There was also a city water system. A circular bandstand of the usual proportions was put up and Sunday afternoon band concerts were a popular pastime in Marble. Suspended on a high tower, a fire bell was installed to warn the town in emergencies. It proved most valuable in 1926 when a disastrous blaze nearly wiped out the town.

Two newspapers flourished during the town's life. One of these was known as the *Marble Booster*. The other was the *Marble City Times*, published in the decade from 1892 until 1902. The *Times* once had a crusading woman editor who attacked a lack of social sensitivity by the Colorado Yule Marble Company. Since this stand threatened the jobs of many of her readers in a prosperous time, her efforts were unpopular.

Over the years, the output of Colorado's quarries met with a remarkable degree of public and official acceptance. Quite an impressive array of public structures utilized Yule marble in their construction. A total of $1,070,000 worth of marble became the Lincoln Memorial, a large number of civic buildings in San Francisco and elsewhere used marble wholly or in part. In Denver, the Customs House, the Colorado National Bank, and the Colorado State Museum were erected from the Treasure Mountain quarries. By far the best known of all was the one-hundred-ton block that became the Tomb of the Unknown Soldier at Arlington National Cemetery near our nation's capital.

Thus far, this single block holds the record for being the largest chunk of monument quality marble that has ever been removed from a quarry anywhere. At the mill it was scaled down from its original weight to fifty-five tons. Old photographs show the huge unfinished piece loaded on a railroad flatcar for removal. At the quarry, slightly more than a year of work was required to remove it from the mountain. Final processing and polishing were done by the Vermont Marble Company at their New England plant before sending it to Washington.

Although the demise of Marble is directly attributable to a combination of high shipping costs coupled with increased use of marble substitutes and veneers, the decline was certainly hastened by the snowslide of 1912 and the catastrophic mud avalanche that nearly buried the town in August of 1941. Some people blame the whole thing on overgrazing by sheep on the alpine slopes above the town. One resident of the valley showed me a photograph of the lush mountaintop rangeland in the early days. Next, he displayed a second picture showing an ugly, barren view of the same region, now nearly devoid of any vegetation, after sheep had grazed there.

In any case there was a cloudburst near the head of Carbon Creek that was not absorbed in the normal manner. Without adequate cover crops the whole mess just slithered off and took the path of least resistance—downward. As the rushing water coursed down the valley of Carbon Creek, it picked up tons of the rain-soaked coal shale. By the time it reached Marble, it had assumed the form of a mass of heavy gray mud. Several blocks of the Main Street business district along the creek were carried away and many private residences were buried. Carbon Creek cut a new channel across Main Street and the bridge that had crossed it was reduced to tinder. The fire warning bell and the community bandstand were inundated. In one house a grand piano was buried. Once again, as it happened at Brownsville, there were those people who recall hearing a tinkling melody as the silt-packed mess pressed down on the keyboard. Can't you just imagine people, in the midst of a tragedy, with nothing better to do than stand about, listening avidly to the accidental musical propensities of a mud slide covering a piano? It is extremely doubtful that any tone as delicate as piano notes could have been heard over the din.

The river cut a block-wide swath, north to south, across the town. Street after street was filled with mud and debris. In addition to damaging the town, the deep mud and silt destroyed the mill. The quarry closed shortly after the flood and never reopened. Actually, it might have folded anyway since the Colorado Yule Marble Company had gone into receivership back in July of 1916. It was out of operation until April of 1922. When work was resumed, things went along spasmodically until 1941. Its Crystal River and San Juan Railroad was taken out in 1942. Another flood dropped more mud onto the town in 1945, and several minor slides have come down in the intervening years.

Several years ago, my family and I had driven across the Scofield Pass Jeep Road into the valley. We spent the night at Marble and had planned to go back out by the same route. During the night it rained and the mud came down across the road between Marble and Crystal City. Two vehicles were buried until bulldozers cleared out the ooze some days later. Needless to say, we revised our plans and left the valley by another route.

In Marble today, the remaining structures shelter a few families during the summer months. A few years ago, Mrs.

Ruby Isler, of Carbondale, wintered up there. Lately, several plans have been considered to find contemporary uses for the still-ample supplies of marble in the valley. Only time can tell what the future holds.

Marble is a very easy place to visit as things stand at present. A new road is now under construction over McClure Pass from Paonia. In addition, State Highway 133 is currently paved from Carbondale to a point some distance beyond Redstone. This highway follows the Crystal River south to Marble. For the more adventuresome there's always the 27 percent grade on the road over Scofield Pass from Crested Butte and Gothic to Marble. Much of the town remains and there are Jeeps available to take you up Yule Creek to the quarries. Limited accommodations are available in the town and there is a beautiful campground west of the highway on the river just north of the town. In a very real sense of the word, it is appropriate to say that Marble wrote its own epitaph with the great quantity of statuary marble now standing in monuments and public buildings all over the United States.*

* In this same general area, see also Scofield City, Crested Butte, and Crystal City.

In this early photograph of Marble the extensive business district
is clearly visible in the valley below the cliffs.

The full extent of the mud slide that buried the commercial portion of Marble
is apparent in this contemporary picture, taken from the same angle.

32.

MONTGOMERY

MORE THAN A CENTURY AGO, gold seekers from the Cherry Creek diggings overflowed into South Park to seek the elusive yellow metal. In the process they established some of the very earliest mining camps in Colorado. One of these was Montgomery. When the ice chunks had stopped floating down from the headwaters of the Middle Fork of the South Platte River and summer breezes warmed the alpine meadows of South Park, gold was discovered here in 1859. In a historical sense, this was nothing particularly new. When Lieutenant Zebulon Montgomery Pike was here in 1806, he met a trapper named James Purcell at Santa Fe who told him about having found gold near the headwaters of the South Platte. But those were relatively prosperous times and there was no economic depression to goad men across far-distant horizons in search of a proverbial pot of gold beneath the terminus of some vague and elusive rainbow.

All things considered, it is rather surprising that a period of two years would elapse between the initial discovery and the founding of a settlement. Nevertheless, an early issue of the *Rocky Mountain News* tells us that the Montgomery district was laid out, defined, and established on August 22, 1861, at the point where the Platte River emerges into its valley from the mountainous western fringe of South Park. Sometime during September of that year, the first log-walled cabin was put up. Allegedly, this first structure became the original post office and general store at a later date.

When the town was laid out, there were three principal

streets. By 1862 there were already more than seventy cabins occupied, and others were in the process of construction.
When the first water-powered sawmill appeared, business was
booming and demands were great. In the final stages, a grand
total of five sawmills was running in the town. A total of
three hotels was built. One of these was a 50x100-foot
structure with a large second story that sometimes doubled
as a public meeting hall until the new theater was completed.
By the time the showhouse was ready in 1862, it was the
largest in the region. Carroll's Minstrels, a popular touring
variety show of the times, played alternately at Buckskin
Joe and at the Montgomery Theatre. When there were no
shows in town, the huge structure doubled as a dance hall
and could also be rented for parties. Of course, Montgomery
had its quota of saloons, and there were several general stores
there as well.

When William N. Byers sent another reporter from his
Rocky Mountain News to the town, the published story
listed an enterprising physician, Dr. Bailey, who also owned
the drugstore and a shoe store at Montgomery. At that same
time a man named Alex Ray was running a bakery and a restaurant. By July of 1862 the town was still growing and
there were now 150 cabins there plus a new stable to care
for the town's livestock. When the townspeople wanted to
show their high regard for President Lincoln, they named
the great peak that rose behind their town in his honor. At
that time it was thought that the new Mount Lincoln was
the highest peak in Colorado Territory. As a token of their
gratitude to the President for having granted territorial status to Colorado, the men at Montgomery also sent a bar of
solid gold ore from their mines to Mr. Lincoln.

To acknowledge the honor, President Lincoln sent Schuyler Colfax, a member of his cabinet and a leading Republican politician of that era, to Colorado. Colfax came to Montgomery, fell in love with the area, and frequently spent va-
cation time there in the years that followed. There is even

an account that relates how Colfax brought his bride-to-be out to Montgomery and proposed to her on the crest of Mount Lincoln. Several puns were made about this elevated occasion but they would not be worth repeating by today's standards. For the record, Colfax was definitely known to have climbed Mount Lincoln.

In later years, both Montgomery and Mr. Colfax fell on evil times. In the case of Montgomery the gold played out later in the 1860's and the town lay dormant for about a decade. Many people became discouraged and moved over the hill to Buckskin Joe. In some instances they even took their cabins with them.

Mr. Colfax became Vice-President of the United States during the first administration of President Ulysses Simpson Grant, 1869-73. Most standard American history texts dwell at some length upon the scandals of these years. Schuyler Colfax was one of those caught with his fingers in the till, having accepted a bribe in the odious Credit Mobilier scandal of 1872. Although it was in a period of decline when Colorado achieved the status of statehood in 1876, the name of Montgomery was considered by the legislature along with Denver and some other cities as a possible state capital. At this time Montgomery was bigger than either Fairplay or Buckskin Joe.

Originally, the mines around Montgomery were included as a part of the Snow-blind Mining District. Then, in the fall of 1861, the name was changed to the Montgomery Mining District. Two years later, the residents of the Montgomery, Jackson, and Independent Districts held a meeting on June 20 and voted to consolidate all three into one. This new aggregation was to be called the Consolidated Montgomery Mining District, sometimes incorrectly referred to as the Montgomery Consolidated Mining District.

Meanwhile, back at the town, the old dumps were reworked often as people hoped for a new boom with the better methods that had become available for refining the ores. From the mountain stronghold far above the town, there suddenly came word of great silver discoveries on the slopes of Mount Lincoln and Mount Bross in 1881. Here, at an altitude of 10,800 feet, Montgomery embarked upon a second boom, becoming a residence center for those who worked in the nearby mines. Outstanding among the several mineral properties was the Robber's Roost which was so vertically situated that it could be reached only by way of a ladder which had something over two hundred rungs. Three other mines were important in the town's life span. They were the Magnolia, Pendleton, and the Montgomery. Two arrastras, crude ore-crushing devices, were at work in the surrounding gulches. In the town, along the river, four steam-powered and two water-propelled quartz mills were in operation from the earlier period.

On the transportation front, wagon trains provided the earliest access to and from the outside world. In the early days all mail came to Montgomery by way of a weekly delivery from the Overland Express Company. Later on there was a daily express line in operation between Montgomery and Buckskin Joe. This afforded a connection with the semiweekly service being operated in Buckskin Joe by the Green and Duncan Express Line. Beginning in July of 1862, W. C. McClellan and Ab Williamson started a four-horse run with Concord coaches. From Denver the line crossed Kenosha Pass to South Park and had stops in both Montgomery and Buckskin Joe. Without a doubt this was the most ambitious undertaking thus far. In addition to passengers, express shipments, mail and commercial parcels were also carried.

Following the repeal of the Sherman Act in 1893, Montgomery's silver boom collapsed, and prophets of doom began carrying on like medieval chroniclers in a plague year. Beyond this, there was a slight revival in 1898. Even with newer refining methods, everything they attempted failed. It was soon clear that Montgomery was finished.

Several years ago, the city of Colorado Springs purchased the old site of Montgomery, cleared out the empty cabins and debris, and built a new reservoir to assure the future of their supply of fresh water. Before it was filled, the graves in the old Montgomery cemetery were disinterred and the remains moved elsewhere.

Colorado State Highway 9 runs north and slightly west from U.S. Highway 285 at Fairplay. Just north of Alma, near the southern foot of Hoosier Pass, a dirt road turns left or west and follows up the valley of the Middle Fork of the South Platte River. When you arrive at the reservoir, there can be little doubt about having reached your destination. Here, beneath the clear, sparkling surface, is the watery grave of old Montgomery.

Montgomery, as photographed by George Wakely in the early 1860's

The watery grave of Montgomery, with Mount Lincoln rising behind the site

33.

MOUND CITY

AFTER MANY YEARS of frustration, Bob Womack found the
El Paso Lode inside the extinct volcanic crater that is now
called the Cripple Creek Basin. The year was 1890. This
single strike gave impetus to the entire Cripple Creek boom
and hundreds of other mines were soon established. In the
process twenty-eight new millionaires made their marks.
Something in excess of $430,000,000 in gold has been pro-
duced over the years. To provide living space, twenty-two
"towns" were started. Many of these were merged later with
some of the bigger ones and lost their identity. Mound City
was one of these.

The earliest beginnings of Mound City date back to 1891
when the ramshackle assortment of log cabins and frame
structures, seen in the accompanying photograph, started
being built. In the valley just northwest of Rosebud Hill,
the elevation measures about 9,360 feet above sea level. Actually, this location is the lower end of Squaw Gulch, named
for the disinterred remains of a female aborigine that had
been "rediscovered" while a mining claim was being excavated. In this single gulch, four towns grew up. These were
Anaconda, Barry, Squaw Gulch, and Mound City.

By the middle of 1893 there were five hundred people
there. During 1894 the community was officially platted.
By the late 1890's, one source tells us that the population had
reached two thousand, a rather high estimate. By 1900, there
were still one thousand people there. In the process of becoming a thriving municipality, three grocery stores opened

up to supply the nutritional essentials of life to the people who lived there. One of these was also a general store. Two meat markets, largely supplied from wholesalers in Cripple Creek, also thrived at Mound City. Inevitably, in a town of this type, two saloons appeared and did a land-office business. To care for the needs of newcomers and transients, there was one hotel, believed to have been the large false-fronted structure in the photograph. Since many riding horses and draft animals were used to perform a multiplicity of functions, the one blacksmith in town was kept busy. One barbershop and one clothing store were also in business at Mound City.

Sitting on the side of nearby Beacon Hill, the El Paso Mine helped the town by providing jobs for many of the residents. By 1951, when it finally closed down, the El Paso had produced $10,800,000 in gold. Its main shaft was 1,300 feet deep. In some records, this mine has been referred to as the Beacon Hill. In any event, it should not be confused with the other El Paso Mine, discovered by Bob Womack, which was later renamed the Gold King. Although Mound City, unlike Victor, for example, was never noted for its profusion of mines, it did achieve a measure of fleeting fame for its two excellent mills. The first of these was the huge Brodie Cyanide Mill, the first of its type in the entire Cripple Creek district. Although it continued to operate until 1900, it could not compete successfully with some of the newer processes that were introduced in the district just prior to the turn of the century. When the Brodie closed down, it contributed one more reason for the decline of Mound City.

The second installation was a French stamp mill called the Rosebud. It, too, was set up and in operation somewhat earlier than most of the Cripple Creek mills. In 1893 Winfield Scott Stratton (see Winfield) tried to run some of the telluride ores from his Washington Mine on Battle Mountain through the Rosebud. Since these ores were not of the oxidized telluride variety, technicians at the Rosebud found that they would not separate easily by the process available to them at that time. Stratton soon abandoned the experiment since high transportation costs were absorbing his profits.

Judge Melville B. Gerry, the jurist who is best known to history for a speech he never made, occupied the bench at the court in Mound City. Gerry, a profound and serious man, became a victim of history as a result of having sentenced Alfred Packer, the man-eater, in 1883. Although his actual pronouncement was a thoughtful and sober one, few people today know about it. Instead, history has preferred to record the profane and ludicrous version that was ululated through the streets of Lake City by Larry Dolan, a bibulous Irish saloonkeeper of the town. In the Doland version, the jurist not only opened up the question of Packer's alleged canine ancestry, but also dragged in partisan politics as well. While Judge Gerry protested this slur on his integrity almost to his dying day, he nevertheless became a creature of history and was never able to shake the spurious skeleton out of the closet. Even today, the Dolan version is quite widely believed.

For those people who sought recreation close to home, there was an organization called the Squaw Gulch Amusement Club which once boasted four hundred members, drawn from Anaconda, Barry, and Mound City. George Carr, proprietor of the original Broken Box Ranch, was its president. For a time, Bob Womack was entrusted with the duties of sergeant at arms. His duties were to exclude undesirables, particularly those female devotees of the "seamier professions." In his magnificent book, *Money Mountain*, Marshall Sprague records that this decision often resulted in a source of consternation to the membership since poor naïve old Bob regarded all women as inherently virtuous. When a club member inferred that a "soiled dove" had somehow slipped in, Bob often took this as a slur on the lady's reputation and was prepared to do battle in defense of the honor of even the most notorious women in the district.

This early photograph shows the short-lived community of Mound City

Here is the site of Mound City in 1966

About 1905 the decline began to set in as people started to move elsewhere: to Goldfield, Victor, or Cripple Creek. By the end of that year, Mound City, Squaw Gulch, and Barry were absorbed by Anaconda and ceased to exist as separate civic entities.

There are very few rewards awaiting the person who wants to see the remains of Mound City today. Practically all signs of former habitation have disappeared with only an occasional scar here and there as nature is in the process of reclaiming the site. State Highway 67 runs southeast from Cripple Creek to Victor. When you round the corner and first see Squaw Gulch below you, start looking for the dim trail where the paved highway crosses the gulch ahead of you. It drops down the spine of the Squaw Gulch and enters the trees. Above you, at the opposite side of the valley, the huge dump and unmistakable log cribbing of the Mary McKinney Mine may be seen. Just below the highway was the site of Anaconda, where only the cornerstone of the jail now remains from what was once a huge town. Our dim trail, in general, follows the original main street of Anaconda. Go on down the hill, following the trail, watching the background mountains as you go. When you reach a point where they correspond to the accompanying photograph, you are in Mound City. All of Squaw Gulch has now been deserted by any forms of human habitation.*

---

* In this same general area, see also Eclipse, Elkton, Gillett, and Goldfield.

34.

MOUNTAIN CITY

FEW AMONG THE multiplicity of Colorado mining camps may boast of the priority in chronological time that can be attributed to Mountain City. No other town can claim the historical preeminence of Mountain City in terms of the mining period and the subsequent settlement of this state. Here, in 1859, John Gregory, of Georgia, made the very first discovery of lode gold, resulting in a vast acceleration of the Pikes Peak gold rush. Mountain City became the first established settlement in the Central City group.

Since the town grew up as a result of finding the Gregory Lode, our story should logically begin with information about the discoverer. John H. Gregory had left his native Georgia in 1858 to work as a government mule driver at Fort Laramie. His real intention was to join up with the prospectors moving to the Fraser River strikes from California. Gregory wintered at the Wyoming post where he was employed not as a driver but as a common laborer.

During that long winter, persistent rumors were heard about gold discoveries along the South Platte. Gregory immediately changed his plans, left the job, and moved south on a general prospecting tour. Within the next few months he had checked most of the favorable mining localities between the Cache la Poudre River and Pikes Peak. On various treks he traced many local streams back up to their sources. Eventually, by a process of elimination, he arrived at the Vasquez Fork of the South Platte River, better known today as Clear Creek.

Alone, Gregory followed the creek, prospecting along the way. Wherever the stream forked, he followed the branch which seemed to show the greatest promise. Using this system, he worked his way up the canyon, being very probably the first white man to invade its solitude. Roughly fourteen miles above Golden Gate City, he reached the division in the stream where today's highways separate to go to Idaho Springs or Central City. Gregory chose to follow the north branch for about seven miles to the gulch that now bears his name.

At this point he left the creek to explore the side canyon along a smaller creek bed. At the point where the little ravine immediately southeast of the Gregory Lode comes in, he prospected once more. Finding it to be the richest of those he had examined, he turned aside into it. As he approached its head, the color grew less and finally faded away entirely. At this point Gregory felt certain that he had struck gold. Before he could explore the lead, however, a heavy spring snow blew in across the mountains. Gregory barely escaped freezing to death. When the weather cleared, he left the discovery and returned to the valley for provisions.

At Golden, Gregory met David K. Wall, a veteran miner with previous experience in California. After hearing the story, Wall supplied him with provisions for a second expedition. Wall is often credited with being the originator of garden farming in this region. Early in the spring of 1859 he had planted two acres of bottomland near what is now the Golden railroad depot. From this venture he realized a tidy profit of about two thousand dollars by selling fresh produce to the miners.

Now amply fortified for his journey, Gregory persuaded Wilkes Defrees, formerly of South Bend, Indiana, and William Ziegler, from Missouri, to accompany him. On the sixth of May, 1859, they arrived in Gregory Gulch. Despite the fact that ice and snow still covered the ground, they began digging. Gregory climbed the hill to about the point where the wash would naturally come down. Here he paused to scratch away the grass and leaves and to fill his gold pan with dirt. When he panned it down his wildest dreams were realized. About four dollars' worth of gold lay at the bottom of the pan, which he dropped immediately.

According to Ovando J. Hollister, Gregory then "summoned all of the Gods of the Egyptians, Indians, Greeks, Hebrews and Christians, to witness his surprising discovery." In the vernacular of the twentieth century, what he said would probably be described with somewhat less delicacy. That night, by his own admission, he never closed his eyes. Defrees fell asleep about three o'clock while Gregory was still talking to himself. History does not record whether he answered his own questions or not. When Defrees awoke shortly after daybreak, Gregory's tongue was still hung in the middle and running at both ends. Between them, they washed out about forty pans of dirt and secured forty dollars before returning to the valley to bring up their friends.

At this point Gregory was already leaving behind the drudgery of common labor for his visions of a princely fortune. "Now my wife can be a lady," he mumbled over and over. The nature of the gold they found convinced Gregory that it must have originated farther up the slope. Abandoning the gulch, they passed along the little ravine that intersects it from the southeast. Upon examining the ground he told Defrees, "dig there because it looks well." Under the surface they found fragments of blossom rock or surface quartz which had been dislodged from the lode by erosion.

At one point where the dirt appeared to be very promising, Defrees filled the pan and Gregory took it down the ravine to wash it. The result was quite astounding. This single pan yielded nearly an ounce of gold. By right of discovery, John Gregory took two claims on the spot. In actual fact the find had been made on the tenth of May but orderly work could not begin until sluices had been completed on the sixteenth. Three days later the erstwhile editor and founder of the *Rocky Mountain News,* William N. Byers, had arrived to see for himself.

Having introduced himself, Byers told Gregory that he had just come over the hill from the Jackson Diggings and wanted some facts concerning what had been happening on this side of the hill. Poor Gregory was a victim of history, still unable to comprehend what had happened to him and how it would change his life. He sat on a log with his head held between his hands. Occasionally he broke forth with incoherent mutterings somehow related to the facts about his previous life.

Byers noted that Gregory had scooped out a place from the hillside for a lodging. Over it he had put up a root and brush roof. The editor noted that he seemed completely dazed by his good fortune and he speculated that Gregory's mind "may have been unsettled while occupied with his dreams of the future." Repeatedly, he spoke of his wife and children back in Georgia, and of the changed destiny awaiting them. More than once, with a distant stare, Gregory speculated, "My wife will be a lady and my children will be educated."

At first he paid little attention to Byers but gradually he softened up and talked. As the two men warmed to each other, the prospector gave the newsman a full account of his progress which has fortunately been preserved for posterity. Reaching out to a nearby bush where his frying pan was turned upside down, he raised it and revealed three large masses of solid gold. Gregory had gathered the samples from his sluices and crudely retorted them in a campfire. Within the space of just three days he had taken out the entire collection now hidden under his pan; valued at roughly a thousand dollars with no confiscatory taxes.

For more than a week, John Gregory had stopped all work to guard his treasure against the possibility of robbery. Scarcely less significant was the fact that his extreme case of anxiety ruled out sleep in any quantity. When editor

Byers visited the gulch, only seventeen other men were there. From then on, as word leaked out, new people came in. By the end of the week 150 men, mostly from Jackson's Bar, had come over the hill to try their luck. An impatient crowd also came pouring up Clear Creek Canyon from Auraria-Denver. From that time on, the influx of people grew almost daily. Some prospectors succeeded abundantly while others complained of "miners' luck."

On June 24 Byers proved to be a true friend in time of need. Taking compassion on Gregory, he loaded a fast team with the treasure, which by this time had grown in value to four thousand dollars, and drove it to Omaha. Fearing robbery, he and a driver traveled day and night, purchasing fresh horses along the route. Fortunately for all concerned, they reached their destination in just twelve days. In this as in so many other similar cases, things got out of hand. Byers still had an office in Omaha. When he exhibited the gold there, it nearly created a panic.

Large crowds gathered to see it. Some, remembering the earlier disappointment occasioned by rumors that had dogged the meager Green Russell discovery, openly declared it a hoax since there was believed to be no gold in the Pikes Peak region. When faced by the need to justify his journey, the editor addressed a public meeting and related the story of the various discoveries that had been made thus far, expressing his own personal confidence in the richness of the country.

In June, Horace Greeley, scrupulously honest owner of the *New York Tribune*, came to Gregory Gulch, also to see for himself. Like a lamb being led to the slaughter, Greeley fell for one of the oldest tricks in the book. Under cover of darkness, the miners loaded a shotgun with gold dust and peppered a dry hole until it literally glittered. Next morning Greeley was given a pan and invited to "see for yourself." What followed hardly deserves comment. The results were as foreordained as a Saturday night wrestling

match. Greeley was amazed! His Gilpin County experiences
doubtless dictated some part of his later, most famous utter-
ance in which he urged the younger generation to, "Go West,
young man, go West, and grow up with the country." That
night in Gregory Gulch he made a less well remembered
speech at Mountain City while pitch-saturated torches blazed
and dynamite explosions rocked the smoky atmosphere. His
oration was typical of the man who would later run for President of the United States. In it he extolled the American
way of life, castigated the local prostitutes and demon rum,
and urged the miners to follow a virtuous life. No shred of
evidence exists in the history of Gilpin County to indicate
that any of his advice was taken seriously but he was cheered
lustily.

Eventually, John Gregory sold his claims for about $21,000
and went to work prospecting for others at a rate of $200
per day, doubtless the finest salary being earned by any person in the United States during that period. In the course of
his work, Gregory struck another lode, an extension of his
original, on the southeast slope of the gulch. Appropriately,
it was named Gregory II. Most of Gregory's clients soon
discovered that gold mining was a business which required
time, a lot of money, experience, energy, and patience.

Thus, in an incredibly short period, about five thousand
people had migrated into the ravine. According to some
contemporary sources, hundreds of others arrived in the
territory each day while Horace Greeley passed tens of
thousands on his way homeward.

Ultimately, cities and towns grew up out of the ramshackle clusters of log and brush shantytowns that adhered
tenaciously to the steep sides of Gregory Gulch. Street over
street, the camps climbed one above the other up the steep
mountainsides behind Clear Creek. Later observers said it
was impossible to tell where one town ended and the next
began. At the foot of the hill was Black Hawk, with its
multiplicity of mills and refineries. Next came Mountain

City, which, of course, grew up around the Gregory discovery. Above it was Central City while still farther up each of two adjacent valleys one might visit Russell Gulch and Nevadaville. Thus in an incredibly short time, the Richest Square Mile on Earth and its environs had a premature taste of the twentieth century population explosion.

Mountain City was laid out by Richard Sopris in the middle of the gulch, almost exactly halfway between Central City and Black Hawk. Like the rungs of a ladder, three streets were cut into the side canyon leading south of Gregory Gulch. Two of these were filled with private residences while the third, Gregory Street, became the false-fronted business district. By the early summer of 1859, Mountain City already had a tent hotel and a log theater in addition to the usual assortment of log cabins, tents, and brush shacks. On July 4, Jerome C. Smiley described the settlement as "A product of the discovery of gold, containing over two hundred dwellings where six weeks before there were none." By August it boasted having had the first show in the mountains at the log theater. Its title was "Cross of Gold."

A number of other notable "firsts" have also been attributed to Mountain City. By August it had the first two newspapers in the mountains, called the *Rocky Mountain Gold Reporter* and the *Mountain City Herald*. Publication was suspended late in October. The first mountain saloon, a dubious distinction, dispensed firewater from unwashed tin cups. The first Masonic hall in Colorado seems to have been there, and the residents boasted the very first church service was held there on June 12, 1859.

In the fascinating diary of Joseph Persons, Jr., thus far unpublished, he wrote the following observation:

Sunday, June 19, 1859.
    There is preaching every sabbath at Mountain City. It is a very peaceable place for so many men. There is in the mountains now about seven thousand men and one woman. Her name is Charly. She dresses in black

pants hickory shirt, vest, and moccasins. Her pants project well behind. Her vest does not want any batting either.

Quite apart from the disparity in spelling, the individual referred to in the foregoing diary excerpt was Mountain Charley, one of the rarest characters to enter Colorado during the initial gold rush. Her name was actually Charlotte and her home had been in Iowa. There she married a man who not only turned out to be a professional gambler but one who soon deserted his new bride for another woman. Directly the pair set out for Colorado in 1859 to help keep the miners' pockets from becoming overloaded.

Charlotte, to assure her own protection, donned male garb and became Charley, joining the Westward rush. According to what she told George West, of Golden, Charley found her husband and his paramour at Mountain City and had her revenge. Later she enlisted with an Iowa regiment during the Civil War and kept her secret from being detected for two years. Disguised [?] as a woman, Charley penetrated Confederate lines as a spy while assigned as a male orderly under Union General Curtis. She later reverted to Charlotte, married again, and raised a family far from Mountain City.

One of the difficulties associated with historical research comes in the area of population statistics. Thus far I have repeated two population estimates in this chapter. A third source, Hall's *History of Colorado,* tells us that there were only one thousand people at Mountain City in the winter of 1859. Without trained census takers and with the highly migratory nature of life in the mining camps, far too many inaccurate, uneducated guesses have been recorded as facts.

Only a small minority of the people who entered the Gregory District could secure a permanent foothold. To make the distribution fair, each lode was subdivided into locations of one hundred feet in length along the vein by fifty feet in width. John Gregory himself finally left for his home in Georgia, carrying about $25,000 in gold, earned during this single season of hard labor.

One of the initial movements for statehood was started at Mountain City in Daniel Doyle's Hall, a saloon which dispensed five-cent whiskey for twenty-five cents a cup. Being somewhat influenced by their environment and after having worshipped copiously at the shrine of the grain, two miners spoke up in denunciation of the government for its indifference to the petitions that had been sent. As the bibulous evening wore on, the men repudiated all allegiance to the laws of Kansas and declared that they would never submit willingly to being included in that jurisdiction. Nothing much came of the meeting and it was nearly forgotten in the excitement that followed involving the gold discovery at California Gulch in April. A virtual stampede of the disappointed ones left Mountain City for the latest Eldorado.

During the Civil War, the speculative boom nearly collapsed. One source tells us that the miners here were saved only by a rapid advance in the price of gold. During this time it mounted to the highest figure known in the nation up to that time. Next came a sudden and almost frantic demand for gold mines and mining stocks. Regardless of actual value, speculators wanted them. Since the hills around Mountain City were literally seamed with fissures, the supply became fully equal to the demand and the excitement was fever-pitched for a while. In fact, many of the titles were wholly or partially fraudulent. In not a few other cases the purchasers were unable to find their property. Nevertheless, the craze extended throughout the winter and into the following April when Lee surrendered to Grant. With the end of the war the bottom fell out of the gold price boom.

As a separate entity, Mountain City had only a few years of life before it was annexed, in 1880, to become the easternmost section of Central City. Curiously, during their years as independent communities, no formal line was ever drawn as a boundary between the two villages.

If you decide to see Mountain City, follow State Highway 119 to Black Hawk. In the middle of town, turn east on the paved road up the hill toward Central City. Roughly halfway up the hill you will see a bronze marker on the left side of the highway. You are now in Mountain City. As you face the marker, you are looking up the gulch, above the road, that once held most of the town. All three of the buildings to your right show in old photographs of the town. Many other buildings, now gone, were built in the main gulch all around the point where you will be standing. Facing the marker again, John Gregory's mine was the big slag pile on your right.

In the course of historical events in the American West, Mountain City will always occupy an extremely important position, for here they found the first lode gold in what is now Colorado. Here was the great discovery that dignified and justified and gave substance to the Pikes Peak gold rush.*

---

* In the same general area, see also Russell Gulch, Perigo, and Forks Creek.

*Stretching up the hillside, above Gregory Gulch, was Mountain City. Note the Colorado
Central train above the town, in the upper right-hand corner of the picture.*

*Mountain City in the winter of 1966. Note the Gregory Lode slash cut
into the hillside to the right of center in both pictures.*

35.

NORTH EMPIRE

WHEN GOOD GOLD DEPOSITS were unearthed in the nearby
creek beds and canyons, Empire City came into being and
went on to enjoy a long life as well as the distinction of having been one of Colorado's earliest gold camps. Slightly more
than a mile away, on the North Fork of Empire Creek, a
second group of discoveries was made. Here Henry DeWitt
Clinton Cowles and Edgar Freeman found wire gold deposits
imbedded in the rocks of both Eureka and Independence
mountains. Rich gold placers were also found on Silver
Mountain, and people began to settle there as early as 1860.
Actually, the main ore body was located farther up the gulch.

To connect Empire City with these new discoveries, "the
longest main street in the county" was built along the hillside grades above North Empire Creek. Quite naturally the
settlement that grew up on the mountainside above Empire
City came to be known as North Empire. Unofficially it was
occasionally referred to as Upper Empire, but the name never
really caught on enough to cause any serious confusion. Built
at an elevation of about nine thousand feet, North Empire
enjoyed a boom that lasted through the 1860's and seventies.
In the beginning a plentiful number of wild game animals
provided a welcome relief from the usual monotony of the
typical miner's larder.

Quite a number of mines were soon in operation and were
providing for the prosperity of North Empire. Among them
were the Ben Franklin, Gold Dirt, Empire, and the huge
Gold Fissure Mine which was made up of five claims. Its

owners had already sunk a two-hundred-foot shaft on the property. Just a short distance above the town stood the Atlantic Mine. Up the valley another mile or so, many North Empire men were employed on the rich Conqueror property, owned by Colonel John Dumont. Superintendent Clark Disbrow closed the operation down for a time after the fire of 1869. In the seventies the Conqueror management hired carpenters to construct a huge two-story white boardinghouse which still stands at the site. In later years, the miners "lived in" and the commuting problem from North Empire was solved.

For many years the Benton Mine produced gold ore that assayed at sixteen dollars to the ton. They also put up a company-owned barracks for the employees and called it the Blue Boarding House. Like the Conqueror structure, it still stands. The Benton property was managed by Fred Bishop. Little more than the shaft house of the once productive Tenth Legion Mine still remains. In addition to wealth from the deep mines, the Negus Placer produced fifty thousand dollars in 1878-79.

During the visit by George Crofutt to North Empire, he recorded the presence of "several" mills. There were at least two. One of these was the Hartford Mill. The other that we are sure of was the Peck Mill, an ambitious structure with twelve stamps.

As the mines continued to spew forth a very respectable torrent of gold, better transportation facilities were contemplated. Suddenly the Great Empire Cable Railroad Company appeared on the scene and announced plans to construct a cable railroad up the hill from Empire to North Empire. Heading up this company as its president was a Dr. Van De Voort. Within a few years the tracks of the Colorado Southern Railroad had been extended into Empire. In 1898 it was bought out by the Colorado Central Railroad. Neither line made any attempt to extend its tracks on up the hill to North Empire but there were always coaches, teams, and saddle horses for rent at Empire.

Obviously the trip back down that long hill was much easier than the trip up. During the long chilly winters, coasting parties were formed to slide down the steep grade on sleds with oxbow runners. On Saturday nights, those miners who imbibed too freely at the saloons in Empire, often found it more than a little difficult to negotiate the sharp grades between the lower town and their homes in North Empire.

Several passes were built, and these contributed in a variety of ways to the lives of both Empire and North Empire. First of all, there was Empire or Union Pass, a short road that switchbacked for two miles over the low mountain range to Georgetown. By 1861, the thirty-mile road over Berthoud Pass, from Empire to Frazer, had been completed. Beyond Georgetown, Argentine Pass crossed the range at a point somewhat above thirteen thousand feet and descended into the valley of Peru Creek. Also from a point west of Georgetown, Loveland Pass was completed and in use by the late 1870's.

When a mining slump set in during the 1880's, North Empire came close to being depopulated. Although it never achieved another boom such as it had enjoyed in the previous two decades, some men stayed on and worked the old properties on an uncertain schedule. This pattern continued until World War II.

Currently, you will find the drive up to North Empire to be an easy and pleasant one. If you are approaching the site from the Denver area or from points to the east, get onto the combined U.S. Highways 6 and 40 west of Idaho Springs. Still going west, these routes divide in a few miles. Turn right at the forks and stay on U.S. 40 for one mile, going toward Berthoud Pass. As you enter Empire, watch for the main intersection in the center of the town.

Here a dirt road crosses the pavement. A left turn will take you up onto the top of what remains of Union Pass.

Collection of Fred and Jo Mazzulla
North Empire, high on a mountainside above present Empire,
was photographed by George Wakely in the 1860's

Photo by Jessie Bingham
With vacant streets, North Empire is now an empty wooded shell of its former self

A right turn will lead you up the hill to North Empire in about a mile. At one point where the road makes a switchback, a huge mine dump can be seen on the left or west side of the canyon. A few cabins lie above and below the road, at a point several yards behind you. Stop and park here on the curve. Walk out on the foot trail along the crest of the big dump. From the end, look back across the valley at the road you used to get up here. You are now facing what remains of North Empire. This is the point from which both of the accompanying photographs were made. Although some structures remain at the site, the town is a mere shadow of its former self. The Conqueror boardinghouse is reached by continuing on up the hill on the same road above North Empire. When last seen, this road was passable as far as the Conqueror. In autumn, this is an especially pretty valley and is well worth the trip.*

---

* In this same general area, see also Gilson Gulch, Freeland, Brownsville, Silver Plume, and Fall River.

36.

ORO CITY

BEFORE 1859, the wide, open valley watered by the upper Arkansas River had not been occupied by white men. For centuries prior to the discovery of precious metals, Indians had used it as a desirable mountain hunting ground and as a secure hiding place for large hunting bands. Apart from this bit of early history, the development of Lake County has been marked by two rather striking periods.

First, there was an enormous influx of a miscellaneous population and the incidental outpouring of gold between 1859 and 1868. Second, there was the disclosure of immense deposits of carbonate of lead in 1874. The second period has been permanent and has resulted in the foundation of Leadville while the first was of brief duration and brought about the beginning of two communities, each known as Oro City.

Except for the Boulder district around Gold Hill, Russell Gulch, and the Gregory diggings, no remarkable gold deposits had been found in the territory. The golden yields of California Gulch proved to be one of the first incentives resulting in attraction of the multitudes of people who came during 1860. On April 25, 1859, there was much excitement resulting from a discovery made by S. Slater and Company. Rich placer gold deposits had been found in the gulch about twenty miles above Kelly's Bar. When the word spread, it caused the usual stampede from the older mining districts to the newer one.

To date, there are two versions which attempt to explain how the gulch got its name. The first tells us that it was due to the immediate influx of a large number of Californians, hence the region took on the name of California Gulch. Another story quotes Abe Lee, an early prospector in the district who, incidentally, was from California. Allegedly, he scooped up a pan of gravel and began washing it. When he saw the quantity of gold dust at the bottom, the startled Lee exclaimed, "Boys, I've got all California in this pan." The site of the original Abe Lee discovery was just below the first Oro City, at about the point where the Rock Mine juts out into the gulch. In any case, the region soon became known as California Gulch.

Some preliminary work was done while the snow was still very deep, indicating that a rich placer probably existed there beneath the thick white cover. In length, the gulch climbs upward for about ten miles. At that time the terrain was filled with clay and decomposed quartz which was high in gold content. In many ways it resembled the decompositions found at the surface of the Gregory Lode and was well adapted to washing by the same methods employed at Mountain City. At the height of the runoff, the available water was about enough to supply five or six lines of sluices. When the extensive nature of these deposits became known, huge numbers of prospectors went over the range from the eastern slope to form a settlement there in the gulch. Panning or sluicing brought enormous returns. Frequently, a man could fill an oyster can with nuggets in a single day of work. Gold, at that time, was worth eighteen dollars an ounce. Beyond this, the placers were among the richest ever opened in the Rocky Mountains, producing great quantities of precious metals.

Oro City has been referred to by a rather wide variety of names. Among them were Sacramento, California Gulch, Sacramento City, Sacramento Flats, Slabtown, and Boughtown. In the early days there were a great many tents at Oro City. One source tells us that tents and wagons extended down the road all the way to Malta. The mining portion of

Courtesy Library, State Historical Society of Colorado
Here, in the early 1860's, was the first and original Oro City.
The site was barely within the limits of present Leadville.

Collection of Robert L. Brown
In May of 1966, lower California Gulch contained this dump. Background buildings are
part of the southern portion of Leadville. The picture was made from a point
among the ruts of the original trail above the present road.

the gulch was about six miles long. In addition to wagons and tents, people also slept on the ground, in outhouses, under packing boxes, or, in fact, anywhere that gave the promise of shelter from the bone-chilling cold.

Wagon roads and tracks extended up both sides of the mountains. Several of these ruts became tributary streets. In many cases wheels were blocked, cargoes packed up, and people lived right in the beds of their wagons.

Gamblers and prostitutes were also there in force, operating in their own tents and wagons. Most gamblers also had their tables stretched out along the trails to the mines, to spare the prospectors those long walks. Three-card monte took in the most money. Some of the larger wagons were used as hotels, after food and dishes had been stacked on the ground between the wheels.

Some other families began by sleeping in their wagons until they could get a quantity of rough slab boards to make tables. This accomplished, they might then take in boarders and serve meals. Among these people were Augusta and Horace A. W. Tabor. Three months were required for the Tabor party to travel from Denver to Oro City. Their route crossed Ute Pass to South Park, then over Trout Creek Pass to the Arkansas River. After surviving a treacherous ford, they followed the Arkansas Valley up to their destination. Several histories have recorded how Augusta took in boarders while Horace received some primary lessons in the highly inexact science of mining. Also busily learning how to acquire gold were quite a number of those hard-bitten old crones who termed themselves "dance hall girls." At one time, Augusta Tabor was described as the only "family type woman" in the gulch. The women's great fortune was delayed until 1879 when the Leadville blanket veins opened up their hidden treasures of silver.

By July of 1860 there were many log and frame buildings, and one source tells us that there were eight thousand people here. Large quantities of gold were being taken out, and many of the claims paid well. No law had been established as yet. Once a circus tent was put up and sleeping space was sold at one dollar per body. Many nights the owners took in one thousand dollars. The streets looked as if most people had built their own cabins without regard to survey. As a result, nearly all streets were very crooked. Wolf Londoner, a pioneer merchant of Oro City, estimated that there were ten thousand people there in 1861.

Along the spine of the gulch was the long, continuous main street which could be followed for the entire distance. Thick with mud from constant reuse, the stream ran down the middle. Most of the business structures were eventually located at one point. Along the north bank, where the hills flatten out beside contemporary Leadville, was the site of this first Oro City. Its chief disadvantage was the previously mentioned water situation. It had been used over and over again, until by the time it reached Oro City and the claims at the lower end of the gulch, it was almost liquid mud.

Father Joseph P. Machebeouf, earliest of the Catholic circuit riders, was the first to hold a religious service in the gulch. The time was early in the summer of 1860. Tom Starr's blacksmith shop was commandeered for the occasion, using an anvil for the altar. Father Machebeouf, best known of the early Colorado Catholic priests, records that he often slept under the stars and sometimes in the snow on his trips from Denver to California Gulch. He once contracted mountain fever in the gulch and was unable to say mass for two months. Both Rev. William Howbert and Rev. John L. Dyer, pioneer Methodist circuit riders, included California Gulch in their territories.

While in session during 1861, the territorial legislature formally organized Lake County and defined its boundaries. Ironically, after 1861, each summer saw fewer and fewer miners returning after spending the winter on the lower plains.

Generally speaking, the mines in the gulch were very productive for about three years. By that time the cream of the harvest had been taken by the original locators and their workers. One shortcoming of these placers was the climate, which prevented them from being worked for more than a short season. Due to the altitude, most mining years were made up of about eight months of winter and four months in the late summer and early fall when life was more pleasant. Despite this, considerable amounts of gold were still secured along the gulch during each successive season until 1870. At that time it was found advisable to enlarge the water supply, necessitating the construction of a canal some twelve miles in length. It extended from the source of the principal stream to the placers.

Three miles farther up the Gulch, Charles Mullen discovered the Printer Boy Lode in 1868. Although it was operated only by the imperfect methods of that period, it still gave some extraordinary returns. Large bodies of soft and porous decomposed quartz were also found in 1868. These carried large masses of free gold in the form of nuggets. Frequently the miners encountered bunches of fantastically formed and matted wires with beautiful crystallization. Many large glass jars were filled with these remarkable specimens and they were exhibited at banks in Denver, Philadelphia, and New York. Mr. J. Marshall Paul, of Philadelphia, owner and manager of the property, realized handsome returns from his rude workings while the rich deposits held out. Although a lot of prospecting was done to develop other mines like it, none of them succeeded.

Life in the upper valley went along peaceably for some years with only an occasional conflict between the settlers and roving bands of stock thieves who preyed upon the flocks and herds. When pursued, the miscreants took refuge in the mountains. There were few formal attempts at law enforcement in the upper gulch during these early years.

Most inhabitants of the earlier Oro City simply moved up

the stream and became residents of the newer town. At this point, just below the Printer Boy, the second Oro City grew up. It was here that the Tabors had a general store. For some years Augusta also operated a restaurant and bakery. Her well-cooked meals and famous pies attracted a wide following. Being popular, Mrs. Tabor was made postmistress for the gulch. A third facet of the Tabor enterprises involved running an express service from Oro City to Denver. Two weeks were required to make the round trip until roads were improved. From then on the time was cut to eight days. Frequently their messengers were robbed.

By the end of 1868, large-scale mining at Oro City was about over. Most stock Colorado histories record the complaints of miners who were unable to cope with the heavy black sands that clogged their sluice boxes, making extraction of the gold difficult. Nevertheless, a twenty-eight ounce gold nugget was found here in 1868. Later, more knowledgeable miners recognized this black sand as carbonate of lead, which was extremely rich in silver. Carbonate kings who grew rich there also founded the city of Leadville, easily one of the West's greatest mining camps, and certainly one of the wildest.

The boom at the new location lasted only two and a half years although there was an Oro City well into the twentieth century. One of the last acts of those remaining in the camp was to pull down the old log gambling house and saloon, to recover from its dirt floor over two thousand dollars in gold dust that had been dropped by drunken patrons.

Both towns are gone now except for a few signs which show some of the locations at the second settlement. Currently, the last remnants of Oro City are the bits and scraps of rusted mining machinery which dot the high meadow, all that managed to survive after the scrap drives of World War II.

To see the site today, drive out of Leadville on East Fourth Street to Toledo Street. Turn east and follow the dirt road into California Gulch. The site of the second Oro City, near the Printer Boy Mine, is marked. Most traces of the first Oro City had disappeared by the turn of the present century. I am told that there were some shacks there until that time but these have long since disappeared. The regular road leads around the upper Printer Boy workings and over into Iowa Gulch. Oro City was the site of one of our very earliest attempts at settlement in the high Colorado Rockies.*

* In this same general area, see also Kokomo.

Collection of Francis B. Rizzari
William H. Jackson, famed pioneer lensman, made this early photograph
of the second Oro City, high up in California Gulch.

Collection of Robert L. Brown
All traces of Oro City are gone now, although signs now indicate
the former locations of a few important buildings.

37.

OURAY

ON THE SLOPES of the high peaks that surround the natural amphitheater where Ouray is now located, prospectors came in search of silver ores as early as 1874. At that time Ute Indians were still in legal possession of the territory. Felix Brunot, who later appeared with his Washington-imposed covenants to hoodwink the aborigines out of their inheritance, was an as yet unforeseen eventuality. In the meantime, those who sought the white metal were either unaware of or completely indifferent to the rights that had been guaranteed to the Utes. Most who came sought to establish claims along the headwaters of the Uncompahgre River or on the slopes that rise above Poughkeepsie Gulch.

As an appropriate name for the community that grew up in the natural basin along the river, the men chose Uncompahgre City. When Chief Ouray and his wife Chipeta arrived unexpectedly in camp one day, the residents were both impressed and fearful for their scalps. The only exception in town was a freighter who had already electrified one band of Indians by removing and replacing his toupee before their astonished eyes. Allegedly, the warriors lost little time in departing, "in several directions at once." Ouray was always a "model" Indian, who had long ago accepted the inevitability of white supremacy. His remarks to the settlers who attended a mass meeting at Uncompahgre City were designed to allay their fears and put their wildest apprehensions at rest. Eventually the settlement was renamed in honor of this most remarkable man.

The setting chosen for Ouray is one of the most beautiful in Colorado, situated at the bottom of a mountain-ringed bowl. To the south, snow-crested Mount Abrams rises sheer from a tumbled mass of surrounding peaks, to form a most majestic backdrop for the town. In size, Ouray measures about a quarter of a mile in width by just over a mile in length. Most records credit its founding to A. W. Begole and Jack Eckles who arrived during the summer of 1875. Both men had entered the San Juan country by crossing lofty Stony Pass. From Cunningham Gulch and Baker City, they had followed Red Mountain Creek over the range to the north before descending into the canyon of the Uncompahgre River. By 1876, the fledgling settlement had been duly incorporated. Before the end of that year, J. D. Crane had freighted in enough goods to open the first store at Ouray.

Due to its fortuitous location, growth was rapid. The *San Juan Sentinel*, Ouray's pioneer newspaper, was first published in 1877. Other imitators lost no time in following up its success. That same year also saw the introduction of the rival *Ouray Times*, which in later years became the *Plaindealer*. In successive years, the *Miner*, the *Pilot*, and the *Argus* all thrived and expired from the newspaper scene at Ouray.

Probably the most singularly colorful newspaper ever to be published in Colorado was the often libelous and always irreverant *Solid Muldoon*, brainchild of the incredibly talented David Frakes Day. Between 1879 and 1892, Ouray alternately seethed in anger and rocked with laughter at the unique opinions and news interpretations penned by the unpredictable Day. Highly placed political factotums who had become too pompous were the most frequent targets of his barbed jibes. His scandalous reporting became so popular that the *Muldoon* was published as a daily after 1882. Most readers were motivated either by morbid curiosity or by fear of what they might find in the *Muldoon*. Under circumstances that are still somewhat vague, Day was "induced" to move his scurrilous sheet to Durango in 1892.

Quite an impressive array of very fine mining properties were developed in the immediate vicinity of Ouray. One of the earliest was the Trout and Fisherman Lode, found by two sportsmen named Logan Whitlock and A. J. Staley, who were just looking for good fishing holes. During the summer of 1875, the Grand View Claim was registered. The Belle of Ouray became a factor in the local economy during 1881. Other good producers were the Clipper and Cedar lodes. Many of the best producers were located high up on the slopes of Mount Sneffels. As early as 1875, with no prior knowledge that a town had been started in the valley far below them, Andy Richardson and William Quinn were busily engaged with prospecting in the Sneffels vicinity. Later, in 1895, as an agent for Tom Walsh, Richardson found the immensely rich Camp Bird gold vein high up in the Imogene Basin (see Camp Bird). Imogene, by the way, was the name of Richardson's wife. Walsh was already a millionaire by 1902. For a time, he and his family made their home in Ouray.

Somewhat earlier, but only a few miles away, the remote Virginius was found in 1877 by William Freeland. Barely a stone's throw away was the Humboldt. Both of these were later merged under a single management. Their location, barely below the treacherous St. Sophia's Ridge, resulted in many summer accidents and all too frequent deaths from snowslides in winter.

Within a few years Ouray became the county seat and the Star Saloon was hastily renovated to serve as the first courthouse. The Fourth of July celebration was always a favorite time at Ouray. In the streets, foot races were run, contests of skill were promoted, quite large sums of money changed hands on the several horse races, huge floats were paraded in the streets, and some celebrants nearly "floated" out of town on their own.

In the early days, the Ashenfelter Packing Company carried most of the equipment and supplies to the surrounding mines and, on the return trip, brought the raw silver down to the smelters at Ouray. Later, as trails were widened, mule drivers rammed their unwieldy steel-tired wagons up and down the steep roads. From the south, the incredible Otto Mears hacked out his cliff-hanging, twenty-six-mile Million Dollar Highway from Silverton up over Red Mountain Pass to Ouray. At Bear Creek Falls he built a toll gate where fees were collected in return for the use of his road. Mears' original grade measured 21 percent and was built at a lower point down in the canyon. Today's Million Dollar Highway is cut higher up on the cliff sides and measures only a 6 percent grade.

Utilizing many of the same grades, Mears began construction of his narrow-gauge Silverton Railroad, the far-famed Rainbow Route. Beginning once more at Silverton in June of 1887, the narrow irons had reached Red Mountain by the fall of 1888. At Ironton, on the north side of the range, construction came to a grinding halt when it was found that the canyon walls were too narrow, steep, and twisting for further railroad construction. With only a few miles to go, Mears had to abandon Ouray as his coveted objective. For a time, rumors were rife that he intended to build a cog railway from Ouray up to Ironton. Like most rumors, this one was groundless.

But Otto Mears was not a man to be easily beaten. If a railroad to Ouray was his objective, then some way would be found to get there. Thus, in an incredibly short time he had started building his Rio Grande Southern around to the south of the range by way of Durango, then north over Lizard Head Pass to Ophir, and through Ridgway to Ouray, Mears was happy and, at last, Ouray had a railroad.

Since Ouray survived the silver crash, it never became a ghost town. Today's visitor will find dozens of interesting things to do and all sorts of wonderful things to see. For many years our family has enjoyed spending a few weeks at Ouray each summer. To reach Ouray, simply follow the fine, paved grades of U.S. Highway No. 550 south from Montrose or north from Durango. Although the elk and mountain sheep of former years no longer graze in the streets, it's still a great place to visit and a wonderful spot where one may "unwind" and forget some of the frustrations of the world outside.*

---

* In this same general area, see also Silverton, Camp Bird, and Dallas City.

Rio Grande Archives
    Looking north from Fifth Avenue in Ouray shortly after the turn of the century

Colleetion of Robert L. Brown
    Several original buildings stand along the business street of picturesque Ouray

38.

PANDORA

AFTER TRAVELING ACROSS the Uncompahgre Plateau and into the San Miguel Valley, early prospectors made a series of mineral discoveries that blazed the way for thousands of pioneers. Following its discovery in 1875, the Pandora Mine played a major role in the mineral development of San Miguel County. Since names are not always a true indication of origins and purposes, the exact derivation of Pandora remains nebulous. In Portuguese and Spanish, Pandora is the name applied to a three-stringed musical instrument. Somewhat more commonly, the word is found in Greek mythology, meaning "hope in the box," from the famed story of Pandora's Box.

Although the early town of Columbia, later called Telluride, already existed at a point only two miles away, a second town was founded near the head of the valley, at the bottom of the natural cup formed by the surrounding gray granite mountains. Initially it was called Newport when it was first started by a small group of hopeful prospectors in 1876. Since some of the men had come west from Newport, Kentucky, the origin of this first name is quite obvious. Postal authorities soon discovered that Colorado already had another Newport and some unfortunate confusion was perpetrated. By request, the name was changed in August of 1881. Pandora has been its designation ever since.

There were listings for Pandora in the Colorado State Business Directory for all of the years between 1882 and 1903. In the early years, until their own post office was established, all mail came in from Telluride. Many good buildings were put up, the homes were well kept with green lawns, and fenced yards were the rule rather than the exception. For many years, Dave Wood distributed nearly all of the coal and wood to the homes at Pandora. Due to the almost vertical cliffs that virtually surround the town on three sides, snowslides were a constant peril on warm spring days. One slide came roaring down in April of 1884 and wrecked the Pandora Sampling Works. In 1902, a tremendous bank of snow broke loose and sent the "white death" surging down toward the town. In some near-miraculous way it was deflected, and came to a stop barely short of Pandora.

Fires also took a fearful toll. On May 19, 1903, a patron of one of the stores threw his cigar stub into a woodbox. By 1:00 a.m. the next morning flames were raging through several structures. A grocery store was destroyed and the stock of E. J. Hawkesworth suffered $1,500 worth of damage.

The population of Pandora has never been large. In 1884 there were about two hundred people there. Between 1885 and 1892 this figure dropped to around twenty-five. Then, in 1902 and 1903, it was back up to one hundred.

In addition to the Pandora Mine itself, several other valuable and well known mineral properties figured prominently in the story of life at Pandora. J. H. Ernest Waters, a professional mining engineer who had been retained by the Imperial Government of China, also acted as an agent in several mining deals for English and Scottish banking houses at Shanghai. Instead of seeking out and developing new locations of their own, Waters' capitalist backers urged him to secure controlling interests in some of the better-known properties around Telluride. With this in mind, he approached the Pandora and Oriental Mining Company in 1888 and purchased the Pandora Mill. Shortly after the transaction had been completed, Waters ordered new equipment and made several changes to facilitate treatment of those ores from the company holdings in the Marshall Basin. At that time, this financial combine either owned or controlled the Mendota, Sheridan, and the combined Smuggler-Union mines.

For many years Pandora was practically a company town. From the great mines on the peaks above, a rather expensive 6,700-foot-long aerial tram was built from the site of the Smuggler-Union down to the flotation mill at Pandora. When it operated at peak efficiency, between three and four hundred tons of ore were moved down to Pandora each day. Powered by electricity, this engineering marvel carried supplies on the return trip back up to the mine in the otherwise empty buckets. Only thirty years ago, visitors could still ride the tram on the twenty-minute trip each way between Pandora and the Smuggler-Union. One condition prevailed, however. The rider must waive all liability in the event of an accident.

During the boom years, Otto Mear's Rio Grande Southern Railroad ran a wye or spur line from Telluride out to Pandora to facilitate the shipment of ores and supplies. For many years the Smuggler-Union maintained managers' quarters at Pandora. During the evening of November 19, 1902, one of their resident managers, Arthur Collins, was sitting by the window in the living room. Viewed in retrospect, this was an unfortunate and careless act on Collins' part. In the course of a particularly bitter labor dispute, acts of personal violence had become common. In any case, a shot came through the window, killing Collins where he sat. Although few people entertained serious doubts about its instigation, the act was never successfully pinned on the Western Federation of Miners.

Following the murder, Colonel Livermore placed Bulkeley Wells in charge as the new manager for the Smuggler-Union. Wells was not only a colorful character in his own right but was also a much-overlooked and rather important person in the affairs of San Miguel County at the turn of the century.

His varied career has been well detailed by Wilson Rockwell in his fine book, *Uncompahgre Country*.

While the company headquarters was at Boston during this period, Wells nevertheless spent considerable time in Colorado. On his frequent visits he always stayed at the same house in which Collins had been murdered. During the 1903 strike, Colorado's governor had sent in the state militia in an effort to restore order. Bulkeley Wells was sworn in as a captain of the militia and a state of martial law was declared. Later, of course, the strike was settled after some unionists had been deported from the district.

Years later, on another of his visits to Pandora, Wells retired for the night on March 28, 1908, choosing to sleep on the second-floor porch of the company-owned residence. During the early morning hours, a time bomb exploded beneath his bed. The blast nearly destroyed one side of the house. Wells was propelled, mattress and all, out into the yard. Miraculously, he managed to ride the mattress down, staying on the top of it and thereby avoiding serious injury.

Next morning, a company employee visited the site after the *Denver Post* had phoned him a report of the incident. In a recent interview he told me about entering the house and what he found there. Wells, it seems, always slept with a loaded revolver beside his bed, a fact that should shed some light on his feelings about the personal safety of Bulkeley Wells at Pandora. Next morning, the gun was observed imbedded, barrel first, handle extending downward, from the porch ceiling. Below the place where the bed had been, a huge hole in the floor made it possible for one to look directly down onto the top of the dining table in the room below.

Today, milling still goes on at Pandora, and a few of the homes are occupied. Actually, Pandora is a most accessible town. Its altitude is only 8,995 feet above sea level and a fine road, State Highway 145, will carry you the two miles southeast from Telluride. From the edge of town, interesting footpaths traverse the cliffs above. One of these goes to the beautiful 365-foot-high Bridal Veil Falls and a breathtaking view of Pandora and the magnificent valley below you.*

---

* In this same general area, see also Tomboy, Vanadium, and Telluride.

Courtesy Wilson Rockwell, author of "Uncompahgre Country"
With many of its neat little cottages, here was Pandora-Newport in its infancy

Collection of Robert L. Brown
A wide variety of mining activities has done much to alter
the present appearance of Pandora.

39.

PERIGO

A. C. GAMBELL had left his home in Ohio to participate in the westward trek of nineteenth-century gold seekers. Prior to his arrival in Colorado, he had mined actively in California. When his luck took a turn for the worse, he joined the throngs of "go-backs" who turned their faces eastward once more. May of 1859 found him among the fresh arrivals at Golden Gate City (present Golden) where he proceeded to organize other miners for a concentrated mineral-seeking expedition. The first of the Pikes Peak boom towns mushroomed into existence in 1859 and in the early sixties as hordes of prospectors like these explored the hills in ever-expanding waves. Placer gold was the object of their search.

Following a few false starts, the Gambell party loaded supplies on their string of pack mules and started prospecting up South Boulder Canyon. In this, as in so many similar instances, the party became enveloped in a spring blizzard. In the face of the blinding snowstorm, their mules were turned loose to fend for themselves, while the men hoisted the packs onto their own shoulders. When the storm abated, they found their way into a high broad mountain meadow, watered by a stream that was tributary to South Boulder Creek. Here they made a primitive camp and threw up an array of hastily devised brush and log shelters.

Since both frost and deep snows often remain rather late at this elevation, Gambell and his men gathered dry wood for fires to thaw the ground. On June 6, 1859, promising deposits of placer gold were found adjacent to the stream bed.

When their quantities of food supplies were nearly depleted, Gambell and a few of the other men set out for Denver to buy hardware and to lay in a new supply of grub. Unfortunately, since hard money was in short supply at that time, the men took out about ninety dollars' worth of their gold dust to pay for the purchases.

In an environment already gone mad with the gold fever, the appearance of such a quantity of dust set off a near riot. Gambell should have known that such a quantity of gold would give him away like a shirt full of fleas. When Gambell and his men responded to questions with understandably vague answers about the source of their riches, antagonisms developed. Under cover of darkness, they slipped out of Denver and made their camp near Golden. When the rays of the morning sun roused them from their slumbers, an angry crowd of Denverites, who had followed along, surrounded them. Too sleepy to defend themselves, Gambell and his crew became prisoners of the impatient mob. The chances for help at this point became as scarce as hiccoughs at a prayer meeting. One thing led to another until the hapless Gambell was forced to tell where he had found the gold. Once the cat was out of the bag, the prisoners were rewarded with a fine breakfast and were released by their captors. Shaken but somewhat wiser for their experience, they returned to what was soon to be known as Gambell Gulch.

Among the variety of incoming migrants was a huge giant of a man named John M. Dumont who had come from Nebraska on a very exhausted mule. Accompanying him was a partner named Perigo. Not content to merely work the placer beds, Dumont and Perigo began searching for the hidden veins from which the placer gold must have washed down. Between them, they uncovered both the Gold Dirt and the Perigo lodes, on opposite sides of the gulch. The Gold Dirt produced somewhere between $30,000 and $2,000,000, depending on which sources one prefers to believe. John Q. A. Rollins once sold a thirty-three foot long claim on the Gold Dirt vein for $250,000.

Up from Black Hawk came W. L. Douglas who also staked out a claim on the same Gold Dirt vein. The profits extracted exceeded his wildest dreams. Douglas amassed a sizable fortune from a combination of hard work and incredible luck. When he sold out and left the district, he carried a roll of bills that enabled him to establish himself as a leading tycoon in the shoe business. In the years that followed, good fortune smiled and the W. L. Douglas Shoe Company of Brockton, Massachusetts, made its namesake both rich and famous. Above town, the Golden Flint Mining Company sank a deep shaft into the earth. Nearby, the Ophir, Savage, Golden Sun, Crown Point, Free Gold, and Virginia, poured out a golden torrent for several years.

As increasing numbers of people entered the gulch and their efforts to devise shelter resulted in the founding of a town big enough to house about five hundred people. At first it was called Gold Dirt, after the rich lode. Its best days were between 1862 and 1864. Nearly all of the buildings were of the conventional log construction. Quite an impressive array of one- and two-room cabins were built. Some housed saloons and stores along what was to become the business street. Later on, there was a mining revival in the 1870's and eighties. When their efforts met with success, they changed the name of the earlier town from Gold Dirt to Perigo.

During this period of renewed activity, more new buildings were put up all along the spine of old Gambell Gulch. Beyond this, some confusion has grown up around the intricate process of town naming. Quite apart from the usually accepted story about how Gold Dirt later became Perigo, another story also exists. This one insists that Gold Dirt and Perigo were actually two completely separate towns which grew up in the same gulch, but which were located about a mile apart. To further complicate things, there is in fact another little town just a mile below Perigo. Judging by the log construction, it is obviously very old. One other reference was found that described several small settlements,

In this early photograph of Perigo we see the settlement with
its clusters of small log cabins.

Except for the background and the curves in the road, Perigo,
today, bears little resemblance to its former self.

strung out for nearly the entire length of the gulch. In any case, the whole thing was known as the Independent Mining District.

In the early days, several arrastras are known to have been in operation here. Later, three different stamp mills were built. The largest and most successful of these was subsequently taken over by Peter McFarlane and Company of Central City, in partnership with Hendrie and Bolthoff of Denver. With a measure of prosperity achieved, Perigo acquired a post office. As time passed and life here assumed its own distinctive characteristics, Perigo became known as a particularly sociable sort of place. An exclusive Perigo Social Club grew up and flourished for many years. Frequent community dances were held to help the residents pass the time. Even legitimate theater was attempted, and serious efforts were made to attract road shows from Denver and Central City.

As time passed, the mines played out, and when the golden sands were exhausted, the miners moved on, leaving little behind to mark their brief stay. A. C. Gambell moved over the hills to mine at Nevadaville. Still later, he tried his luck once more in Middle Park. Concluding a very long and full life, he died in Denver on September 10, 1908. Today, his name has been victimized by contemporary misspelling and the site of his discovery is now known as Gamble Gulch.

To see this area, drive south of Rollinsville on Colorado State Highway 119 toward Black Hawk. Just under a mile outside the town, the road bends around a hill and Rollinsville is out of sight. From this point, take the first dirt road on your right and head up the gulch. At the only fork, keep to your left. The distance from the pavement to Perigo is almost exactly three miles of very passable dirt road. Most of Perigo is gone now. It was never a very large town, but its priority in time and its brief life have combined to furnish us with a true ghost town.*

---

* In the same general area, see also Russell Gulch, Mountain City, and Forks Creek.

40.

PITKIN

LATE IN JANUARY, 1879, a small band of prospectors carefully picked their way up into the heavily wooded and snow-filled valley of Quartz Creek, a branch of Tomichi Creek. There were already a number of locations where rich mineral float had been obtained along the banks of this same stream. Further prospecting convinced the party that they were in an area which might potentially rival and possibly even surpass the rich Leadville district. At a point roughly twenty-seven miles northeast of Gunnison, on the north bank of Quartz Creek, they made their camp. For several weeks they prospected. At last they decided that this location was, in fact, going to be a good one, and a crude building was started in the dead of winter. On George Washington's birthday, February 22, 1879, they located their town. Roughly thirty men stayed in camp that first winter. In addition to their tents, a few cabins with dirt roofs were put up. There was also a tent hotel which charged fifty cents per body per night. For a name, they chose Quartzville, although some in the party preferred just plain Quartz or Quartz Camp.

By April, with heavy snows all around and not much else to do, the men grew tired of the original name. Frank Curtiss, a miner, was a close friend of Frederick W. Pitkin, popular governor of Colorado. After some discussion, they decided to call their town Pitkin in honor of the chief executive of the state. A. J. Sparks surveyed the townsite but neglected to file his plot at Gunnison until July 16, 1879.

As Pitkin, the town was formally incorporated in April of 1880. By May of that year there were fifteen hotels and boardinghouses. Best known among them were the Pitkin Hotel and the European House. Soon a post office was established and, to no one's surprise, Frank Curtiss became the first postmaster, proving once again that it's not so much what you know as who you know. Prior to this, all mail had been carried in on horseback from Alpine.

As the town grew, the business district started to fill up. There were the usual stores and saloons, a bank, a sampling works to test the quality of new ore discoveries, two schools, and several churches. The first formal sermon was preached in the town on June 6, 1880. On the surface, this would seem to be a rather imposing array of enterprises for a new town, but you can't win them all. When a reporter for the *Ouray Times* was in town, one disgruntled resident complained as follows: "There are only three women, seven children, one hundred and eighty dogs, one cat, two burros, and three fiddlers in Pitkin. What we need is a newspaper and a saw mill." On July 23, the paper published this account in full.

Before the year was up, Pitkin had acquired both of its "needs." A weekly newspaper, the *Pitkin Independent,* was a reality beginning on July 1, 1880. Frank Sheafor was the founder, owner, publisher, and chief reporter. Well before the first snow fell there were also five sawmills running in the town. About seventy-five new prospectors per day had come in during the summer of 1880 to seek their fortunes. In this early phase, Pitkin was a rather rough and tumble place. Work crews from the Alpine Tunnel descended onto the town every weekend and kept the saloons and dance halls humming. When these toughs were in town, the respectable citizens locked their doors and went to bed.

Although there was an abundant supply of wild game, local cooks demanded, and got, more variety. All foods and most other supplies were freighted up from Alamosa until the railroad was finished. Hay sold at $100 a ton and flour

cost 80¢ per pound. Ham and beefsteak were more reasonable at 18¢ and 20¢ per pound respectively. Eggs sold for
40¢ a dozen. Later there was daily stagecoach service from
Gunnison. After the Alpine Tunnel was completed, the first
train steamed down into the newly erected station on July 12,
1882. In fact, Pitkin became the first permanent settlement
on the Denver, South Park and Pacific Railway on the western slope of the main range. From a distance standpoint, Pitkin is twelve miles below the Alpine Tunnel, twenty-five
miles northeast of Gunnison, and about forty-two miles from
Buena Vista, as the crow flies.

When Frank Fossett visited the town in 1880, he was
quite well impressed. He described it as a "lively and pop-
ulous mining town with many civilized institutions." The
population of Pitkin was fairly stable. It had 1,050 people
in 1880, about 1,500 in 1881, and could still boast of 1,881
souls in 1893.

Mining claims were almost as numerous as the people. An
accidental discovery in 1878 revealed the presence of wire
silver and started the Fairview, Pitkin's first mine. It continued to ship increasing quantities of good ore to market
until 1893. When mining interest declined in Gunnison
County, Pitkin suffered along with the rest of its contemporaries. Prestige was restored a few years later when the deposits were better understood and subsequently were worked
by more experienced miners. Among the more prominent
mines were the Red Jacket, the Silver Islet (or Eyelet),
which produced 744-ounce silver bricks, and the Sacramento which was worked almost continuously after 1890.
It was made up of twenty-three claims on the same gold belt
and was located about three miles northwest of Pitkin.

Most of the mines around Pitkin produced both gold and
silver. In general, they produced ores that assayed out at
from $60 to $20,000 to the ton, a rather wide range in
values. For many years the roster of mines around Pitkin
was an extensive one. It carried names like the Iron Cap,

Little Per Cent, Sultana, Silent Friend, Chloride King, Terrible, Nest Egg, Sulton, Wampum, Tycoon, Little Nellie, and Silver Age. Some among them were fine producers. Each new discovery was heralded as a great bonanza and sent hordes of people into deep shafts to chip away the mountainsides, a pound at a time. A few succeeded abundantly and accumulated generous fortunes over the years.

For the most part mining was suspended after 1893. Here, as elsewhere, the reason was Grover Cleveland's interest in tariff reform and in preserving the credit of the government. On August 7, 1893, he called the Congress into extra session and asked for an immediate repeal of the Sherman Silver Purchase Act. In late October, after extended wrangling in the Senate, he got his wish. Gold production around Pitkin continued sporadically but silver mining went into an eclipse. A new city hall was built in 1901, and the first telephones in town were installed in 1904.

So, gradually, other activities than mining began to dominate the local economy. Two years previously, in 1891, a State Fish Hatchery was built just below Pitkin. Still in operation, it now produces about 91,000 tons of trout annually. Here, where the altitude is 9,220 feet, fine timber stands grow. In the 1890's a lumbering industry was started. Presently, sawmills account for much of the town's prosperity. Many families left as a result of the depression of 1925. At that time the only industry in town was cutting timber for railroad ties.

Pitkin is a beautiful mountain spot. To see it, drive to Parlin on U.S. Highway 50, west of Monarch Pass. Turn northwest at this point and go nine miles to Ohio City. From there, go on for seven more miles to Pitkin. Just north of the town there is a beautiful campground. Nearby is the new road to the west side of the Alpine Tunnel. Fishing is usually good in the nearby streams and there are many attractions in the Quartz Creek Valley to make your stay enjoyable.*

---

* In the same general area, see also Alpine.

Collection of Velma Churchill
 An early picture of Pitkin, looking toward the northeast

Collection of Robert L. Brown
 Pitkin, today, is a busy logging camp

41.

PLATORO

UNLIKE THE OBSCURE NAMES of its immediate neighbors, Stunner and Jasper, we know the origins of the name of Platoro. Quite simply, it was contracted from two Spanish words, *plata* for silver and *oro* for gold. Fortunately, limited quantities of both metals were found here. To pinpoint its location on a map, look at southern Colorado, in the central part. Platoro is twenty-two miles north and about fifteen miles west of Conejos. Here, in the high meadow which was chosen as a townsite, the elevation is 9,700 feet.

Although some earlier prospecting was done in the neighborhood, most accounts agree on 1882 as the actual year in which Platoro began to be built. During that year some claims were worked on the eastern slope of Conejos peak. Hall's *History of Colorado* specifically mentions the Peoria and Eurydice lodes and says that they were southwest of town. Whether both of my sources were referring to the same mineralization or not is unclear. From another quarter comes mention of the Parole and the Mammoth mines and their contributions to the wealth of Platoro. Also prominently mentioned were the Anchor, Merrimac, Chief, Mammoth, Puzzler, and the inevitable Last Chance mines. Spanning a somewhat more extended time schedule than that occupied by most of its neighbors, Platoro seems to have been a relatively stable district with new gold and silver claims recorded as late as 1901 and 1902.

Population statistics fluctuated typically through the eighties, with 1888 and 1889 listed as the peak years. After that things seem to have settled down somewhat since the population was reported at three hundred people in both 1890 and again in 1895. Transportation, or the lack of it, played a dominant role in the history of Platoro. Good roads were the greatest need from the start. During 1888 a wagon road was built toward the southwest from Del Norte. Late that year it reached Summitville and crested the range. Following an already established trail, it descended the southern slopes and followed the Conejos River into Platoro.

Being built in the wide meadow cut by the Conejos River presented both advantages and problems. The advantages are too common and too obvious to be worthy of mention. One of the problems is obvious from the accompanying pictures. During those years when heavy snowpacks built up on the peaks above the town, warm spring days sometimes brought a flood rushing down into the town, overflowing the banks of the river. Three separate floods have inundated Platoro during its recorded history. When the town was barely two years old the Conejos spilled over its banks for the first time. Old records say that the flood of 1884 reached a "record high" but fail to give any statistics. When history repeated itself on June 10, 1905, the *Del Norte Prospector* carried an item calling Platoro's water level the "highest in twenty years." Again, no depth figures were supplied. On October 5 and 6, 1911, Platoro got its feet and foundations wet for the third and final time. A recently constructed reservoir nearby seems to have decreased the chances of a recurrence in the immediate future.

Further relief on the transportation front seemed in sight when the Platoro Toll Road Company filed their articles of incorporation on July 14, 1890. Almost at once they began to construct a road from McDonald's Ranch, on the Alamosa River, over the mountains to Platoro. Immediate work not only improved the mineral prospects but assured winter access to the district beginning during 1891. Before it was completed, this formidable undertaking ran up a bill of eighteen thousand dollars. Even today the grades are still there and are known locally as the Silver Lakes Road.

Over the long haul, most of the factors that had contributed to the demise of nearby Stunner helped to spell out the final act at Platoro. Although many of the "mines were still doing relatively well, Platoro was just too isolated for full development under these circumstances and at this time in history. At another time the story might have been different.

In its contemporary existence, Platoro is a sleepy little resort village where vacationers and sportsmen come to get away from it all, to pursue the wily trout or just to relax. A ranger station and good accommodations are available in the town.

Platoro may be visited by driving west on Highway 17 from Conejos and then north along the Conejos River to the town. It is also accessible by the road that goes southwest from Del Norte through Summitville and over Stunner Pass. From atop the pass, Platoro is clearly visible in the high meadow below you. My favorite route follows the same instructions given in the chapters about Jasper and Stunner. Briefly, follow Highway 15 south of Monte Vista for twelve miles. Here the pavement stops. From this point a graded road leads directly west. All along the way, frequently spaced signs direct you to the Platoro Reservoir. The town is beside it, surrounded by pretty mountains, and nestled in a quiet, restful, historically rich environment.*

---

* In this same general area, see also Stunner and Jasper.

Looking along the main street of Platoro, with Stunner Pass in the background

A few original structures still line the old road through Platoro

42.

PUMA CITY

IN 1896 A VETERAN GOLD SEEKER, known to history only as Rocky Mountain Jim, had been prospecting in the Tarryall country. Jim was an experienced miner who had cut his eye-teeth on the Cripple Creek excitement. On this occasion he made camp on an outcropping of porphyritic quartz that had attracted his attention. At the time he had failed to stake a formal claim. Four days later, he thought better of his actions, gathered up his two partners, and returned to the site. His associates were Sam Swingley and W. H. Preston, the clerk and treasurer, respectively, of the city of Victor. This edition of Rocky Mountain Jim should not be confused with the original Rocky Mountain Jim, James Nugent, who was murdered near Estes Park in 1874.

On this second trip the proper claims were filed around the outcroppings in the midst of a large, open meadow at an elevation of 8,500 feet. Soon the word was out and the ensuing rush resulted in the founding of Puma City. Within a few weeks C. W. Gilman had laid out the plat for a town covering approximately forty acres of placer ground. By the time winter snow fell, there were about fifty houses, log cabins, and tents. Roughly twenty-six of these were spread out along both sides of Simmons Avenue, the principal business street.

One newspaper, the *Puma Ledger,* told the outside world about life in the new camp. Two sawmills were kept busy turning out rough planks and finished lumber for the grow-ing construction demands at the town. Five saloons also enjoyed a flourishing business. Several restaurants took care of the hopes of a migrant population for a more substantial fare. Among the stores one could find a general merchandise, a hardware store, and a meat market. Lodging houses did a good business and there was also a dance hall which was never in want of customers.

Three hotels kept their doors open during the boom. One of these was a large structure with many rooms that had been torn down and moved from Cripple Creek. At its previous location this building had been known as Casey's Flats, a bordello in the red-light district on notorious Myers Avenue.

By 1896 the Tarryall post office had been established to better serve the three hundred people who had settled there. When 1897 rolled around, this number had grown to one thousand. Most accounts agree that Puma City had reached the peak of its boom. An estimated fifty newcomers poured into the camp daily during that year. Lots of others must have pulled out during this same period—otherwise the population would have soared astronomically.

A daily stagecoach brought in both passengers and mail from Lake George, thirteen miles to the south. The same line also ran on to Florissant and Cripple Creek. From the latter point, the distance was forty miles and the time required to ride from there to Puma City was eight hours. The nearest railroad connection was at Lake George where the Colorado Midland could be boarded for the ride to either Colorado Springs or Cripple Creek.

Because the climate was relatively mild here, people remained at the site all year and the mines stayed open through the winter. Among them were the Boomer, which had a shaft only forty feet deep. Nevertheless, it was shipping ore that assayed between $85 and $100 to the ton in gold, silver, and lead. The Comstock produced less valuable ores that were worth only $10 to $18 in gold. J. V. Malone, who may have been the Puma City Rocky Mountain Jim according to one source, located the June Mine on June 1,

1895. It actually adjoined the Puma City townsite. The Tarryall Prince had a naturally formed round chimney of ore, a geological rarity.

On Scheppe Hill, the No Name Mine was owned by A. K. Bay, of Denver. It had a one-hundred-foot-deep shaft with a ninety-five-foot crosscut. Their assays ran $25 to $58 in gold. Nearby, the Louisa group had only a fifty-foot shaft and was not nearly as rich as its neighbor. A Chicago syndicate owned the Hammond group of mines and their 2,200-foot-long Big 6 Tunnel. Another tunnel, the Bonnie H, was only 110 feet long. It was owned by Mr. H. Webb, of Milwaukee. Ore shipments from the Sunday Mine assayed $47 at the Grant Smelter in Denver.

The Colonel Sellers Lode was worked by the firm of Walsh and Scott, under bond for $11,000. Edward Parker, of Colorado Springs, owned a property called the Hard to Beat. From Omaha, C. M. Hunt came west and operated the Redskin Mining Company. In addition there were the Climax, Tenderfoot, Allie S, Electric, Plymouth, and Barnaby. Quite apart from the extraction of the more precious metals, many of these mines also shipped copper ores which were worth an average of thirty dollars a ton. Between fifteen and twenty properties were shipping ore on a year-around basis. Using this number, the newspaper pleaded for a mill in 1898.

The decline of Puma City is attributable to nothing more sophisticated than a wholesale collapse of the mining boom. One account says the whole show came dangerously close to a hoax anyway and that the mining estimates were rather inflated. When the true facts became known, the whole thing just collapsed like a house of cards. In any event, its life span was a very short one.

In the present century, old Puma City has taken the name of its post office and is now officially called Tarryall. It is reached by a good dirt road that runs northwest from Lake George on U.S. 24. The dirt road passes through Tarryall, cuts up through South Park and ends at Jefferson on U.S.

This early picture of Puma City shows some of the typical Western architecture

*Puma City is now called Tarryall. The old city is adjacent
to the contemporary community.*

285. Access is equally good from the north or Jefferson end of the road. The original Puma City was barely west of the present town of Tarryall, in the open meadow toward the mountains. Only a few traces of it remain.*

---

* In this same general area, see also Alma, Buckskin Joe, Fairplay, Quartzville, Montgomery, Leavick, and Sacramento.

43.

QUARTZVILLE

IN POINT OF TIME, Quartzville dates from the very earliest phases of Colorado's mining period. For three years disappointed miners from Denver, Gregory Gulch, the Blue River district, and California Gulch had been combing the promising terrain of South Park. As a result, towns such as Montgomery, Tarryall, Hamilton, and Buckskin Joe had grown up around a variety of rich gold deposits. Almost inevitably, other strikes would be made. Before the mining period ended, a grand total of something over twenty-five gold and silver camps came into existence in and around South Park.

In the process of prospecting among the towering peaks of the Mosquito Range at the western extremity of the park, promising quartz lodes were unearthed on the high, subalpine slopes of 14,163-foot-high Mount Bross. There, on the eastern face, a sheltered, cuplike depression was found just below timberline. In this bowl or sunken meadow, the miners hastily erected a collection of log dwellings. One early account tells us that there were fifty cabins in 1861, plus an assortment of tents.

Shortly after the initial discovery had been made, the miners came together in a common meeting and formed the Independent Mining District. For most of the remainder of that year, the population of Quartzville hovered between sixty and one hundred men. In his book *The Snow-Shoe Itinerant* the Rev. John L. Dyer recalled a trip up Mount Bross to the 11,300-foot elevation where Quartzville was cinched down tight to the mountainside. There, in August of 1861, Father Dyer preached his doctrine of salvation to about thirty attentive listeners. His sermon was calculated to keep them from the alluring and, under the bone-chilling circumstances prevalent at this high altitude, utterly desirable flames of Hades. Dyer said that he "felt that the Lord was with us indeed." Following the service, he walked back sixteen miles and held two other services at unspecified locations. Incidentally, at that time Rev. Dyer referred to Mount Bross as Quartz Hill.

Later that year there was a decline in local mining fortunes, but there was also a revival before the end of 1861. At that time silver was discovered in the Moose Mine, high above the town, and Quartzville entered a second phase of life as a silver camp. As an interesting sidelight, the entrance to the main tunnel of the Moose was situated at an elevation of nearly fourteen thousand feet above sea level. The Moose was also the only property on the peak that was worked during the winters of 1871 and 1872. Over the years, the combined Moose and Russia mines turned out ores worth something over three million dollars.

Other mines that contributed to the economy of Quartzville included the Putman Lode, which had actually been the first discovery, the Hail group which were located in 1871, and the Democrat, which was a gold producer. Inevitably, many claims changed hands over the years. In most instances the prices of claims in the Independent Mining District ranged between one and two thousand dollars.

Shortly after the camp was founded, some placer mining was attempted but in general it was not a successful proposition. At one point there were also a few arrastras in operation but these, too, were abandoned. Some of the silver ores were of a type that was difficult to treat locally. In this, as in so many such cases, the ores were shipped overseas to Swansea, Wales, for refinement. Much ore from the Montezuma–Saints John area of Summit County was also sent to Swansea.

More cabins were built during the early 1870's and by the

Here are some of the ten or fifteen remaining structures at Quartzville

Here is Quartzville, under a mantle of fresh snow

summer of 1872, over two hundred people were living there. Once more the fortunes of the town began to fade in 1878 or 1879, and the town was abandoned once again. But Quartz-ville steadfastly refused to die. A third revival was effected in 1884 when the Quartzville Tunnel had been excavated. For the pioneers who returned, life went on as usual for some years but the peak had been passed. Some traffic, principally ore and supply wagons, moved up and down the old wagon road from Dudley. In winter, jack teams hauled supplies up the mountain and packed the unrefined ores down to the mills around Alma and Fairplay. Finally, the repeal of the Sherman Silver Purchase Act in 1893 succeeded in emptying Quartzville for the last time.

From the empty site of Dudley, just northwest of Alma, the old original wagon road leads off to the left from State Highway No. 9 as you drive north. Dudley, was just beyond the point where the highway crosses the Platte River. From the Placer Valley settlement that now follows the river up to the site of Montgomery and the Colorado Springs Reservoir, a new road leads off across the stream and goes directly up the mountain to Quartzville. Both of these are four-wheel-drive roads and should not be attempted before July in most cases. At Quartzville today, the tumbled-down remains of several cabins may still be seen, nestled in one of the wildest and most beautiful of high-altitude mountain settings, a truly remote and nearly forgotten relic of the period when gold and silver held the promise of Colorado's future.*

---

* In this same general area, see also Alma, Buckskin Joe, Fairplay, Puma City, Montgomery, Leavick, and Sacramento.

44.

RUBY

FOR THE PIONEER postmasters of Colorado, life must have been confusing indeed. In several instances the same names were chosen for different and often widely separated communities. For many years Ruby was one of these. Although the town of Ruby in Gunnison County was often called Ruby-Irwin, some confusion has resulted over the years. All of the material in this chapter will deal with the town of Ruby near Aspen, in Pitkin County but close to the edge of Chaffee County.

Quite apart from some published information which places the town's chronology in the 1890's, the area's beginnings should be moved back to about a decade earlier. In the course of seeking out good mineral prospects, unemployed argonauts from Independence (not the Independence by Cripple Creek, but the one on Independence Pass) explored the possibilities of a variety of streams tributary to the Roaring Fork River. After negotiating a crossing of nearby Green Mountain, they prospected up Lincoln Gulch, following the stream back into the high country.

In the spring of 1880 they found several veins of good ruby silver ore at a point about ten miles south of Independence. This distance should be regarded with an "as the crow flies" computation since by road or trail the actual distance one must travel to get there was and is considerably greater. In reality, the two towns are just over the mountain from each other.

Inevitably, when the news spread, a small rush came rolling

up the creek bed. Most of the early mines were holed in at the head of the gulch, barely below timberline. And wherever there was a mine, a settlement sprang up. The largest and most prominent of these early attempts at colonization was known as Hurst's Camp. Among the early claims were the Scottish Chief, Lone Bay, Jennie Larson (or Larsen), Windsor, North Star, and Tenderfoot.

Before the first snows fell, the miners got together and decided to set up a mining district. Its name was chosen from the nearby creek and the Lincoln Mining District came into existence. Although most of the organizers seem to have come from Hurst's Camp, the name of South Independence appears to have been in rather general use at about this time.

Changing the name of one's town to fill the idle hours was a highly favored form of pioneer recreation. Nearby Independence went through a grand total of five completely different names before it finally settled down. Seemingly the only deterrent to this continuing practice was exhaustion of the mineral deposits and abandonment of the towns.

From the beginnings, perceptive persons should have been able to predict causes for the town's eventual demise. Actually, poor roads and high transportation costs killed the town. Most of the mines were relatively good producers, capable of returning a fair share for a day's work. In the beginning most of the unrefined ores were transported out by burro packtrains to Leadville. No refineries were erected at South Independence in this earlier period.

Their trail led out over Red Mountain (another multiple namesake), through Taylor Park to Everett, and ultimately to Leadville. For many years this long haul cut deeply into profits. Thus, in the course of time, mining operations at Ruby tended to grow less and less attractive to risk capital. When a new trail was built to the site in 1900, it improved matters somewhat but in general it was described as "too little, too late."

Quite apart from the difficulties imposed by the natural

or geographical environment, the town's name now underwent its third and final change. From then on, Ruby became
its official designation, derived from its close proximity to
Red Mountain or to the presence of ruby silver, the accounts
vary. In another source it was stated that the name Ruby
was assumed in 1900 when the Ruby Mines and Development
Company (or Corporation) began operating in the valley.
Physically, the town was composed of a single, rather steep,
principal street which stretched up the mountainside for
approximately a mile. Along both its sides, log structures
of various sizes and shapes, lined the solitary thoroughfare.

Apart from stores and a few other commercial houses,
log-sided cabins that were homes for the miners were about
the only structures in the town. Down near the trail one
may still see the old stable and a moderately good-sized
boardinghouse that usually sheltered about forty or fifty
unmarried miners. No particularly notorious saloons or
gambling dens are described in the old records. There were
never any churches at Ruby either. An occasional circuit
rider sometimes found time to conduct services in private
homes, however.

In 1900 the Ruby Mining and Development Company put
up a fifty-ton concentrator which was equipped with a
crusher and shaker tables. Scarcely less significant was the
long tunnel they drilled deep under Red Mountain. To better supply the miners' wants, a better wagon road was built
up from the original Roaring Fork road in 1906. Taken as
a whole, the activities of the company showed signs of pro-
longing the life of Ruby. With the transportation problem
temporarily whipped, large quantities of the ore were hauled
out to Aspen for shipment.

For more than six years the future seemed assured. New
people migrated to Ruby to try their luck in the mines.
Wherever the miners went, shopkeepers, lawyers, and all the
other multitudinous elements that combine to bring that pe-
culiar state of affairs we call civilization, followed along and

the future appeared promising. With a grubstake, shovel, pick and washing pan strapped to a mule's back, the prospectors came up the new trail. Few obstacles could have checked their enthusiasm. A few succeeded abundantly, but taken as a whole the new activity merely forestalled the inevitable decline for a few more years.

Like so many fine projects, Ruby's tiny boom amounted to little. The impatient crowd of prospectors, traders, miners, and gamblers were doomed to disappointment. By the close of 1912 the handwriting was on the wall. Although the new road was an improvement, it wasn't enough. The long hauls soon ate up the meager profits that were left after meeting increased milling costs.

When the Barnes brothers, last of the operators at Ruby, gave it up in the face of minimal profits, the exodus began. Over the years several individuals leased the properties and tried to buck the tide. But in general most traffic now led back down the hill.

At this writing Ruby is a completely dead town, far advanced toward the process of complete decay. Although several scattered buildings may still be seen at the site, all of them show the marks of decades of neglect.

From the Twin Lakes Reservoir near U.S. Highway 24, north of Buena Vista, State Highway 82 starts its journey northwest over Independence Pass toward Glenwood Springs. Well down the western side toward Aspen, one may enjoy a choice of several attractive campgrounds. Among these is the Lincoln Gulch campground, situated on the south side of the road.

This site is the key to finding Ruby. As you enter this facility, a fork in the road offers you a choice of turning left to the campsites or turning right on an unmarked road that crosses a small bridge. The latter road will carry you to Ruby. Although several roads intersect along the way, stay on the one that is marked to Grizzly Reservoir. Where intersections are not marked, stay on the well-worn trail. When you

The old town of Ruby had a mile-long street leading up this hill and among the trees

Photo by Dick Lindvall
Being able to observe Colorado bighorn sheep in their natural habitat is one of the
fringe benefits that accrues from exploring the back country.

reach the reservoir, drive to the far end where a trail starts up the hill to your left.

Athough a battered sign was standing at this corner during our last visit in 1964, I have heard that it is now gone. It used to show the mileage to Ruby. From this point on, proceed with caution, particularly if there has been any rain in the preceding week or two.

Within the past few years I have heard several times of people who drove their cars to Ruby. We took our Jeep and were glad that we had not chosen to expose our conventional car to this particular road. Many soft spots, sharp dips, and considerable water may be found along the way. Just remember that the greatest problem to the pioneers was that of maintaining a decent road to Ruby and that the same elements still combine to keep this trail primitive.

While you may certainly expect to drive to Grizzly Reservoir without incident, my advice is caution if you choose to drive on up the trail to Ruby. Better yet, why not park and enjoy a beautiful hike up the trail to a most picturesque old ghost town?

45.

RUSSELL GULCH

IN MOST INSTANCES the westward migration that settled the trans-Mississippi country proceeded along in a fairly orderly progression. Then came the discovery of gold in California, and the whole tier of what would become the Rocky Mountain states was literally jumped over in the process of getting to Sutter's Mill as quickly as possible. Those Western states ranging from Nevada eastward to the Great Plains were settled in a virtual backwash of disappointed argonauts who had failed in California. Colorado, peopled a full decade after the California rush, was one of these states, and William Greenberry Russell was one of the unsuccessful gold seekers who gave it up and returned homeward, as fate would have it, by way of Colorado.

Green Russell was a native of Auraria in Lumpkin County, Georgia. He considered himself a professional prospector as a result of his having taken part in the 1827 gold rush in northwestern Georgia. Here a pattern was set that would be followed innumerable times during the settlement of the American West. The gold discoveries were on Cherokee Indian land and Russell was part Cherokee. His wife was a full-blooded member of the tribe. When the presence of gold was positively established, "Indian troubles" inevitably developed and the tribes were excluded from Georgia in 1830.

Following some abortive attempts to regain their land in Lumpkin County, Russell and his brother got out and started for Sutter's Mill with the hundreds of other Forty-niners. Enough gold was found to finance another return to Georgia and one more unsuccessful attempt to regain the family estate. By the 1857 financial panic, the Russell family was again impoverished.

Being financially embarrassed and having no place to go, Russell thought back again to his journeys through the Platte River Basin. His prospecting propensities caused him to suspect the existence of gold here. With his brothers he set out in 1858 for the Rocky Mountains. As the men moved westward, others joined them. By the time they had reached the Platte, there were about fifty in the party, mostly Cherokee Indians. To further their search, the men split up and worked both banks of the river. Both Cherry and Ralston creeks were also worked. No thought was given to deep or lode gold at this time. Their efforts were directed toward the recovery of placer gold or "dust."

When a war party of Plains Indians came by, the Georgians scattered to avoid a fight. Some loose gold was found on Dry Creek at a point about ten miles from their camp, prompting the men to work the Platte up to its source in South Park. Meanwhile, with cold weather approaching, Russell started north toward Fort Laramie to purchase supplies for the winter. Upon his return he discovered that a second party had arrived, from Lawrence, Kansas, and had appropriated his campsite. Hastily the Kansans threw together a handful of log cabins and called their settlement Montana City. Russell put up a cabin to shelter the members of his party who planned to spend the winter here while he returned to Georgia to recruit more help. He soon became aware of a growing interest in himself wherever he went. As so often happens, an unfounded rumor was spreading eastward ahead of Russell, describing eloquently how he had found gold. Being an honest man, he tried to squelch these stories of the "Russell Bonanza," only to find that people suspected his motives and figured he wanted to keep it all for himself.

In a shameless conspiracy to turn a tidy profit in the midst of a depression, Midwestern newspapers and businessmen embellished upon the story until Russell was powerless to stop them. The gold rush to Pikes Peak was on, and Green Russell became a hapless victim of history. Before he could return from Georgia, the residents of Montana City moved up to the junction of Cherry Creek and the South Platte River to start another town which they called St. Charles. Across Cherry Creek, a second settlement called Auraria came to life. St. Charles became Denver City and eventually absorbed Auraria, Montana City, and a third community off to the west called Highlands. The whole thing consisted of an amazing collection of tents, sod houses, log cabins, tepees, and mud.

By the summer of 1859, John Gregory and George Jackson had made gold discoveries in the mountains west of Denver, miraculously justifying the Pikes Peak gold rush. Green Russell suspected that the placer gold he had found in Dry Creek had washed down from the hills. At once he started into the mountains to seek the original lode. Instead of seeking his fortune at one of the established diggings, Russell made his way up Clear Creek Canyon, past the Gregory diggings, to a point three or four miles higher up the gulch. Apparently Gregory and Russell had experienced some misunderstanding back in their native Georgia. When they subsequently met in the gulch, they passed each other without a word.

Along the base of what is now known as Russell Gulch, Green Russell hit it again with the discovery of free gold. Word of his find leaked out, causing another stampede into the hills. As a settlement began to grow beside his discovery, the stream bisecting the townsite was worked for both dust and nuggets. Both sluices and waterwheels were used. Before the winter of 1859-60 moved in, a set of covenants for the Russell Mining District were drawn up. In several ways these were rather remarkable documents. For one thing, women were given equal rights with men. Another provision allowed claims to be held by anyone, except children who were under ten years of age.

By September, about eight hundred people had settled at Russell Gulch. Census figures for 1860 show 2,500 residents there. The town was built of log cabins, with a few frame homes of dressed lumber here and there in the large open meadow to the south of Quartz Hill. Soon there was a school, and fourteen pupils were in regular attendance in 1860. Eventually a brick schoolhouse was built. There was also a brick Federal hall in the town, plus the usual assortment of assay offices, general stores, and other business firms. The *Rocky Mountain News* reported on November 14, 1860, that Sunday services were being held at Russell Gulch. The article went on to state that a Dr. Rankin had preached to a crowded congregation; crowded since the house in which services were held was small, not because of the numbers present. Later, a frame-construction Methodist church was built on the hillside above the gulch.

During 1859 the miners took out about $20,000 in placer gold. By the next summer this sum was up to an average of $35,000 per week. After three or four years of work, the placers were abandoned. Moderately successful deep mining occupied the residents during the next twenty years. By 1881, the population was down to four hundred. Russell himself had left town back in 1862 for an enlistment in the Confederate Army. After the war he came back to Colorado and was a familiar figure until about 1875. At that time he left to accompany his wife and the other Cherokees to the reservation in Oklahoma.

Although Russell Gulch has declined in the twentieth century, it is not a deserted ghost town since there are still a few families living there. Also, a uranium boom in the 1920's attracted a population of about one hundred people. During the last depression, local bootleggers sought to circumvent the prohibition law by hiding their bootleg whiskey in the mine shafts. On one occasion the underworld

Russell Gulch was once a busy and prosperous place

To match these pictures, start with the outline of the hills against the sky

members themselves hid out down in the tunnels until the heat was off.

To see Russell Gulch today, drive up through Central City to the Triangle Parking Lot. From here several roads fan out. The extreme left one going up the hill past old wooden sidewalks leads to the Virginia Canyon Road which passes right through Russell Gulch on the way to Idaho Springs. From the other end, start at Idaho Springs and follow Virginia Canyon in reverse.

Russell Gulch was a particularly important pioneer settlement in early Colorado. It was important not only because it was one of the very earliest mining settlements, but also because it bears the name of one of Colorado's most distinguished pioneers.*

---

* In the same general area, see also Mountain City, Perigo, and Forks Creek.

46.

SACRAMENTO

CHRONOLOGICALLY, Sacramento dates from the discovery of silver ores and the location of six claims on October 22, 1878. Their names were Sacramento, October, Lark, Anniboby, Ada, and Watacka. The lucky prospectors were Charles W. Dwelle, a former manager of the Water Company of Denver; W. M. Tobie; D. B. Mullen; Napoleon P. La Duc; and C. J. Birdzell. On November 12, an adjoining claim, the Jessie, was located by A. J. Wells and Peter Hanson. Of this group, only Dwelle retained a long association with Sacramento.

Just across the range, very close as the crow flies, were the great silver mines surrounding the Leadville area. It seemed logical to mining men that the Leadville formation of blue limestone probably extended across to the South Park side of the range. Both Sacramento and Horseshoe gulches are capped with blue limestone. The well-known London Fault is only about four thousand feet west of the spot where the Sacramento Mine was located by careful and systematic explorations on the exposed parts of this blue limestone. The mine was capitalized at one hundred thousand dollars, with principal offices at Sacramento in Park County.

The Sacramento was duly incorporated and La Duc signed his articles with an "X." In January of 1879, stocks in the company were divided five ways. By far the greatest proportion of the original twenty cabins was built during this first year. All were of log construction but some sported an upper story and at least one had multiple gables on its roof.

Back in the trees one may still see a tremendous structure with a double roof, one above the other with air space in between. Perhaps the first one leaked.

In 1879, D. B. Mullen, by now the vice-president of the Sacramento Mining Company, carried a lump of sulphurets the size of his fist into Fairplay. Such an unorthodox and theatrical display threw the local people into a frenzy of excitement. He boasted at that time the ore body was four feet thick and very extensive. The sample assayed at $1.40 a pound in silver. Before 1879 had ended, a large two-story boardinghouse, a 26' x 30' office building, and a few new cabins had been erected at the site.

During 1880 a number of profitable new drifts were opened up and capitalists from Nevada, California, the Lake Superior region and elsewhere, bought into the Sacramento. A Congressman from Michigan and a son of Governor John Evans of Colorado also invested. As prosperity continued, a New York office was opened at 62 Broadway. During the month of July stocks in the Sacramento were on sale at the Hathaway Bank in Fairplay at five dollars a share.

The bonanza period of greatest production seems to have ended in 1881 but work continued into 1882. The ore had been of very high grade but was frequently spotty. Most of the production had come from a single stope at the west end of the mine. Once this main deposit was exhausted, no real ore was found thereafter. This, rather than low-grade ore, caused the decline of Sacramento. Gross profits from the Sacramento have been pegged at $175,000, including 1882. After that year several lessees worked the property from time to time but production was small.

Whether or not you can drive to Sacramento depends in large part upon the condition of the old trails at any given time. Start south from Fairplay and drive about a mile on the paved road. When you reach the top of the first hill, turn right (west) on the good dirt road that follows the old railroad grade. This is known locally as the Horseshoe Road or

Fourmile Creek Road, since it followed the creek and led up through the now empty meadow where a town called Horseshoe once existed. At this writing, a black and white metal sign with the name "Horseshoe" is tacked on a fence post at the point where the road leaves Highway 285. There is also a section of old rail ties in the vicinity of Horseshoe.

The road is always passable to Horseshoe. At this point a narrow trail takes off to the right and follows the original grade of the stagecoach road from Fairplay. Stay on the main road, disregard the two dim trails leading off to the left, until you have driven to the fork where the road again divides with the right branch seeming to enter a high, open meadow. Forking sharply to the left, the other branch stays in the timber and climbs gradually upward toward Sacramento. When last seen, a Forest Service sign marked this intersection with the distance back to Horseshoe. The wooded road up through the timber gets rough in spots and emerges into two or three meadows where huge gray stumps show evidence of extensive lumbering operations.

The miles seem long here since this road hasn't seen maintenance crews since the turn of the century and your progress will be slow. If it's any comfort, station wagons have successfully negotiated this road. Some of the newer cars with long rear overhangs and tiny wheels may have trouble now, however. The only rule of thumb here, or on any comparable road, is to know how much your car will clear since this terrain can hardly be called flat.

A few miles farther and you will emerge into another clearing where a stream bed, shallow or dry in summer, can be seen to your right. This is Spring Valley. Across it, to the north, near the trees, is an old cabin. From the cabin you can see a dim trail up through the trees. This leads without detour to Sacramento and the distance is less than a half mile. Cars have crossed the previously mentioned meadow at its lower or east end. Once across the stream, it's easy to drive north for fifty yards or so to the cabin. Cars have made it all the way up to Sacramento but a short hike might be safer from this point. If you drive, the road is not steep but there is an eroded crosscut near the point of a climbing turn which should be driven at an opposite angle. The road leads generally north and then west to the town which sits at an elevation of about 11,250 feet.

There are several cabins at Sacramento, scattered among the trees and along streets that have long since disappeared. On the downhill side of the town is another group of cabins, not visible from the main cluster of buildings. Continuing up the trail for a short distance, the Sacramento Mine is just off to the left. From the top of its dump one may enjoy a fine panorama including Fairplay and the extensive dredging operations in South Park.

Since Sacramento never progressed beyond the log-cabin stage, all of its structures are of that type. Due to the density of evergreen growth here, pictures including more than two or three buildings are difficult to take. A wide-angle lens helps. If time permits, the lower road from the last meadow below Sacramento may be followed by Jeep for several more miles until it disappears on top of the tundra. From this point the tops of several mountains are accessible, rendering a fine view of Mount Sherman and Mount Sheridan. The ghost town of Leavick is nestled in the valley far down below. At the present time, however, there is no road down the other side and it is necessary to return by the same way you came up.

One source, published not long ago, showed Sacramento as being located on Sacramento Creek, high up in Sacramento Gulch. This is logical enough but is untrue. Its actual location is one more range to the south.

The ride from Fairplay to Sacramento is not a long one and none of the distances is great. The scenery is fine and well worth your efforts.*

---

* In the same general area, see also Alma, Buckskin Joe, Fairplay, Puma City, Quartzville, Montgomery, and Leavick.

A rock retaining wall held these two houses up above the main road

These crumbled buildings are typical of the remains of Sacramento

47.

SALINA

IN POINT OF TIME, the first discovery of precious metals in Gold Run Gulch dates back to 1859 but it failed to produce a settlement. Although Gold Hill, two miles north, got started in this same year, no population overflow to speak of spilled down into the winding canyon. Another flurry of excitement resulted from a placer discovery in 1872, but once again people preferred to live elsewhere and commute up or down the gorge from other settlements.

The task of colonization devolved upon O. P. Hamilton and a party of six men from Salina, Kansas. Shortly after noon on April 27, 1874, they pitched their tents in Gold Run Gorge, below some old placer diggings. Apart from Gold Hill, the nearest settlement was Boulder, some ten miles to the southeast. Enough good tellurium ore was found to warrant their further attention. From then on things started looking up. Some among the party grew nostalgic and began referring to their cluster of tents as Camp Salina. Quite apart from their hometown as the source of the name, the word Salina is also a Spanish one meaning "salt mine," or "salt pit." Later, of course, the "camp" was dropped and the name Salina has persisted since that time.

Here, as elsewhere, the mines built the town. About thirty families showed up and prepared to settle here during the first year. By 1875 the population had reached one hundred. A telegraph line was extended from Boulder that same year. Cordial greetings from Boulder to Salina constituted the first message to be carried over the "Singing wires." The date was

January 15, 1875. By the end of the year Salina had eight thousand dollars' worth of new construction in place or going up along the crooked street that followed the twisting contours of Gold Run. In the beginning all mail was picked up at Boulder. Later, a post office was established at Salina. G. F. Mayer was the postmaster.

At first there was only one general store in the gulch. Later, as the town grew, so did the business district. In addition to the usual saloons, Salina also had its own assay office and soon there was a full-time blacksmith shop. Both William Hunt and H. C. Sartore opened up general merchandise stores. For the ladies, B. A. Bigger established Salina's first and only dry-goods store. Transients could find lodgings in the Salina House Hotel. Three boardinghouses sheltered and fed the bachelor contingent. One early newspaper account noted that there were many bachelors in town, a common condition in most mining camps. A town well was dug to provide water for most household purposes.

Unlike many of its contemporaries, Salina had a church of its own. In addition, a fine frame school building, which still stands and is shown in the accompanying photographs, held classes during a six-month term every year. When George Crofutt visited the town he mentioned that there were three mills in operation. Mr. Crofutt also spoke disparagingly of Salina's "high priced toll gate."

Without rich mines, the town could not have justified its existence. There were several good properties in the surrounding hills and gulches. The Melvina was probably the best of the lot. It was found almost on the top of Salina Mountain. Below the town, nearby in the creek bed, the Black Swan also turned out good ores. Many of the claims reflected a wistful yearning for home. Among these were the Kansas and the Salina mines. In addition there were the Leona, Baron, Ohio, Melonia, Emancipation, Ingram, Richmond, Victoria, Antioch, Tambourine, Great Eastern, Bessie Turner, and Mayflower properties.

Up until 1881 many people spent their time just washing gold from the creek. At first, most of the ores were hauled over the hills to the smelter in Black Hawk. Large numbers of oxen, horses, and mules were kept to pull the heavy ore wagons. When faced by the need to save transportation costs, the Ohio and Colorado Reduction and Mining Company installed a chlorination mill at the town late in 1875. This brought sufficient prosperity to justify another chlorination mill, owned by Mayer, Penn and Company. Salina boomed on tellurium ores from 1874 through 1876 but mining continued on a lesser scale for many more years.

A daily stagecoach service was operated out of Boulder, up the canyon through Salina, to Sunshine, just a mile over the hill. The line then went on and terminated at Gold Hill. Between 1881 and 1886 passengers could make connections to ride the little narrow-gauge trains over the Greeley, Salt Lake, and Pacific, later known as the "Switzerland Trail," to a variety of other Boulder County mining towns. Between 1881 and 1886 the line was operated by the Union Pacific until a flood washed out the tracks and necessitated abandonment. With the revival of mining, the right-of-way was acquired by the Denver, Boulder and Western. This, in turn, was later reorganized as the Colorado and Northwestern until its abandonment in 1919.

From the standpoint of population, Salina was never large. An impatient crowd of roughly one hundred people had crowded into the gulch by the end of 1877. Beginning with a few tents and four cabins, the town soon expanded to include twenty houses before the first year had ended. At the beginning of 1879, there were three hundred souls there and several more homes had been built along the hillsides. Shortly afterwards, people began to leave; but Salina still had about two hundred residents in 1883. By 1888 the records showed only 150 still holding out.

Then things started looking up a bit with 175 people there in 1897. Another gain was registered as mining interest was

*J. B. Sturtevant, early photographer of Boulder County,
took this fine old photograph of Salina.*

*By September of 1965, a growth of trees had done much to obscure
the view of Salina from this angle.*

renewed enough to attract still more people so that an all-time high of 350 was reached by 1899. Then there was another slump, but seventy-five people were still holding on once more in 1920. Even today, there is still a small resident population that swells slightly in summer and declines between September and June. Many houses, some original, still stand at the site, along with the fine little schoolhouse which is no longer used.

To see this pretty little mountain community, you should drive west out of Boulder on State Highway 119. Shortly after you enter Boulder Canyon, an unpaved road turns right and there is a sign about directions to Gold Hill. When the pavement stops, a well-graded dirt road goes on to Salina. If in doubt, follow the signs to Gold Hill; Salina is at the bottom of the hill just before you start up to Summerville and Gold Hill. If the little church happens to be open, take the time to set your emergency brake on the steep hill and go inside for a look at its minute interior and beautiful antique organ.

In a historical sense and in point of time, Salina has been fortunate enough to avoid the fate of becoming a ghost town. With the booming economy of Boulder County, the chances seem to be good that Salina will continue to be a live town with a promising future.*

---

* In this same general area, see also Tungsten, Camp Frances, and Eldora.

48.

SCOFIELD CITY

AS THE WARMING RAYS of the rising sun crept slowly over the lofty ridges of the Elk Mountains, Joseph Evans crawled reluctantly out of his warm blanket roll to face the early morning chill that pervaded his high valley campsite. Although it was August, a thin frost that had formed in the night melted rapidly from the firewood as he slowly prepared his monotonous morning repast. Cautiously he scanned the immediate surroundings for hostile Utes. This was 1879, and Evans was an unwelcome trespasser deep within a hostile territory. Before the sun could retire that night, he would stake out an illegal townsite on the crest of one of the high ridges of the Elk Range.

Evans had been retained by S. H. Baker, Daniel Haines, B. F. Scofield, H. G. Ferris, William Aggee, E. D. Baker, G. Edwards, and A. H. Slossen to survey and plot a townsite on Rock Creek between Crystal City and the Elko Basin. Quite commonly a new location took the name of one of its early pioneers and somehow it was decided that the name of B. F. Scofield belonged on the handsome alpine park that Evans had selected, and on the fledging community as well. Before long a wagon road bisected the terrain and its nearby crest became Scofield Pass.

Some silver had been found on Rock Creek as early as 1872 but fear of Ute reprisals and an economic panic after 1873 served to retard permanent settlement until Evans selected the site near Galena and Crystal mountains. Although initially isolated, the Scofield group soon had company. Some eight miles to the southeast, another band of trespassers was founding Gothic. By 1879, Chief Ouray was busy quieting the Utes, making exploration somewhat safer but nevertheless technically illegal. To avoid possible confusion, Rock Creek is designated on contemporary maps as the Crystal River.

Almost overnight a ramshackle array of fifty to sixty foundationless log cabins sprang up near the edge of the meadow, exactly the right architectural environment for the birthplace of aspiring presidential candidates. Only one President, however, was ever associated with Scofield and he wasn't born here. Several sources have been at great pains to describe the more humorous aspects of a visit to Scofield by President Ulysses S. Grant. These accounts contain some discrepencies that ought to be cleared up. The date of his visit seems to have been 1880. This date seems correct since Grant's visit to nearby Gothic and Ruby-Irwin are also recorded in 1880. He rode into camp on a white mule, accompanied by ex-Governor John L. Routt, last territorial governor and first chief executive of the new state of Colorado. During his stay, E. E. Riland dug deep in his valise and concocted some home brew. This was done after the failure of some elements in the camp who had tried to sell Grant shares in a mine, and after they had failed, to "lose" some shares to him in a poker game. Now they hoped to get him drunk and give the claims to him so that they could boast of the President owning a mine at Scofield.

Prior to his departure, Grant's hosts showed him the Devil's Punch Bowl, a sheer cliff with a waterfall which drops into a deep hole of the Crystal River. For his benefit they identified it as S.O.B. Canyon or Gulch, the accounts do not agree. Needless to say, the initials were not employed, the full name was flamboyantly used. Grant roared his approval and shouted the name appreciatively across the canyon several times. At this point things get confusing. From one source we learn that Grant suggested renaming the spot Schultz

Canyon since he was running for reelection and this was the name of his opponent. It makes a good story but Grant was already out of the White House in 1880. His years as President were between 1869 and 1877. Furthermore, he never ran against anyone named Schultz. His opponent in 1868 was Horatio Seymour and in 1872 he defeated Horace Greeley.

Grant may have said or meant Carl Schurz, who once led an unsuccessful splinter rebellion within Grant's own Republican party with the slogan, "Anything to Beat Grant!" If any basis for the S.O.B. story exists at all, this may be its source. It is entirely possible that the old warrior had become confused, or muddled, imagining that he was back in the political arena. If so, certain conclusions seem in order with reference to the potency of the Riland brewing recipe. Fortunately for Scofield, the General was not regressed to the Civil War. Folklore and history make a dangerous, but often amusing, combination.

Somewhere between two hundred and three hundred miners came to seek their fortunes at Scofield, quite apart from the fallacious source that would have us believe two thousand souls resided there. Counting transients might have swelled the figure but not to such an extent. During the peak year of 1882, we find records of the usual assortment of commercial enterprises that were indigenous to most Western mining camps. They had a post office, a hotel run by a woman from Illinois, one restaurant with problems when they tried to boil water at this nearly ten-thousand-foot elevation, a general store, carpenter shop, a barbershop, one blacksmith shop, and several saloons. Perhaps one of these was operated by Riland the bootlegger. Daily mail service was afforded by the stagecoach from Crested Butte which came pounding up the stony right-of-way. To provide better service, a stagecoach station was included at Scofield.

Taken as a whole, Scofield was one of the best developed camps in the district. From Quincy, Illinois, came a group

of people with plans to install a forty-ton smelter at the
park in 1880. Whether or not this was the same mill that
was erected in 1881 cannot be resolved at this time. In all
the surrounding gulches, men were busy digging for rich
ores. Unfortunately, most of it was low grade. Although
some good galena was found, the inaccessible location, coupled with high transportation costs, soon drained off the
profits.

By 1885 the peak had passed and the post office had closed.
All things considered, Scofield enjoyed between twelve and
fourteen years of life before the real decline began in 1892.
Some of the people moved on down the valley to start Crystal City at one of the prettiest spots in the West. Others
left for newer boom towns elsewhere in the state.

Another contributing factor in the Scofield exodus was
the almost annual presence of eight to fifteen feet of snow,
lasting eight months of the year. Two-hundred-foot-deep
slides were recorded more than once, and a forty-foot-deep
drift once buried the town. The snowfall was particularly
severe during the winter of 1896-97. Although the town
was already deserted, a few miners had remained in the park
to rework some of the outlying properties. Snowshoes were
the order of the day for these men during almost the entire
winter.

Scofield Park today is a wonderful spot. Our daughter
received her first driving lesson there and can boast of learning to drive on top of a mountain pass. Our son found it
the best of all possible places in which to fly his model air-
plane with no obstructions. The town is gone, except for
a few rubble piles, and the area is flat, open, and green.

Only one route to Scofield is completely satisfactory. Drive
north from Gunnison through Almont to Crested Butte. At
the south edge of the latter town, turn right and stay on the
main dirt road through Gothic and up the steep hill past
Emerald Lake. You are now on the Scofield Pass road. From
this point on, observe caution. While some cars and many

Scofield, high above the Crystal River Canyon in Gunnison County

Only a few scattered foundations now remain to mark the site of old Scofield

pickups have driven all the way to Scofield, it depends a lot on road conditions of the moment. A walk from Emerald Lake is not out of the question. After crossing the pass, the town was in the next open meadow, just a short distance away.

Conventional cars sometimes go down from here to the Crystal Valley but none come back up. A 25 percent grade on slide rock precludes this being anything but a Jeep road. Hot brakes are no rarity at the bottom and few people go back for seconds. With a Jeep, this trip is simple for even the beginning driver. Under any circumstances, barring bad weather, this will be a rewarding trip, one that will long be remembered and discussed during the long, cold winters that lie ahead.*

---

* In this same general area, see also Crested Butte, Crystal City, and Marble.

49.

SILVER CLIFF

FOR MANY YEARS after 1877, the carbonate craze extended all over the mountains, excited by the finds at Leadville, in Chaffee, Lake, Gunnison, and Summit counties. Most prospectors were searching for carbonates, and if what they found bore any resemblance to the ores at Leadville, it was at once proclaimed as a wonderful discovery.

To a decisive degree, silver mining dominated the second and third decades of mining in Colorado. The circumstances that resulted in the discovery and naming of Silver Cliff came about when R. J. Edwards, a transplanted prospector from Racine, Wisconsin, led two friends on a trip near the eastern foot of the Sangre de Cristo Mountains. Robert Powell and George Hofford, along with Edwards, had prospected and leased a number of mines around Rosita. All three men were living in Rosita at the time. Hofford had crossed the plains with the multitude during the original Pikes Peak gold rush of 1859, pushing a wheelbarrow that contained his blanket and provisions.

Three separate dates have been given for the discovery that they made. These are July of 1877, August of 1877, and June 29, 1878. A low, black-faced cliff, roughly thirty feet high, stood alone on the prairie near an old trail that crossed the Wet Mountain Valley from Oak Creek Canyon to Grape Creek. Such a conspicuous prominence could hardly have avoided attracting the attention of prospectors. On this occasion Edwards and his friends rediscovered it and broke off some of the black substance which they carried home to

Rosita for assaying. One sample showed 24¾ ounces of horn silver to the ton. This was a new metal to Edwards. Another sample turned out to have twenty ounces of gold to the ton. Although the gold figure was discovered to be in error, the word got out and there was a rush that nearly depleted both Rosita and Querida. When no other gold was found, the prospectors returned home.

Meanwhile, Edwards, Powell, and Hofford kept their silver discovery a secret. Hofford owned a team which they outfitted for a prolonged journey. While camped at the base of the cliff, they located the source of the horn silver and staked out their claim. At the beginning of the next summer Edwards returned and began to develop two locations. These became the Silver Cliff and the Racine Boy mines. One source states that both locations were found on June 20, 1878. Over the years, both mines were developed to a high degree. Some of the samples taken out during the second year showed 740 ounces to the ton in silver. When word leaked out, there was another rush, sending a stream of humanity into the Wet Mountain Valley, and a large town was hastily built near the base of the rich cliff.

Silver Cliff burst forth upon the Colorado scene soon after Leadville. It was pleasantly situated on the flats between Grape Creek and Round Mountain, at an elevation of 7,920 feet. Most people were confident that it would become a large and permanent city. The first house was built by two men named McIlhenny and Wilson in September of 1878. It was a small frame building that contained a general store and the first primitive post office. There were five thousand people there in 1880 and ten thousand at the peak of the boom a few years later. Ten miles of streets were built and maintained by a chain gang from the local jail. Evergreens and flowers were planted around the homes. W. H. Holmes laid out the townsite on 320 acres and patented it with the authorities on December 8, 1879. Following an election held the next February, the first set of town officers took over.

As the population grew, a water works was constructed, complete with twenty-nine fire hydrants by 1880. In the early days, water from the nearby springs were hawked through the streets at forty cents a barrel.

At first there were no churches. When families started to arrive, all that changed. The Episcopalians put up the first house of worship, followed closely by the Baptists, Seventh-Day Adventists, Presbyterians, Catholics and Methodists. After the churches, schools were soon built and then the other usual businesses followed. The county was divided into twenty school districts and there were some 1,400 children of school age. H. A. McIntyre purchased the interior fixtures of the old Boyd and Stewart Bank at Rosita and then opened a bank of his own at Silver Cliff. Two men named Reynolds and DeWalt bought him out and reopened under the name of the Merchants and Miners Bank. Later, a second bank was opened to handle the growing number of accounts. The Western and Cliff House hotels were soon followed by eight other hostelries, all eager to house those who had migrated to the Wet Mountain Valley.

By 1881, Silver Cliff had become the third largest city in Colorado. There were twenty grocery stores and ten dry-goods establishments in operation. Three sawmills were busy almost constantly, trying to keep up with growing demands for lumber. Cheap Charlie's Clothing Store and seven other similar outlets provided wearing apparel for the residents of the new city. There were seven meat markets, six barber-shops, and for the ladies, five hairdressers.

At one time or another, seven newspapers have flourished at Silver Cliff. W. L. Stevens began by publishing the *Silver Cliff Miner* in 1878. Next came the *Silver Cliff Weekly Prospector* on May 5, 1879. Just a month later it dropped one word from the title and came out as a daily. The *Republican* first went to press on April 1, 1880, followed by the *Mining Gazette* in November of that same year. Two years later, Will C. Ferril established the *Daily Herald*. Incidentally, Mr. Ferril was the father of Colorado's distinguished poet-author-publisher, Thomas Hornsby Ferril. Finally, in the 1890's, the *Wet Mountain Tribune* and the *Silver Cliff Rustler* appeared.

Shortly after the town was started, an active night life began to develop. For many years there were five theaters in town. Most notable of the group was the Gem Novelty Theatre. In addition to an unspecified number of dance halls, there were also twenty-five very busy saloons. One of these is known to have cleared two thousand dollars in a single ten-week period. They were so busy that the bar glasses were washed only once each day, whether they needed it or not. The well-known antiseptic qualities of alcohol probably saved the day and the customers as well. To assure a steady flow of customers for the rowdy part of town a parade was sometimes held at 6:00 P.M. Leading off in the finest "Pied Piper" tradition was a brass band. Next came marchers, sometimes slightly tipsy, carrying advertising placards and banners for the several sponsoring establishments. Finally, the big treat appeared. Horse-drawn buckboards, filled with the more presentable "dance hall girls," clattered down the street. Invitations were tendered, knowing winks exchanged, and another night was under way.

At the beginning there had been just a few mines on the cliff. With the passage of time, several more appeared. Speculation ran riot, mines were staked, bonded, and sold on the flimsiest evidence, often without development. Among the new mines that had appeared by the mid-1880's were the Island City, Lady Franklin, Plata Verda, Alta Verda, Crescent, Vanderbilt, Songbird, St. Mary's, Terrible, Rambler and Milkmaid. Several sampling works, four stamp mills and two smelters ran on a busy schedule. Most of these mines were rich in horn silver and were worked at the grass-roots level. On the other hand, the Racine Boy was a deep mine. Also in this latter category were the Bull and Domingo properties, in such close proximity to each other that, inevitably, lawsuits followed. In the courts, decisions went to both parties in a long series of trials. Attorneys for the Bull once pursued the harried judge while he was out fishing. With the help of copious libations from one of those twenty-five saloons, they got an order ousting the Domingo owners from their own property. Instead of fleeing, the Domingo group girded themselves for battle.

That night, following a brisk flurry, Bull men captured the surface buildings and boarded up the mouth of the tunnel while twenty-five Domingo miners were still at work far below. To add insult to injury, the Bull men hurled burning wads of waste, soaked with ammonia, sulphur, and arsenic, down into the hole. Fear of permanent respiratory damage or worse drove the men to the surface. Finally, both sides agreed to sell out to an eastern syndicate and the mines were merged to become the Bull-Domingo. Armed guards were placed on the property to keep out nocturnal highgraders and claim jumpers.

Like so many booming towns, Silver Cliff wanted to become the county seat. Custer County had two bitter controversies over this question. Rosita, which had the coveted designation, contested the upstart claims of Silver Cliff. The first election was held in 1882 and Silver Cliff amassed a majority of the votes cast. Some of the records and a few county officials moved across the valley. Quite apart from the results of the balloting, Rosita now began to advance the claim that a majority of two thirds of the votes was required to move a county seat. When the dispute was carried up the line, the State Supreme Court decided in favor of Rosita.

By 1886, Silver Cliff was ready for round two. This time nearby Westcliffe, one and one half miles away, came in as an ally and the necessary majority was racked up. Still licking its wounds, Rosita refused to give up the records until a Vigilante group was formed to forcibly wrest the coveted documents and records from a reluctant Rosita. To assure future peace, a new courthouse was built halfway between Westcliffe and Silver Cliff.

By May of 1881 the Denver and Rio Grande Railway had completed its Grape Creek extension line into Westcliffe from Canon City. No effort was made to extend the line on to Silver Cliff. There was plenty of trouble just maintaining the line that they had. A stagecoach line maintained connections between the two towns. With improved transportation facilities, Silver Cliff suddenly became a mecca for British remittance men. Thus in an incredibly short time English country houses began to sprout all over the place. Almost at once the valley resounded to the ridiculous tootling of hunting trumpets and the coyote and gopher populations were sent scuttling away to avoid the newest common enemy.

Although the railroad stimulated much local interest, the tracks were a source of vast expense to the company. Freak washouts from Grape Creek disrupted traffic and necessitated costly repairs. One storm, on August 18, 1889, entirely destroyed about five miles of the roadbed. The company became discouraged and abandoned the line altogether. By 1890 the rails had been torn out. Although the withdrawal of the railroad greatly retarded the prosperity of the area, it inevitably benefited local farmers and stockmen. While the railroad was in operation, they had purchased their hay, oats and corn from Denver, paying extra to have these commodities shipped in. Now they raised their own crops at home on their own farms.

Silver Cliff had a fire in 1880 and another in 1882. A volunteer fire department, such as most towns had, functioned efficiently. After the 1882 blaze, a new two-story fire house was built. That same year, Silver Cliff played host to the State Fireman's Tournament.

With the passing of the mining boom, the settlers began to rely on other sources of income. Some people feel that mining declined sharply after 1882. Certainly the silver crash of 1893 finished the job. In the intervening years, many

This was Silver Cliff in the 1890's. The background mountains are the Sangre de Cristos

Here is Silver Cliff in 1966

residents moved to the new town of Westcliffe to avoid high taxes. Some cut down trees, trimmed them into logs, and rolled their houses over to the more favored location of the moment.

Westcliffe had been established in 1885 and owed its beginning to the railroad. The two towns of Silver Cliff and Westcliffe were very close to each other and were often regarded as being one. In most instances they worked together for their mutual interests. At the turn of the century there were still over five hundred people there. Small resident populations are still found at both places and there is even a fine little weekly newspaper.

From U.S. Highway 50, west of Canon City, State Highway 69 drops south through Hillside to Westcliffe and Silver Cliff. A somewhat longer, more involved but much prettier route can be followed in from State Highway 115 running south out of Colorado Springs to Florence. From there, State Highway 67 runs through Wetmore and Querida. Then follow State Highway 96 to Silver Cliff, a delightful little hamlet that still retains much of the original flavor that made it one of the truly great mining camps of Colorado's colorful past.*

---

* In this same general area, see also Custer City.

50.

SILVER PLUME

FOUNDED IN 1870, Silver Plume is about the only town in Clear Creek County where the origin of the name is definitely known. Commodore Stephen Decatur, shirttail relative of the great hero of the War of 1812, bestowed the name. Each passing year seems to bring additional hindsight versions of what he had in mind. Although amusing, these stories are far too numerous for repetition here. Allegedly, the date of Decatur's act was July 28, 1870. "The Plume" is located about two miles above Georgetown, and a thousand feet higher, at the base of Sherman and Republican mountains. Denver is fifty-four miles away and nearly a mile lower.

It was a silver and lead discovery by Owen Feenan in 1868 that started things moving in the valley and eventually resulted in the building of a town. Feenan called his discovery the Pelican and kept the event pretty much to himself. When a serious illness made his death seem imminent, Owen confided his secret to a couple of friends. With such friends, he needed no enemies. Within a few days, the two men had stealthily opened the vein. When poor, trusting Owen miraculously recovered in 1871, he found that the tables had been turned and that he had been squeezed out of the partnership at what had formerly been his own mine.

In the course of their history, the mines here produced copper and gold in addition to silver and lead. With very few exceptions, the mines were close to the town. Narrow zigzag trails were cut out on the mountainsides above the settlement to enable the jack trains to carry ore down to Silver Plume. Among the better properties were the Pelican, Dives, Dundenburg, Baxter, Dunkirk, Terrible, and Consolidated-Payrock. Many of these were in clear view of the town. Within a comparatively short time the Pelican and the Dives properties had combined. From the beginning, the shafts of the companies had been close together. Each mine had been working only a short distance from the other on the very same eight-foot silver vein. Inevitably, each felt that the other had been stealing and some very spirited battles were fought below ground from time to time. Most of Clear Creek County took sides as lawsuits and countersuits were filed by the contesting parties. The poor beleaguered judge, who wished he could be elsewhere, actually kept a pistol on the bench.

Suddenly the pot boiled over when Jack Bishop, a hired mercenary on the Dives payroll, followed a Pelican official into Silver Plume and murdered him in a stable. Another version says it was done on a public street. A newspaper report gives the name of the dead man as J. H. McMurdy although Hall's *History of Colorado* says it was Jacob Snider. Since Bishop would not have been allowed to remain at large to do interesting things and since other items in both stories correlate, there is no doubt that both accounts were describing the same event. In any case the issue was solved when the aforementioned merger took place. W. A. Hammil, of Georgetown, purchased both mines and the Pelican-Dives became the best known, and one of the most valuable properties in the district. Hammil eventually sold out for five million dollars.

Despite the fact that it had been founded a full decade earlier, the first settlers were rather remiss in their duties and the town was not formally incorporated until September 24, 1880. Life in Silver Plume followed about the same patterns as those of its contemporary mining camps. Colonel Charles Baldwin and Jane Huff erected the first buildings in town. Two churches, a Catholic and a Methodist, appeared eventually and are still standing, although the Catholic structure is no longer used. Since the village expanded rather rapidly, little time was lost in building a school, which burned in 1893, and in establishing the inevitable post office. In an incredibly short time the business district had expanded to include a grocery store, a meat market, several general stores, many stables, a drugstore and a dry-goods store.

On the second floor of one of the larger structures, Silver Plume's first theater was established. Seating for three hundred patrons was provided. Covering the stage was a handpainted drop curtain which sported a view of the Bay of Naples and Mount Vesuvius. Most of the traveling shows of the day, from musicals to Shakespeare, played at the Opera House in Silver Plume. In addition, local talent groups produced minstrel shows and occasional serious dramatic efforts which are replayed today as melodramas. To fill a social void, the Silver Plume Social Dancing Club was organized by a group of young townsmen. Tickets to their functions were sold at one dollar each.

Five hotels ministered to the creature comforts of large numbers of migrants while nine saloons took care of some other needs. Over the years a total of six mills was kept busy crushing and refining the ores that were brought down the hill from the mines. For the building trade, a shingle mill and a brick kiln went into production. Near the edge of town, a stone quarry was opened up. Before closing, it supplied some of the material used to erect the new state capitol edifice in Denver.

After a fire department had been established, hose cart races became a common attraction, with keen competition between the local runners and those from Georgetown, Central City, and Denver. Rock drilling contests were also a source of much local interest. An active baseball team was formed to play against teams from nearby camps. Their athletic field was the vacant lot across the street from the now-abandoned second school. From the Payrock Mine came a fine community band. In 1904, a circular bandstand was erected near the center of town. Although it is no longer used, it still stands.

Transportation at the Plume began with somewhat less effort for the residents since the town was built in a meadow adjacent to the Bakerville Road. Later, in 1879, this same grade became the Ten Mile Toll Road, described by its contemporaries as "dry and dusty." Daily mails and stagecoaches came up from and went down to Georgetown. One of the earliest operators was W. P. Ferris who ran an omnibus line to Georgetown and Brownsville. In 1874, his first year, Ferris cleared $9,135.

Railroad connections arrived in town by way of the incredible Georgetown Loop. Although Georgetown is only two miles or so away, as the crow flies, it is a full thousand feet lower than Silver Plume. To gain the necessary altitude and connect the two villages, a tremendous loop of track was built, filling the valley and circling back across its own lower grade. It took five years to construct the necessary trestles that held the four miles of track. By 1884 it was completed and six locomotives each day came whistling and puffing into Silver Plume. Geography texts of the nineteenth century commonly showed the Georgetown Loop alongside the Grand Canyon and Niagara Falls as examples of the wonders of America. Before the tracks were torn out in 1939, a thoroughly amusing but extremely jumpy motion picture was made, showing a ride over the loop. In nearly every scene, ridiculously attired tourists fill every window of the cars, waving white handkerchiefs at the photographer as the tiny engine hauled its load up to the 9,175-foot elevation of the Plume.

In 1905, Silver Plume acquired its second railroad. Edward Wilcox, a former Methodist clergyman, discovered that there was more money in Colorado mining than in the salvation of souls. On August 1, he started construction of the Argentine Central line to Waldorf and eventually on to the crest of Mount McClelland. In deference to his former calling, this became the only railroad in the United States that never operated on Sundays.

Population statistics seem to have run the usual gamut with 175 to 200 reported here in 1875. Four years later a figure of 600 was given, with a winter population drop to 120 people. When George Crofutt came to town in 1881, he reported that about 600 lived there. By far the most exaggerated statistic encountered was a figure of 2,000 as early as 1875, a completely irresponsible estimate.

Catastrophes of the usual sort also figure in the story of life at Silver Plume. Fire swept the town for the first time in November of 1884. Shortly after midnight, an overheated stove in the back room of Pat Barrett's saloon got out of control. Pat was burned to death and some fifty buildings in the business district went up in smoke before control was effected. No waterworks had yet been installed. A brigade, wielding one hundred leather water buckets, formed a line from the stream and put up a good fight. Fortunately, a pumper and crew came up the hill from Georgetown. They were able to stop the fire just short of the church. Silver Plume purchased its first pumper from St. Louis in 1885. It is still stored in town. Until recent years it was often sent to participate in parades around the state.

By far the most serious catastrophe in Silver Plume's history was the avalanche that struck on February 12, 1899, a Sunday morning. Both the slopes and crests of the surrounding mountains were blanketed by drifts that averaged three feet in depth. Unexpectedly, a thaw materialized and caused huge masses of snow and ice to detach themselves. Down it came; picking up trees, rocks, and loose materials. Pushing a massive wall of debris before it, the slide gained momentum, stopping with a resounding crash when the base of the canyon was reached.

Large numbers of miners of Italian extraction had built

their homes high on the steep mountainsides above the valley. Zigzag paths led up the rocky slopes from the town. A straight line path to any of these houses would have been impossible to negotiate. It was in this declivity that the slide ran. Obviously, the victims had no warning. As it was, nearly all were caught in their cabins. Most were buried, after first being carried two or three hundred feet down the mountain.

One version tells us that there were actually two slides which ran simultaneously, moving several hundred feet before combining above where the shanties were struck. In extent, both masses were about four hundred to five hundred yards long and about half as wide. The near-impossibility of extracting people from the slide, either dead or alive, becomes apparent when we realize that the solidly packed mass was upward of ten feet deep at the point where it stopped. Rescue parties did succeed in taking out a few badly mangled people. Miraculously, most of them recovered.

The exact number of dead was unknown until summer when the snow had melted. At first, it was thought that about a dozen persons had perished. When the mass melted, revealing its victims, the final tally was around twenty.

Great damage to mining property also resulted. Huge shaft houses from several mines were swept away and the mouths of most tunnels were filled with snow, rocks, and uprooted trees. Ten days later, a second slide came down. A partial precaution for the people was to keep out of the probable path of an avalanche. Regrettably, it was often difficult to tell where those tracks would be.

In the March 23 issue of *Leslie's Weekly* for that year there was a report detailing how the Rockies had been covered with one of the heaviest snows ever known. Those railroads which ran into the mountains lost thousands of dollars. Both tracks and marooned trains were shoveled or plowed out

Collection of Fred and Jo Mazzulla
Silver Plume as it looked prior to the turn of the century

Collection of Robert L. Brown
Silver Plume in June of 1965

time and again, only to be snowed in the next time there was a storm, and the whole process had to be repeated.

Silver Plume is a quiet, peaceful village, just off to the side of Interstate Highway 70, west of Georgetown where the grades begin to incline upwards toward Loveland Pass. In winter it is often possible to watch herds of mountain sheep who come down close to the town in search of forage. When hungry, one may sometimes approach them close enough for photographs. In the town, a small local museum and many original buildings establish a pleasant tie with the past for those who enjoy firsthand exploration of nineteenth-century history.*

---

* In this same general area, see also Fall River, North Empire, Gilson Gulch, Freeland, and Brownsville.

51.

SILVERTON

CAPTAIN CHARLES BAKER was a restless sort of frontiersman who had spent a considerable amount of time just knocking about from one mining camp to another. In the course of his wanderings Baker frequently heard Ute Indian rumors to the effect that gold had been found in the San Juan Mountains. Consequently, Baker assembled a party of six men and set out for southwestern Colorado in July of 1860. His employer, S. B. Kellogg of Oro City, had become infected by Baker's enthusiasm and had agreed to underwrite the expedition financially. The party traveled south down the Arkansas Valley, took on provisions at Fort Garland, and then turned straight west toward the high San Juan Range. Inevitably, word got out and they were followed. After crossing the towering eastern peaks, Baker's party dropped down to a beautiful, 9,200-foot-high alpine park, situated on an elevated level plain, a two-mile-wide tract of land above the Animas River that was completely encircled by high, snow-capped mountains.

To shelter themselves, a series of rude log and brush huts was hastily thrown up and the whole thing was called Baker City. Here they wintered, living in almost constant dread of the Utes since, at best, they were little better than trespassers on the Indian lands. With this settlement as a sort of headquarters, they worked their way up the Animas Canyon, panning for gold as they went. Some gold was actually found at a point roughly corresponding to the later location of the city of Eureka. Although the actual returns were rather meager, gross exaggerations found their way to the outside world and a small migration devolved upon Baker City. When the true facts became apparent, Baker was blamed and put on trial by the miners. The *New York Times* carried an account of the trial in which Baker pulled a "Perry Mason" and won acquittal from the threat of hanging by panning some gold on the spot.

When word of the Civil War filtered in, Baker made his exit via Fort Garland and returned to fight for his native Virginia. By 1868 he was back, only to lose his life at the hands of Indians near the mouth of the Little Colorado River. Inevitably, others also returned, following in Baker's footsteps. Baker City expanded. The Brunot Treaty of 1874 ended the Indian problem and opened the land for settlement. Somewhere along the line the name was changed to Silverton. When F. V. Hayden was there during his monumental survey of 1874, he recorded the presence of twelve houses. Although it occupied the older site of Baker City, the beginning of Silverton is ordinarily dated from 1874.

A tremendous number of rich silver properties was found in the area. This resulted in a influx of population that one source estimated as 4,000 people by the end of 1874. A more reliable source records only 3,000 people at Silverton during the peak of its boom several years later. When George Crofutt was there in the 1870's, he reported only 850 residents. At that time springwater was hawked through the streets at fifty cents per bucket. The mail was brought in from Antelope Springs. Dogsleds brought in the freight in winter. After each trip the dogs were rewarded with a shot of whiskey. In winter, Silverton was often isolated by snowslides.

As the town grew, all of the usual improvements arrived. There were stores, saloons, stables, restaurants, three sawmills, schools, a Masonic Lodge, Order of the Eastern Star, Eagles, and an Odd Fellows Lodge. The First National Bank of Silverton and one other did huge businesses. Isaac Grant operated the first hotel in town, the Grand, opened in 1882. It

---

later became the Grand Imperial and was taken over by W. S. Thompson, an Englishman. Later, the Walker and Silverton Hotels were opened. The *La Plata Miner*, Silverton's first newspaper, appeared in July of 1875. At a later date it became the *Silverton Miner*. A second paper, the *Silverton Standard*, came along a few years later.

Greene Street became the principal business artery while Blair Street, just a block south, became the "Honky Tonk" district. Many dance halls and gambling houses were scattered in among the thirty-seven saloons that lined the street. At one period the underworld gained control of Silverton and ran the town from their dens on Blair Street. When vigilante groups were formed and failed in their attempts to restore order, Bat Masterson was hired to come in from Dodge City and was placed in charge of the Police Department. Although Masterson failed to close Blair Street because he enjoyed partaking of the creature comforts available there, he did tame things down a bit. The taming process was furthered by the arrival of families and the establishment of churches. By the 1880's there were four: a Congregational, an Episcopal, a Methodist, and a Catholic church. Some other diversions were provided by boxing matches and a racetrack.

The list of mines that contributed to the prosperity of Silverton is nearly endless. Among the better known were the Pelican, Victor, Terrible, Silver Crown, North Star, Aspen, Titusville, Idaho, Susquehanna, Gray Eagle, King Solomon, Mammoth, Parker City, Lackawanna, Prospector, Seymour, Dakota, Pompeii, Isle of Beauty, Cleveland, Creedmore, Belcher, Potomac, and the great Shenandoah-Dives. Several refineries of one sort or another kept up a busy schedule. The Walsh Smelter was situated at the entrance to Cement Creek and the Green and Company Smelter was at the edge of the city. Nearby were the Silver Lake-Aspen, North Star Mill, Martha Rose Smelter, Shenandoah-Dives Mill, Kendrick and Gelder Smelter, and the Silver Lake Mill which started up in 1907.

Silverton's economy really gained in prosperity when the Denver and Rio Grande Railway built north up the canyon of the Animas River from Durango, arriving at Silverton in July of 1882. An impatient crowd went wild and Silverton was caught up in the throes of a giddy celebration. Otto Mears also started three narrow-gauge lines from Silverton. His famed Rainbow Route, the Silverton Railroad, went up over Red Mountain Pass to Ironton. The Silverton, Gladstone and Northerly went up Cement Creek to Gladstone, and his Silverton Northern climbed up the Animas River Canyon to Eureka and Animas Forks. In all, four railroads served Silverton. One of these, the Denver and Rio Grande, still makes daily trips up from Durango during the summer months, traversing one of the most spectacularly beautiful canyons in North America. If you choose to make this run, get your tickets well in advance. This, incidentally, is the only regularly scheduled narrow-gauge railroad in the United States and it has been widely used by Hollywood film makers in recent years. Access for other kinds of traffic was provided by way of Stony, Cinnamon, Red Mountain, and Poughkeepsie passes.

After the silver crash of 1893, gold was found and Silverton was spared the final indignity of becoming a ghost town. Over the years, something in excess of a quarter of a billion dollars in precious metals has been taken out of the Silverton area. In addition to being designated as a National Historical Site, Silverton also has the distinction of possessing the first city-owned public utility system in the United States. Although Silverton has been generally lucky, there have been a few sad times, too. For example, a flu epidemic in 1918 took the lives of nearly a third of the townspeople.

To see Silverton today, simply follow U.S. Highway 550 south from Montrose or north from Durango. There, just twenty-six miles south of Ouray, you will find one of the prettiest and most historic mountain-ringed communities in all of North America.*

---

* In this same general area, see also Camp Bird, Dallas City, and Ouray.

Rio Grande Archives
*With Sultan Mountain as a backdrop, Silverton looked prosperous
in 1909 with its new City Hall, then just a year old.*

Collection of Robert L. Brown
*Greene Street in August of 1965 showed **many changes** and **many points of comparison***

52.

STUNNER

WHEN THE FIRST PROSPECTORS sought to extract precious metals from the mountain ranges south of Del Norte in 1879, no town had yet been established at the location which is to be the subject of this chapter. Initial prospects were found in the valley of Cat Creek or Cat Gulch. Because the current maps published by the U.S. Forest Service show no Cat Creek in the vicinity, this may have been "Gato Creek," since this is a Spanish translation of the word cat.

Most of the rather meager sources of information about Stunner tell us that the first construction at the site occurred in 1882. Here, as in so many early camps, more than one name was tried before they found one that lasted. Probably because it was barely across the line between Conejos and Rio Grande counties, Stunner first kited the name of Conejos Camp. Conejos is another Spanish word, meaning rabbit. Later, this name was dropped and for several years the town was known as Loynton. Thus far I have been unable to find any reason for this change. Finally, in 1887, it became Stunner, an equally obscure name. It seems possible that Stunner might have been the optimistic reaction of some miner to his claim of the moment although this is sheer speculation of the most reckless sort.

Geographically speaking, the townsite was located about forty-five miles southwest of Alamosa, just below the headwaters of the Conejos River. Both gold and silver properties were found and worked in the neighborhood but the sheer remoteness of the camp prevented optimum development. Notable among the better properties were the Merrimac, Log Cabin, Eurydice, Pass-Me-By and Snow Storm lodes. Population statistics for the town fluctuated considerably. The earliest figure encountered tells us of 150 people who settled there by 1889. Between 1892 and 1894 this total seems to have dropped to 100 souls. In between these two estimates was one that showed only 20 people there in 1891.

An item in the library files of the Colorado State Historical Society indicates that 1886 was the best year the town ever had. One other account tells us that the Denver and Rio Grande Railway built a line into Stunner but the report is simply not true. It was, however, reached by a fine toll road constructed by the Le Duc and Sanchez Toll Road Company. Papers for this undertaking were filed at Conejos on July 2, 1884. With few exceptions, the road followed the Conejos River from Antonito, passing through Platoro which was on the north side of the water. Since mountains separate these two towns, a series of switchbacks was cut out to enable the road to cross over to Stunner. The total distance was about forty-five miles. Where the road topped the range between the Conejos and Alamosa Rivers, it was named Stunner Pass and still carries a Forest Service marker to that effect on its crest. Despite this, maps published by the Colorado State Highway Department have labeled the crossing as Celeste Pass for the past several years. Its elevation is 10,500 feet.

When the Colorado General Assembly met in 1891, an appropriation for $12,000 was passed for the purpose of cutting a wagon road across the range by way of Platoro and Stunner. Beyond this, very little information is available. Whether it used the already existing grades of Stunner Pass, or whether this became 11,775-foot Elwood Pass, is not clear.

During 1890, a United States post office was established at Stunner but the town lasted only a few more years. A shortage of any really rich ores, good enough to absorb the high transportation costs, doomed the town. By the turn of the century there was nothing stunning about Stunner. The nearness of Summitville on the other side of the range made better ores available at a lower cost. Both transportation and communication facilities for Summitville were also much better developed.

Before you decide on a trip to Stunner, it might be well to look carefully at the accompanying contemporary photograph. With the exception of four early log structures on the hillside across the creek from the road, the town has almost completely vanished. Stunner is about as ghostly a ghost town as anyone could want.

Follow the same directions given in the chapter on Jasper as far as access roads are concerned. I prefer the twelve miles of paved road, State Highway 15, south of Monte Vista. Where the blacktop stops, turn right and follow the signs toward the Platoro Reservoir. This good dirt road passed through Jasper and reaches Stunner just before the roads fork to Elwood and Stunner passes. Platoro and Summitville are over the hills. Stunner was in the wide, open valley where the routes divide.

Currently, the Forest Service has a ranger station here and maintains a very beautifully located new campground facility just below the road to Elwood Pass. Called the Stunner Campground, it barely misses being on the exact site of the old town. It is also the home of some of the most vicious and numerous mosquitos that ever plagued a lover of the great outdoors.*

---

* In this same general area, see also Jasper and Platoro.

Stunner, photographed by George Beam when it was trying to be a prosperous mining camp

Stunner today. The road at the right leads over Stunner Pass to Platoro

53.

TARRYALL AND HAMILTON

FROM THE STANDPOINT of community images, Tarryall probably suffered the worst set of public relations ever to devolve upon a mining camp. Without a single exception, all stock Colorado history texts to date have dwelled at some length upon the covetousness and downright greed of the town's original inhabitants. Also noted was the manner in which any newcomers were discouraged from settling there and how all promising claims had already been preempted. With such dismal prospects for the future and in view of their inhospitable treatment, the late arrivals moved on a few more miles across Red Hill and established a town of their own, called Fairplay, in mockery of their feelings about Tarryall. More often, they bitterly referred to it as "Grab-All."

Historically, many people have speculated that Tarryall was the site of that first nebulous gold discovery in South Park by James Purcell. While he was being detained by the Spanish at Sante Fe in 1807, Lieutenant Zebulon Pike heard the story firsthand from Purcell, an early fur trapper. In any case, during July of 1859, a party of eight disenchanted argonauts from Gregory Gulch decided to journey deeper into the mountains to try their luck a second time. Actually they had another purpose in mind, too. Just a month earlier five other prospectors from Gregory Gulch had been killed by Indians near Kenosha Pass. William Holman and Earl Hamilton were now leading a party into South Park to punish the Indians. At present Kenosha Pass they were joined

by six men from Wisconsin who promptly named the crossing for their home city. Venturing down the other side into
South Park, they succeeded in raising color on Tarryall Creek
at Deadwood Gulch. Little time was lost in establishing a
pick and shovel camp two miles downstream which they
named Tarryall. William Holman, one of the founders, first
called the place Pound's Diggings, in honor of Daniel Pound,
who, it was rumored, had found scales of gold as big as watermelon seeds there. The name was misinterpreted and
many thought it simply meant that one could take out "a
pound a day."

Inevitably the word spread and hordes of men from the
Denver area, Gregory Gulch, and other locations started for
South Park. Soon both banks of the creek were lined with
tents. It was a reaction to this unexpected influx that the
original settlers became jealous and began running off in-
dignant newcomers. Winter finished the job and really deserted the camp. By the spring of 1860, most of the people
were back and had already resumed work. About 150 men
had worked there in 1859. During 1860, some three hundred
log houses were built. Irving Howbert, later a capitalist at
Cripple Creek, moved to Tarryall with his Methodist clergy-
man father in 1860.

Another winter depleted the town once more but the
spring of 1861 saw another revival of interest in full swing.
An attitude of permanence now pervaded the area and steps
were taken that led to the formal laying out of a town in
1861. One hotel, the Dunbar House, seems to have opened
its doors that summer. The Parsons Mint also went into
production here in the summer of 1861. Both $2.50 and
$5.00 rectangular gold slugs were minted. I have also seen
twenty-dollar pieces from the Parsons Mint. At this point
it might be advisable to explain that privately minted
coins were entirely legal as media of exchange, provided that
the gold content of each coin was equal to that of the fed-
erally minted variety. Not until June 8, 1864, was private

coinage outlawed. After that date all such operations constituted a counterfeiting operation.

Almost concurrently with the beginnings of Tarryall, a second town called Hamilton was started on the south side of the creek by some of the other people who had been driven out of Grab-All. Earl Hamilton, one of the original founders of Tarryall, led the dissidents and was the source of the town's name. Although the two communities were easily within shouting distance of each other, separated only by a narrow creek, rivalry between them was understandably intense. Despite the fact that many contemporaries spoke of Tarryall-Hamilton in the same breath, the towns steadfastly refused to merge. When Governor William Gilpin visited Hamilton in 1861, a hastily contrived excuse to visit Tarryall was fabricated and trouble was narrowly averted. At one point when Tarryall received the designation as the seat of Park County, several Hamiltonites nearly succumbed with apoplexy.

One visitor described Hamilton as consisting of one long narrow street running parallel to the creek. There were no sidewalks. Constant traffic from oxteams made this thoroughfare a dust bowl in summer and a mudhole in the spring and fall. Something between 3,000 and 6,000 people are alleged to have lived at Hamilton. If the latter figure is accepted, surely Tarryall must have been included in the estimate. Among the commercial enterprises were several saloons and gambling houses, a post office, the St. Vrain and Esterday General Store, three boardinghouses, a drugstore, six grocery stores, a meat market, two physicians, a sawmill, one hotel, an attorney and a justice of the peace.

W. N. Byers, founder of the *Rocky Mountain News,* once started a newspaper at Hamilton which he called the *Miner's Record.* Byers assigned O. J. Goldrick as a roving reporter and the actual printing was done in Tarryall. Curiously, only eleven issues were published. Hamilton also had a theater that managed to attract a variety of the traveling shows that crossed Colorado's frontier. Gambling was always a popular pastime but the professional merchants of chance usually deserted the mountains each winter, even after the towns were established on a year-around basis. Since gold was plentiful, life was both hard and exciting at Hamilton and Tarryall.

During the summer rushes that swelled both of these embryonic communities in the beginning years, the old original Indian trail across Kenosha Pass proved to be inadequate for the immense volume of wagon traffic. Consequently, most traffic from Denver and the east traveled south on the old Santa Fe road, east of the Front Range. Just north of Pikes Peak, the primitive wagon road up Ute Pass provided access to South Park. Merchants at Colorado City spent $1,400 on bridges and road improvements to make the route more attractive. In the process, migrants kept Colorado City green by bringing money. Generally, this route paralleled the present U.S. Highway 24 to Lake George. There the trail turned north up Tarryall Creek into South Park. Twice each week, the Central Overland California and Pikes Peak Express Company ran four-mule coaches over this route from Denver to Tarryall and Ute Pass. The C.O.C. and P.P. was often maligned by its employees as standing for "Clean out of Cash and Poor Pay."

Although placer deposits are rarely satisfactory producers of long-term wealth, those at Tarryall-Hamilton were exceptional. The best locations were found along both sides of the old creek channel, extending westward all the way to the mountains. Beginning in the summer of 1859, gold flakes as large as watermelon seeds were recovered regularly. In value, these were worth anywhere from $.35 to $1.25 each. Most men took out gold that was worth between $2.50 and $25 per day per man. Thirteen hydraulic installations were already at work by July of 1861. One source also reports the presence of primitive ore-crushing arrastras. One particularly rich placer claim was worked by 150 men during a single winter and earned the name of Whiskey Hole. Here, allegedly, a thirsty man could always pan out the price of a drink, providing he spent it in the local saloons.

For many years after the coming of white men to South Park, both the Utes and Arapaho Indians fought for the privilege of hunting among the game herds at the south end of the park. Sometimes, when they grew tired of giving each other their lumps, both tribes would travel jointly up Tarryall Creek, pitching their lodges among the cabins of Hamilton and Tarryall. All animosity was forgotten as they watched in amazement while the white man alternately dug and panned the yellow metal from Tarryall Creek. One such encampment is shown in the accompanying photograph. For a time, aboriginal social and aesthetic aspirations were submerged while the warriors licked their wounds and attempted to figure out the intricacies of this gold business. Finally, in despair, they would journey southward again to resume the more practical aspects of their warfare around the buffalo and elk herds.

Although Tarryall Creek yielded two million dollars in gold between 1859 and 1872, trouble began as early as the water shortage that first became apparent in the fall of 1861. By 1872, Tarryall was dead. Ten families still resided in the valley but all made their homes in Hamilton. While the shortage of water was a factor in the abandonment, a more compelling reason was the end of profitable placering in 1875. When the Denver, South Park and Pacific Railway entered South Park in 1879, it bypassed the towns completely and the last residents moved a few miles south to Como. When George Crofutt was here again in the 1880's, he mentioned only Hamilton and referred to it as a station on the Denver, South Park, and Pacific with one hundred and fifty people in residence, indicating a possible short revival as a railroad town. Later, when much of South Park was subjected to extensive dredging, the sites of Tarryall and Hamilton were

This photograph shows some of the structures of Tarrvall and Hamilton in 1880

Here is the empty site, of the two towns in 1967. Boreas Pass crosses the mountain at the right of the picture.

buried under tons of rock. Such is the status of the towns at present.

To see the site today, take U.S. Highway 285 across South Park to Como. Drive through Como for two miles on the road toward Boreas Pass. At the point where the road drops sharply down to Tarryall Creek, huge piles of boulders will be seen on every side. Look north (left) toward Mount Silverheels. Hamilton and Tarryall are under the tons of rock that now fill the valley. This is also the point from which the accompanying photographs were made. A brief moment to compare these pictures with the actual site will quickly reveal the approximate locations of two of Colorado's earliest mining settlements, Hamilton and Tarryall.*

---

* In this same general area, see also Boreas, Como, Dyersville, and King City.

54.

TELLURIDE

IT SHOULD BE MADE CLEAR right at the start that Telluride is not a ghost town in any sense of the word. It is, however, one of the most beautifully located small cities in Colorado, and one with a history that reaches far back into the silver- and gold-mining history of Colorado. In addition, it is my own opinion that Telluride is one of the most friendly communities in the state.

Familiarly known as the "City of Gold," life began here in 1878, although one source places the founding two years earlier. Certainly there was mining here in 1875 and people had to have a place to live. Many people came over the range from Silverton to work in the San Miguel River placers. Some of them appear to have arrived as early as 1874. In those days it was known as Columbia and at that time it was a part of Ouray County. The altitude here is 8,300 feet and Columbia was built just a mile up the road from the earlier community of San Miguel City. The initial head count showed one hundred people there although one source kites it to three hundred. During those early years, commercial and mining supplies were all brought in by oxteams, mule packtrains, or by horses and freight wagons. Under such conditions, costs were almost prohibitively high.

Columbia became Telluride in either 1881 or 1883; two dates have been found. In February of the latter year, San Miguel County was carved out of Ouray County and Telluride became the county seat. The new name for the town was derived from the prevalence of tellurous ores found

Photo by Dr. Gerald G. Coon
The author and his son Marshall are shown here on the sheer ledge over the vertical cliffs above Telluride. They are heading down the Black Bear Road toward the town, visible at the extreme left in the valley far below.

Rio Grande Archives
Taken from across the valley, the zigzag switchbacks of the Black Bear Road are clearly visible. The mill and town of Pandora can be seen in the lower right corner.

nearby. Quite a number of excellent mineral-producing properties were found among the mountains above Telluride. Among them were such famous names as the Liberty Bell, found by W. L. Cornett in 1876, and the great Tomboy, which was located in 1888, high up on the Savage Fork of the Marshall Basin. Other good producers were the Alta and Gold King, over the crest of Boomerang Hill; the Cimarron, Columbia, Japan, Black Bear, Argentine, Snow Drift, Cleveland, Red Cloud, Bullion, Hidden Treasure, Champion, Ajax, Emerald, Andrews, and the incredible Smuggler-Union. John Fallon made the initial discovery on the Sheridan claim, a fabulously rich property that included the Smuggler-Union and the Mendota, all on the same tract. In August of 1875, he took out ores that were worth $1,200 to the ton. Beneath the mines, something in the neighborhood of 275 miles of underground tunnels were dug. Although they are still there, most are now unsafe and should be avoided. By 1909 the combined production of gold, silver, lead, zinc, and copper had reached $60,000,000. In the intervening years this total has been pushed upward beyond the $300,-000,000 mark.

When L. L. Nunn built a power plant near Ames to supply electricity to the Gold King Mine, an extension was strung over the hill to Telluride and it is still in service. This became the first long-distance high-voltage alternating current line in the world. With a ready supply of electrical power, Telluride began to achieve its potential. The population soon reached five thousand. A courthouse, school, and opera house were built. In the early days, religious services for the Congregational, Catholic, and Methodist faiths were held in the courthouse. After 1890, these three put up church buildings of their own. In addition to the usual businesses, a water-powered sawmill was erected on the San Miguel River.

Telluride became so prosperous that twenty-six saloons were located there. In addition there were eight bawdy houses and a dozen dance halls. Business was so good that license fees and "fines" from these establishments produced enough money to run the municipal government for many years without a general tax levy. Some of these now-empty establishments are still standing on Pacific Avenue but twenty-one of the saloons were destroyed in a big fire and Telluride's city government is now supported by a more conventional tax structure.

Telluride really boomed when Otto Mears, pioneer road builder of the San Juans, built his narrow-gauge Rio Grande Southern Railroad from Durango, around the southern tip of the range and up to Rico, and all deliveries became much faster. Prosperity had arrived at last.

Over the years, three factors operated to the detriment of Telluride. First, because of its beautiful location at the bottom of sheer canyon walls, the city has been unusually prone to damage from snowslides. One of these even carried off the Liberty Bell Mine Buildings, leaving only an ugly scar in its wake. On several occasions the community itself sustained extensive damage. Second, there were bloody labor troubles in 1901. Peace was not restored until Governor James Peabody sent in the state militia under Major Z. T. Hill in January of 1904. This event is detailed in the chapter on Tomboy. The prolonged strikes opened many wounds that were slow to heal. Third, Telluride was badly hurt by the effects of the panic of 1893 and the slump in silver mining. However, unlike many places, gold was found here and a gradual recovery was made.

Telluride today is a prosperous and pleasant little community. The huge new mill of the Idarado Mining Company processes 1,800 tons of crude ore daily. This is the largest installation of its kind in Colorado. On at least two occasions, Hollywood motion picture companies have gone on location here and have taken advantage of the unparalleled scenery. To visit Telluride, take State Highway 145 in southwestern Colorado. It leads directly into the town. A fine campground, good fishing, hair-raising Jeep trips, and many other activities may be combined to make you wish that you could stay longer.*

---

* In this same general area, see also Pandora, Tomboy, and Vanadium.

Rio Grande Archives
  Pack mules, loaded with timbers, crossing Main Street in Telluride

Collection of Robert L. Brown
  Today, Telluride still has most of the original structures seen in the picture above

55.

TOMBOY

When the ice chunks stopped floating down the San Miguel River and warming breezes blew across the deep valley, a golden treasure was tapped on the peaks above Telluride. In this mountain stronghold, more than three thousand feet above the town, the rich Tomboy vein was first located in 1880. But in the decade or so that followed, the San Juan country was caught up in the throes of a monumental silver boom and this above-timberline strike on the Savage Fork of the windswept Marshall Basin was somewhat neglected for the moment. Many chapters in this book have ended with the demonetization of silver in 1893; this story begins with that unhappy event.

The cry of "gold" at Cripple Creek and in the San Juans electrified the depressed state with news that the much-sought yellow metal had once again been found in paying quantities. When the news seeped out, it sent a fresh new stream of humanity into San Miguel County, stirred by the desire for adventure and by their own acquisitiveness. Off they swarmed, across Colorado's eastern prairies, into the canyons and mountain passes, risking their resources and even their lives on a search for subterranean riches. Before the end of the 1893-94 winter, hundreds of gold seekers were already on the trail to southwestern Colorado.

To shelter those who came in search of a livelihood, a small settlement was started near the mine in this unlikely location. Although it was never formally incorporated as a city or town in its own right, all the necessary elements were there.

As a first designation, it was called Savage Basin Camp. Several stores were established, many sturdy cabins were built, and there was even a school. Two livery stables supplied mules and horses for the hair-raising ride on the cliff-hanging trail to or from Telluride.

The Tomboy name seems to have come into more general use during the 1894 gold boom when production was heaviest. During that year the property was sold for $100,000. It was later resold to the Rothschilds of London in 1897. The price was a cool $2,000,000. Regardless of ownership, the name was usually the same: The Tomboy Gold Mines Company. Less than a half mile away, the Columbia and Japan lodes were found. Many of the men who worked in these shafts also lived in the Tomboy area.

L. L. Nunn built a transmission line across lofty, 13,114-foot-high Imogene Pass, which crosses the range in a saddle between Telluride Peak and Imogene Peak. Through the Savage Basin to the top, then down into the Imogene Basin on the east side, early scouts had blazed the way for the hundreds who would follow. By air, the distance is a scant four miles from Sneffels to Telluride. By the old trail, the distance is much longer. Early packtrains, loaded with ore, coal, and supplies, wound their way across from the Camp Bird Mine, then down to Ouray and Silverton. As prosperity continued, a daily stagecoach brought both passengers and mail from Telluride by way of the narrow road that still zigzags its way up and then runs along the face of a vertical cliff. Frequent but narrow turnouts and a tunnel help somewhat to quell anxieties among the uninitiated. Among the miners, ever alert for new thrills, a unique practice was tried on this road for just one winter. Wings were installed on toboggans for a faster "schuss" down to Telluride. Needless to say, frequent wrecks discouraged the practice.

Beginning in 1890, the Rio Grande Southern Railroad had established service in and out of Telluride. Their station still stands beside the San Miguel River. From here supplies and ores from the Tomboy and other nearby locations could be shipped in or out of the district.

Another unusual means of transportation became a reality when a tram was built down the steep mountainside to the Smuggler-Union Mill at Pandora. Visitors who rode this conveyance were required to waive all claims to liability. In 1919 the Tomboy Gold Mines Company of Telluride bought up a total of sixty claims from the Revenue Tunnel Mining Company, at Sneffels, on the mountainside above Canyon Creek. About twenty-one of these claims were on the Ouray side of the range. To connect these extensive holdings, a vast amount of traffic was carried over the wild road across Imogene Pass.

In the years immediately following the turn of the century, labor troubles characterized the manner of life at Tomboy. The Western Federation of Miners had officially espoused a belief in Socialism during this period. In 1901 they called their first strike in the Telluride district on the issue of the contract work system. Here, as at Cripple Creek, the union won its opening battle. In a hard-fought, hand-to-hand battle, the nonunion men lost and were herded out of the district across Imogene Pass. The hated contract system was abolished.

Later, when the Tomboy Mill began using nonunion laborers, a second strike was called on October 31, 1903. About one hundred workers from the Tomboy walked out. On November 5, members of the Mine Owners' Association asked Governor James H. Peabody, a conservative Republican ex-banker, to send in the state militia. This, they figured, would enable them to reopen the mines with nonunion help. When nothing happened, they issued a second request on November 17. On the eighteenth, Peabody asked President Theodore Roosevelt to send Federal troops to restore order. But in the days that followed, no help from Washington was forthcoming. It became increasingly certain that

This picture shows both sides of the medal that was awarded to members of the
Colorado National Guard following the turn of the century labor wars.

Collection of Robert L. Brown
Above Tomboy, visible at the left of the cliff, is the 13,114-foot crest of Imogene Pass.
Chicago Peak is in the foreground and Mount Sneffels is visible in the right background.

the burden for any action was back on the shoulders of Governor Peabody.

Under the command of Major Z. T. Hill, state troopers arrived in the troubled San Miguel Valley. During January, the troops arrested twenty-two union troublemakers and lodged them in jail. Even more ruthlessly, Hill loaded the agitators onto the train and deported them to Ridgway with a "don't ever come back" warning. Meantime, Major Hill took another step and imposed a military censorship on the press. Next he took over control of the telephone and telegraph lines. With most means of communication with the outside world under his thumb, Hill ordered beatings for the more obnoxious union leaders and for some of the miners as well. In one case, a union leader was publicly chained to a telephone pole on the streets of Telluride.

On March 14, 1904, about one hundred men from a group that called itself the Citizens' Alliance, conducted an armed search of the town. Their investigation flushed sixty unionists and some sympathizers who were kept incognito in a vacant store until it was dark. After midnight they were marched at gunpoint to the railroad depot beside the river. All were packed into two coaches, given the admonition about what would happen if they returned, and shipped off to Ridgway.

Meanwhile, up at Denver, Union President "Big Bill" Haywood boarded the train for Ouray with Harry Orchard, as foul an assassin as ever skulked across the pages of Western history. For a price, Orchard did the union's "dirty work" for them. Among others, he murdered Governor Frank Steunenberg, of Idaho, who had been unfortunate enough to incur the wrath of the Western Federation of Miners during labor troubles in the Coeur d'Alene district. As a start, Orchard doctored up some dynamite to make it resemble lumps of coal. Little time was lost in adding these fiendish contrivances to the fuel piles at the Tomboy and other mills. He next debated the pros and cons of poisoning Telluride's

Evelyn Brown and a friend at Fort Peabody, above Imogene Pass

Ghost town souvenirs. From the collection of Evelyn Brown

water supply with potassium cyanide but his one experience with poisons had been such a disappointment to his personal pride that he remained a career dynamite man ever after. Rubbing his hands with anticipation, Orchard gleefully considered rolling dynamite down the steep mountainsides into Telluride while it was under military rule. Before he could do anything about it, Haywood sent Harry back to Denver to assassinate Governor Peabody. Orchard had few failures and served his masters well. Peabody was one of the failures. An unfortunate newsboy tripped over the wire and was blown sky-high. Peabody lived to a ripe old age. Meanwhile, Harry was getting hot, so the union shipped him off to Cripple Creek where he performed magnificently, in his own way, during that strike.

By April 5, the Telluride Mine Owners' Association was tasting the fruits of victory. They issued a remarkable document which declared that there was no strike in the district and nothing to settle. Unanimously, they refused to negotiate with the Western Federation of Miners and agreed to recognize no union in Telluride. Unlike the results of the 1901 strike, this one broke the power of the union. High on the peaks above, work was resumed at the Tomboy, and at other properties, with nonunion labor.

In one of the accompanying photographs you may see both sides of a medal that now reposes in my collection. Originally these were given to all members of the state militia who had served in any of the four cities listed on the top plate, above the ribbon. In each location there were strikes which required the use of troops. The pendant carried a likeness of Governor Peabody on one side and the State Seal on its reverse. Among union men, these medals became the most hated pieces of hardware in Colorado. Years later, there were instances of wearers being put off trains, assaulted, or publicly insulted. As the years passed, fewer and fewer of the veterans of the Colorado labor wars chose to wear their citations publicly.

Rio Grande Archives
Beyond the Smuggler-Union Mine (in the foreground), there was the Tomboy, in Savage Basin above Telluride, at an elevation of 11,500 feet.

Collection of Robert L. Brown
Empty ruins mark the Tomboy site, at the end of a thrilling, cliff-hanging road

To see the Tomboy, why not start off where many of the pioneers did? From Telluride, get on the zigzag county road at the north side of town. Aside from a "Jeeps only" turn to the left that goes to the Marshall Basin, you can't get off this road. Along the way you will be treated to some of the most throat-clutching vistas in Colorado. The road is still a narrow cliff-hanger and the valley below you seems to grow progressively deeper. Ahead of you, the tunnel is still there, as are several of the old turnouts in case you meet another car. For the record, I have seen conventional cars at the Tomboy many times. As your climb continues, the Smuggler Mill at Pandora can be seen far below. Among the other sights is a view of Bridal Veil Falls and the treacherous Black Bear road across the canyon to the southeast.

Extensive ruins cover the Tomboy site today, along with a number of original buildings. Beyond it, a four-wheel-drive road goes on up and stops at the top of Imogene Pass, from which you may enjoy a magnificent panorama of the surrounding ranges. For the experienced hiker, this will be a worthwhile jaunt. For the rest of us, it is a challenging walk. Long after the return home, you will remember the trip to Tomboy as a real road to high adventure.*

---

* In this same general area, see also Vanadium, Telluride, and Pandora.

56.

TUNGSTEN

LIKE SO MANY of the towns written about in this book, Tungsten started out as a gold- and silver-mining camp dating from the period of the Nederland boom. Although good strikes were being made all around it, no really outstanding finds were discovered to justify the existence of this new town. In the beginning the settlement was known as Stevens Camp, named for Eugene Stevens, an early-day resident and prominent mining personality of the district. This name, rather than the later designation of Tungsten, will be noted on the accompanying photograph. Following a decline of the surrounding mining territories, Stevens Camp underwent a slump for several years. When it reemerged under a new identity, a completely new substance was being mined there. In the meantime, Barker Dam was built in 1910 just to the west of the old and temporarily abandoned townsite.

When magnetic iron oxide was first discovered, it was called magnatite. Later, the hard, white, heavy, metallic element was found to be useful in the manufacture of filaments for electric lamp bulbs. With the addition of 18 percent quantities of tungstic oxide, a yellow powder, it was found that tool grade steel could be hardened much more effectively. When these uses were discovered and tungsten was found in the nearby hills of Boulder County, little time was lost in reactivating the old town. Although the presence of tungsten had been a well-known fact during the earlier mining boom, nothing had been done about it since there had been no market for the stuff. Actually, the first tungsten discovery in this area dates from 1900. Now, all that was changed. In the meantime, World War I had started, providing a tremendous demand for tungsten and a real shot in the arm for Boulder County's sagging mining industry. By 1917, tungsten claims covered an area of twelve square miles, extending from Boulder Canyon to Magnolia.

In the midst of all this profitable excitement, the Boulder Tungsten Production Company invested $30,000 in opening up the old town and for installing milling facilities. Their investment paid for itself in just thirty days. During the peak of the war years, population for the town reached 5,000, with 20,000 given for the total number who worked there. Laborers commuted to Tungsten from Eldora, Hessie, and Nederland. An influenza epidemic in 1917 brought the town to a standstill, but not for long.

When the wheels started turning again, there were seventeen mills running in the town. Many of them were in operation on an around the clock basis. Among them were the Colorado Tungsten Corporation, the Tungsten Mining and Milling Company, the Primos Company, the Boulder County Mining Company, and the Wolfe Tongue. While the town was booming, new people came in to seek jobs. From Boulder, fleets of Stanley Steamers were used to transport the incoming migrants up to the tungsten mines. The Stanley Steamer was used because it was one of the few automobiles capable of making the long pull up Boulder Canyon.

After the war ended, the demand for tungsten declined and took the fortunes of the town along with it. For a variety of reasons, the price of tungsten increased on the domestic market. In the face of boosted prices, American steel companies began to import the cheaper tungstens from abroad, particularly from China. Almost overnight the Boulder County mines closed, the mills suspended their operations, and the people moved away.

To see Tungsten today, drive up Colorado State Highway

Collection of Florence and Bob Staadt
A panoramic view of the settlement of Tungsten

Collection of Robert L. Brown
From just below the highway, barely east of Barker Dam, one may match the view with
that in the picture above. Note the enlarged dump and the
rock outcroppings on the background hill.

119 from Boulder toward Nederland. Just a mile east of Nederland, and at the foot of Barker Dam, was Tungsten. An equally pleasant ride will take you up State Highway 119 from U.S. Highway 6 west of Golden, through Black Hawk and Rollinsville to Nederland, and finally to Tungsten.*

---

* In this same general area, see also Camp Frances, Eldora, and Salina.

57.

TURRET

FOR MANY YEARS prior to the discovery of precious metals in the valley of Cat Creek, a sawmill stood on the future site of Turret. There are records of extensive timbering operations here as early as 1885, a full dozen years before the discoveries in the summer of 1897 that ultimately brought settlers to this high and remote valley. When fall came, tents, cabins, houses, and about a hundred anxious people were already there. In point of time, the settlement was platted in September of 1897 as Camp Austin. After a very brief period of use, the name was discontinued in favor of Turret. Although the town was actually built on the south side of Nipple Mountain, a spur of Turret Mountain, the more picturesque name was chosen. One source went a step farther and referred to the infant camp as "Turret City."

By 1898 there was a huge demand for building lots in the growing town. New homes and business structures were going up as fast as freshly sawed green lumber became available. Rather large amounts of Cripple Creek money were invested in both real estate and in the mines around Turret. Daily mail service became a reality in 1898 when a post office was established in the town. Across the main street from it stood the Hotel Gregory, a rather pretentious two-story building with a front balcony on the second floor. Just a few doors away, the inevitable saloon had been established. Scattered about in the business district were several stores, a couple of assay offices, and the usual number of restaurants.

One butcher shop supplied the hungry populace with fresh meat and poultry.

By May of 1898, the peak year, there were three hundred people there according to the *Rocky Mountain News*. Later, of course, a one-room school was built. During that same year, Turret got its own newspaper, the *Gold Belt*. From another source we hear that 1899 was also the peak year. That same article tells us that there were only five hundred people there at the time. The disparity between the 1898 and 1899 population statistics is difficult to reconcile. As noted elsewhere in this book, such figures were rather irresponsibly handled, a factor that was completely beyond the control of the newspapers which published these accounts. In the early years of the town, a stagecoach came up twice each week from Salida. By 1899 the service had been expanded to a daily run.

For the pioneers who came to Turret, there were employment possibilities in any of the several mines that contributed to the well-being of the settlement. The Gold Bug was owned by a group of Salida businessmen. It had a 200-foot tunnel and a 50-foot side shaft. Gold, silver, and copper ores from this property assayed at $60 to the ton. Its main vein pinched out rather early in the game. Two men named Crosby and Miller discovered the Vivandiere Mine in 1896 and later operated it on an $18,000 lease. Jasper quartz worth $43 to the ton, was taken out of the Last Chance property.

Both the Golden Wonder and the Monongahela Mine were owned by the same syndicate. The Mollie Gibson property was close to the upper end of the town. Ore from the Altman shaft was regularly sent to the cyanide works at Florence for refinement. Three men named Martin, Welch, and Hart, from Goldfield, operated the M. W. Lode. A three-ton shipment from their holdings netted them only fifty dollars to the ton. At first the Deerhorn seemed to show promise and it was worked through the winter of 1897-98 but the high hopes were soon shattered. The Copper King and the Inde-

C. E. Skinner, of Salida, made this early picture of Turret

Empty ruins now mark the site of Turret, west of Salida

pendence shipped their output to one of the smelters at Pueblo. From the Turret Copper Mining and Reduction Company, came shipments of copper and gold which continued as late as 1916. Other properties in the vicinity of the town were the Hattie, Cashier, Monterey, Little Jack, Anaconda, and the Lady Du Bois, which was being worked on a $25,000 lease.

The decline of Turret seems to have started about 1900. From time to time there were resurgences of interest but nothing that became permanent. Enough people stayed on so that postal authorities did not discontinue the post office until 1941. No particularly sophisticated reasons are attributable to the decline of Turret. It was just another mining slump.

A good dirt road that once bore the designation of State Highway 180 runs northeast from the gasoline storage tanks on the northern fringe of Salida. Cross the railroad tracks and follow the main road for twelve miles to Turret. Keep to your left at any main intersections. From time to time there have been Forest Service signs along the road with posted distances to Turret. Those other roads that turn off to the right go to the empty site of Calumet and to the handful of cabins that was once the town of Whitehorn.

Quite a few buildings still stand at Turret, nestled among a quantity of weirdly shaped rock formations. There's more of the town around the corner to the right and one of the mines can be seen at the end of this road. On my last several visits, the town had been completely deserted. If you happen to have camping facilities with you, this is a fine spot for a rest and the chance to get the dust and smoke out of your lungs. If you go in summer, keep a wary eye out for rattlesnakes. After the sun goes down, the wind whistles cool all night, smelling of pine trees and rain and sometimes of snow from the high Collegiate Peaks.*

---

* In this same general area, see also Bonanza and Crestone.

58.

VANADIUM

MOST TOWNS ARE NAMED for their founders, for prominent people who once lived there, for nearby mountains and streams, or for geographical features. This one was named for the rare substance that was mined there. Quite apart from the fact that Vanadium is a completely abandoned ghost town today, its period of life came about later than that of most of the other somewhat obscure communities written about in this book. Vanadium occupied a rather brief spot-in-the-sun during the era surrounding our participation in two World Wars.

When mining first began here, the name of Newmire was initially attached to the small cluster of cabins that sprang up in the vicinity. Essentially this deposit was an extension of the Hermosa-Barlow Creek Lode that apexed west of Telluride. Because the area was quite remote at that time, all of the early output was packed in by horses or on pack mule teams. There are stories in circulation which infer that the ores used by Marie Curie when she isolated the element of radium came from here, but details are nebulous. In view of the chronological disparity, this seems an unlikely possibility. It is entirely possible, however, that materials for their later research could have come from the Uncompahgre Plateau.

Shortly after the start of World War II, the name was changed from Newmire to Vanadium. Over the years, population figures have fluctuated between seventy-five and four hundred people who lived and worked there. The town's location is in San Miguel County, at an altitude of 7,700 feet upon the plateau, roughly eight miles northwest of Telluride. When the Vanadium Corporation of America took over a total of seventy-two claims in southwestern Colorado and Utah, a reduction plant was erected at Vanadium.

To supply the miners' needs, there was at least one general store here. Within it, the inevitable post office was established. For those families with small children, a single-room log schoolhouse was built and used for thirty years. During the New Deal era of the 1930's it was replaced by another one-room structure, but this was built of native stone and was financed from PWA funds. Incidentally, the Vanadium school district was composed of 13,000 acres, presumably the extent of the mineral holdings of the company. For many years, Otto Mears' narrow-gauge Rio Grande Southern Railroad served Vanadium. In fact, a small station house, with facilities for a passenger and freight agent, was built here. Much of the ore was shipped to the refinery at Durango until an unexpected cloudburst sent a wall of water coursing down the San Miguel River and washed out the tracks.

Vanadium, the mineral element, is the source of bombastic uranium as well as the source of radium. Fissionable materials used in America's first atomic bomb are definitely known to have come from here. Additionally, vanadium was classified as a critical and essential material during both of our World Wars. Found near the tops of high mesas, below the slick rims, vanadium is one of the finest steel alloys the science of metallurgy has developed. During both wars, it was widely used to harden the steel used in rapid-fire gun barrels and in making armor plating. Demands for accelerated output of all strategic materials were increased, particularly during World War II.

After the first atomic bomb had been detonated, Major General Leslie Groves made a personal congratulatory telephone call to Blair Burwell, vice-president of the Vanadium

Vanadium, on the Rio Grande Southern Railroad north of Telluride

Vanadium is now an empty shell beside the highway

Corporation of America. The date was August of 1945. This call ripped the veil of secrecy from the furtive activities around Vanadium. Prior to this, the presence of armed soldiers, elaborate secrecy precautions, and very little positive information had effectively kept people in the dark about what it had all been about. Quite unwittingly, the residents of the remote San Miguel Valley had played a small role in the faraway events that suddenly catapulted America into the Atomic Age.

Quite ironically, the site of Vanadium today looks somewhat like a miniature Hiroshima. Nearly all of the surface buildings are gone. Those that remain have been severely gutted. The railroad grade has been all but obliterated. Only a gigantic ugly scar on the plateau side remains, almost as if a bomb had removed Vanadium from the face of the earth. To see the site, drive northwest out of Telluride on State Highway 145 for about eight miles. Vanadium was above the road on the right side and will be recognizable from the accompanying photographs which were made from a point facing northwest. If you reach Saw Pit, you have missed your destination. Turn around and retrace your route for three miles to see Vanadium, an honest-to-goodness twentieth-century ghost town.*

---

* In this same general area, see also Telluride, Pandora, and Tomboy.

59.

VIRGINIA DALE

FOR WELL OVER A YEAR after the discovery of gold in Colorado the incidents connected with settling a frontier had been passing quietly into history. Then, in 1861, the country was severely divided as men took up arms against one another in a major Civil War that lasted four years. Generally speaking, this drew few complaints from the Plains Indians who relaxed and watched with profound pleasure as the whites counted coup on each other. Under the circumstances neither the North nor the South could spare troops for large campaigns against the aborigines.

Hardly a clean page exists in the entire record of our dealings with the American Indian. Taken as a whole, the trail of broken promises and systematic mistreatment was far too long. Probably the growing tribal restiveness had nothing to do with any grand Indian plot hatched to take advantage of the nation's preoccupation with its fraternal war. Nearly everything they attempted in the way of intertribal cooperation met with failure. Burying the hatchet was a fine practice, just so long as it was buried in some other Indian's skull. Preoccupation with religious trivia and cultural differences that shouldn't have made a difference served to keep the tribes divided.

Nevertheless, sporadic raiding and pillaging began to reach serious proportions in the summer of 1862. Such groups as the "Dog Soldiers" of the Cheyennes struck at isolated ranches, poorly guarded wagon trains, and at the vulnerable stagecoach relay stations. One particularly troublesome spot was in southern Wyoming. Here the stagecoaches on the Overland Route to California were using the old original Oregon Trail. Ben Holladay, erstwhile "stagecoach king," was forced to reroute his stages because of the Indians. From the Oregon Trail his new route headed south through Wyoming, across the Colorado line, and then along the South Platte River to Denver. On the return, it went north through La Porte and on to rejoin the Oregon Trail through Fort Bridger and Salt Lake City.

Virginia Dale was established on this cutoff in the summer of 1862. Actually, the route was not particularly new. General William Ashley had used this low pass on his fur trading expedition of 1824-25. Again in 1843 it saw use when John C. Frémont and his expedition are known to have traversed it. By 1849 it had a name; the Cherokee Trail. When faced by the need to change the stagecoach route, Joseph A. (Jack) Slade was chosen to supervise the building of several stagecoach stations along the way to Denver. He named this one for his wife, Virginia Dale Slade.

To assure protection from the Indians, Slade also constructed a stone tower on top of the ridge east of the station. From this point, a lookout could keep a sharp eye on any approaching hostiles. Through 1867, the station was also used by about fifty to one hundred emigrant wagons every day. It became a favorite campground and the Overland Stage people never discouraged the practice since there was safety in numbers.

In the annals of the American West, Jack Slade is best known as a notorious gunfighter. In this, as in so many confused records, he is credited with having killed somewhere between two and forty-five men. Mark Twain credited him with twenty-six. Under Slade's administration, Virginia Dale inevitably became a notorious rendezvous for desperados. Their lookout point on the mountain to the northeast is still known as Robbers' Roost. Slade, of course, knew when loads of rich bullion were due in or out of Denver on the coaches. Working closely with the desperados, Slade tipped them off and shared in the loot from their robberies.

At one time Schuyler Colfax, later Vice-President of the United States, 1869-73, was detained at Virginia Dale with his party. This particular event transpired during the severe Indian raids of 1865. Apart from visits by a few notables, Indian depredations, and the drunken behavior of Slade, life was quiet here. His affinity for the grape eventually caused Ben Holladay to fire Slade. His replacement at Virginia Dale was Robert J. Spotswood who later achieved a well-deserved measure of fame when he ran stagecoaches across South Park between Denver and Leadville.

Fortunately for all concerned, the firing of Jack Slade by Holladay did not result in the violence that accompanied another firing with which Slade was connected. During the spring of 1860 Jules Beni (or Reni), founder of Julesburg, ran the Leavenworth and Pikes Peak Express Company station at that location. The record seems to indicate that he operated pretty much to suit himself. Among other things, mail deliveries often went to the wrong destinations. After a prolonged feud, Slade fired Beni.

Old Jules brooded and bided his time until his tormentor came through Julesburg on a routine inspection tour. Amazingly, Slade was unarmed. Jules met him at the door and promptly emptied the contents of a Colt cap and ball pistol into him. Without the assistance of liquor, Slade staggered around the building. By this time Beni had a double-barrel shotgun loaded with pistol balls which he also discharged at his wounded adversary. Either treatment would have killed most men.

When the physician arrived from Fort Laramie he recovered a handful of pistol balls from Slade's body. Miraculously Jack recovered and at once vowed to rid society of old Jules. When the spring of 1861 rolled around Beni was at Cold Springs, east of Fort Laramie. One version would now have us believe that his friends tied Beni to a post until Slade arrived, drunk, and shot away various parts of his victim's anatomy. Afterwards Slade cut off Beni's ears and wore them for watch charms. The other story says Slade killed him with two shots in an honorable fight, and then cut off the ears.

Later, after his connections with Virginia Dale, Slade left Colorado and continued his alcoholic career in Montana where he made a general nuisance of himself in Virginia City. Finally, the Vigilantes hanged him for a crime he did not commit, thus ending his "eary" career.

For many years stagecoaches continued to run beside Dale Creek in the Cache la Poudre Valley. When Indian raids threatened the well-being of Virginia Dale or the other stations, the operators sometimes tried running two coaches at a time for protection. The full name of the company that operated stages along this route was the Central Overland California and Pikes Peak Express Company.

So, gradually, as Indian raids diminished after 1867, Virginia Dale was abandoned and activities other than transportation came to the forefront. Today the Poudre Valley is a prime agricultural district.

Taken as a whole, the ride to what remains of Virginia Dale is an easy and a pleasant one. Drive northwest out of Fort Collins on U.S. 287 toward Laramie. Just five miles south of the Colorado-Wyoming border is the Virginia Dale sign by a filling station. This is not the early Virginia Dale. Just north of the sign is the Colorado State Historical Society marker. A few feet north of its stone foundation, a good dirt road takes off to the northeast. Follow this road, staying on the most-used section and disregarding the tributary roads. The rocky base is rough in spots but not dangerous. Any car can make it on this good, short farm road. Winding around and up and down over the uneven terrain, the grade drops into and across Dale Creek on an old bridge. Shortly the destination is in sight. Since this is private property, ask

Collection of Fred and Jo Mazzulla
William H. Jackson made this early plate of Virginia Dale

Collection of Robert L. Brown
Virginia Dale, a bit off the beaten path, is still there

permission before you start looking around. The stable is gone now but the old station house with its huge fireplace is still here. Few historic spots can boast of a more unusual background than Virginia Dale with its Indians, stage-coaches, and characters.

60.

ROADS TO HIGH ADVENTURE

AT THIS POINT a few notes on the early roads and trails of the state would seem to be appropriate. An occasional digression away from the neon and asphalt along any of our Colorado pioneer trails can be a pleasing and unforgettable journey into the past as you retrace the routes of the gold seekers. Our motives today are quite different from the grim purposes that impelled brave men and women to strike out into the uncharted wilderness. Currently, the United States Forest Service estimates that there are some 12,500 miles of back-country trails in Colorado alone. Many of these came into being during the mining period.

Since the birth of our nation, Indian trails have served as our earliest roads. More than a century ago, argonauts reblazed many of these trails by notching the trees that bordered them. For miles on end, summit roads and passes slithered around over most of the ranges of our Colorado Rockies. In fact, three fourths of America's real estate above ten thousand feet lies within the borders of Colorado. In general, Colorado's mining boom occupied the second half of the nineteenth century, leaving a heritage of old roads and trails among the timber. Through the foothills and into the high interior ranges, early settlers and scouts blazed the way for the thousands of pioneers who would follow.

From well-worn Indian trails, more than one of these routes have developed into our most important pioneer roads. Bullwhackers and mule skinners rammed their wagons and packtrains across hundreds of scorching miles. With the passage of time, many of the original trails were widened and improved. As new areas opened up, new roads met the need for getting people to Tin Cup or Leadville or Cripple Creek.

Since there was no State Highway Department in those days, private citizens secured a charter for five dollars and built their own grades. In such instances, many, like the intrepid Otto Mears, adopted the toll road motif to defray expenses and turn a tidy profit as well. Within a few years, many prime roads were sold and subsequently became railroad beds. The heyday of railroad sight-seeing came during the mining boom. Most of the larger mining towns were served by one or two day loop railroad excursions. Other early trails became stagecoach routes, lumbering, or freight roads to the early mining camps.

With each chapter in this book, specific instructions have been given for reaching your individual destinations. Most of these roads, except where noted, are accessible by private car. For the others, a four-wheel-drive unit of some sort is desirable, but there are other ways. To see those more remote spots, horses can often be rented. With sturdy footwear and adequate clothing, short hikes to some of the old towns can be pleasurable. We often leave our Jeep and walk the last few miles, just for the enjoyment of it.

In winter, except for those valleys where snowslides constitute a peril, snowshoeing is an invigorating diversion. Our family of four often spends the winter weekends in this way. For example, the short one and a half miles up to Saints John from Montezuma is an excellent first trip and the scenery above the deep snow is majestic. Snowshoes can be rented at a nominal fee from a variety of places. Although slower, this is a safer way to see the backcountry under its mantle of white.

If you are the sort of person who perpetually wonders what is at the end of this or that unmarked road, a few suggestions may be of some help. Highly detailed quadrangle

Photo by Ron Ruhoff
A snowshoe trip makes for an interesting method of visiting ghost towns in winter

Collection of Robert L. Brown
On a hiking trail to a ghost town

maps are available for a most reasonable sum from the United States Geological Survey offices. In my own opinion these are unsurpassed for information about the more remote regions. A fine book, *Guide to the Colorado Mountains*, by Robert M. Ormes, is published by Sage Books for the Colorado Mountain Club. In size and weight, the book is easily carried and contains a remarkable amount of information. Marshall Sprague's fine book, *The Great Gates*, is a monumental contribution, the most comprehensive book on the early mountain passes at this time. He covers not only Colorado but the other Western States as well.

Furthermore, any of the following trails offers a chance to get away from it all, look at handsome mountains and at a road that is rich in history. In only a few instances will you find these passes on oil company maps. Most are much too old and far too remote for that. From the reservoir west of Georgetown, a road branches off the main road and goes up to the old town of Waldorf. In the early days Argentine Pass crossed the peaks above Waldorf at an elevation well above thirteen thousand feet to the Argentine-Chihuahua mining district in the valley of Peru Creek. From Waldorf, the approach twists up across the above-timberline tundra. Although Jeeps can still make it, many people walk the remaining miles from Waldorf. The west approach, from Peru Creek, is now gone. Also from Waldorf, a second road follows the old grade of the Argentine Central Railroad to the top of Mount McClellan and a picture-postcard view of Grays and Torreys peaks.

Not far away, as the crow flies, is Webster Pass. From Montezuma, drive on through town and up the Snake River Valley to the United States Forest Service sign. Turn left here. Regular cars have made this one at times. At the top, you must turn around since the road on the other side washed away years ago. From the top, much of Summit County is visible.

Between Fairplay and Alma, a dirt road turns west to Mos-

quito Pass, highest crossing in the United States. For the past
few years, passenger cars have been getting across the steep
cuts and exposed talus slopes to Leadville but the experience
is a far cry from driving over Loveland or Berthoud passes.
In the early days, Father Dyer crossed the Mosquito Range on
snowshoes. During the Leadville boom, it became one of
the busiest roads in Colorado with regularly scheduled stagecoaches, ore wagons, and pack outfits moving in both directions.

Southwest of Buena Vista, from Nathrop, the Chalk Creek
road leads to St. Elmo. From there, a good dirt road for passenger cars goes to the top of Tin Cup Pass, 12,154 feet above
sea level. The west side, however, is a wild Jeep road down
Willow Creek past Mirror Lake to the early town of Tin Cup
in Taylor Park. Tin Cup Pass dates from the early 1880's.
Only the east side is now maintained. Back at St. Elmo again,
a second road goes up to Hancock and then traverses Hancock Pass. On its westward descent to Pitkin, it passes the
trail to the Alpine Tunnel. The actual top of the pass itself
remains a Jeep road, crossing a handsome panorama of tumbled peaks above Brittle Silver Basin.

Scofield Pass is only 10,700 feet high. From time to time
a conventional car gets over it from the west side although
this is certainly not a recommended procedure. From Crested
Butte, go up the valley of the East River to the old ghost
town of Gothic. At the opposite end of town from the way
you came in, the road climbs up and passes Emerald Lake.
In the open meadow at the top is the site of Scofield. Here
the Crystal River begins its descent to the northwest, cutting deeply into the beautiful Crystal Valley. At one point
there is a twenty-seven-degree grade, hardly to be recommended for the family sedan. Crystal City and Marble are
on this road. Soon afterwards you will come to pavement
and access to Carbondale and Glenwood Springs.

Southwestern Colorado contains the finest assortment of
old passes in the state, located among one of the most mag-

nificent settings to be found anywhere. Four of the better
ones will be noted here.

On U.S. Highway 550, at a point five miles south of Red
Mountain Pass, a dirt road branches left to Ophir Pass and
Telluride. Originally opened as a toll road in 1880, Ophir
never kept up with progress and remains as a four-wheel-
drive road today, with extensive and potentially treacherous
talus slopes on its western approach. Although Ophir only
reaches a height of 11,700 feet, the scenery that unfolds before you at the top is magnificent. Among others, Lizard
Head Peak, Wilson Peak, and Mount Wilson tower above
the valley spread out below you. From Ophir's base, good
roads lead to Telluride, Rico, or Dolores.

Stony Pass was once the main route to the San Juans. Today it is a rather long and time-consuming trail from Cunningham Gulch, above Silverton, to the extreme upper headwaters of the Rio Grande River on the Del Norte side of the
range. At the Rio Grande Reservoir, a fine campground will
be found. Stony Pass was completely inaccessible for many
years. Roughly a decade ago, it was cleared to permit four-
wheel-drive vehicles to cross its 12,594-foot-high summit.

Anyone who has crossed Cinnamon Pass will remember it
as one of the most stimulating journeys in Colorado. At its
crest, Cinnamon crosses the range at 13,009 feet.

From a well-worn Indian trail, this pass developed into one
of our most important pioneer roads. Later on, it was used
by the Hayden Survey party. Still later, it was widened for
use with wagons. In its existence as a true road, it was both
built and allowed to decay during the final quarter of the
nineteenth century. From Lake City, a high, twisting shelf
road climbs sharply above Lake San Cristobal and the Lake
Fork of the Gunnison River. Along the way you may see
remains from the towns of Sherman, Whitecross, and Bur-
rows Park. On the western side, a sharp descent puts you
down into the upper reaches of the canyon of the Animas
River. Here at the foot of the pass is old Animas Forks, and
below it are Eureka, Howardsville, and Silverton.

Rio Grande Archives
Cinnamon Pass was first used by Charles Baker in 1860. Enos Hotchkiss widened the crossing into a wagon road in 1877.

Collection of Robert L. Brown
In August of 1965 the east side of Cinnamon Pass showed little change from what was recorded in the photograph above.

Beginning back at Lake City once more, Otto Mears blazed another trail over the range and called it Engineer Pass. On August 10, 1877, the first stagecoach crossed its 12,800-foot-high crest and connected Lake City with Animas Forks, twenty-five miles away. Below the crest on the western side, the trail forks, allowing passengers for Animas Forks or Silverton to go by that route. A turn to the right and you drop sharply down to Ouray by way of the upper Uncompahgre River and Mineral Creek. When followed by Jeep today, this route offers some of the most breathtaking travel in Colorado.

More than a century ago, pioneers spent many weeks or even months traveling these trails into the unknown recesses of the Colorado Rockies. Today, in a four-wheel-drive vehicle you can telescope those journeys into a one- or two-day trip that will long be remembered. For the hiker with a well-planned pack and sturdy boots, the possibilities are limitless.

In some instances, major highways parallel or cut across several of the historic trails that have played important roles in the development of Colorado. For the lover of the great out-of-doors, these early roads offer access to scenic beauty so remote that the American national flower, "Kleenexus Americanus," does not even bloom here. In most instances the beer can and other contemporary highway markers are also conspicuous by their absence. Why not start off like many of the pioneers did? In this way you may still see some of the best of Colorado, reliving history as you go, seeing the old and all-but-forgotten ghost towns. Gone now are the lawns, the beds of flowers, and the tidy streets that once fringed the cabins that stood among sun-dappled groves of aspen trees. In their place one now finds long rows of dilapidated little cabins falling into ruin. Beside the quiet stream beds that once held miles of ditches, are the remains of rotting sluice boxes among the tons of rock and gravel. Hundreds of these deserted hamlets may yet be seen along the thousands of miles of backcountry roads to high adventure.

Courtesy Library, State Historical Society of Colorado
Engineer Pass was constructed by Otto Mears and first opened
to traffic in August, 1877.

Collection of Robert L. Brown
This vastly improved Jeep road now traverses Eng'neer Pass

INDEX